GUTENBERG AND THE IMPACT OF PRINTING

STEPHAN FÜSSEL

Gutenberg
AND THE IMPACT OF PRINTING

TRANSLATED FROM THE GERMAN BY
DOUGLAS MARTIN

ASHGATE

The translator acknowledges the willing and expert help of
Hans Eckert, librarian, of Rüsselsheim. He would also like to thank
Erika Gaffney at Burlington, VT, and Kirsten Weißenberg at Aldershot
for valued advice and encouragement.

This book was first published in German in 1999 under the title
Gutenberg und seine Wirkung by Insel Verlag Frankfurt am Main and Leipzig
The English edition first published 2003 by
Scolar Press, Ashgate Publishing Limited
Gower House, Croft Road, Aldershot, Hampshire GU11 3HR
and Ashgate Publishing Company
Suite 420, 101 Cherry Street, Burlington, Vermont 05401-4405

The German text copyright © Stephan Füssel 1999, 2005
The English translation copyright © Douglas Martin 2005

The publisher acknowledges a grant for the translation from Stiftung Moses

Designed and typeset in df︎TYPE Rialto by Douglas Martin
Printed and made in Great Britain by MPG Books, Bodmin, Cornwall

British Library Cataloguing-in-Publication Data
Füssel, Stephan
Gutenberg and the impact of printing
1. Gutenberg, Johann, 1397?–1468. 2. Printers – Germany – Biography.
3. Printing – History – Origins and antecedents
I.Title
686.2'092
ISBN 0-7546-3537-6

Library of Congress Cataloging-in-Publication Data
Füssel, Stephan
[Gutenberg und seine Wirkung. English]
Gutenberg and the impact of printing / Stephan Füssel;
translated from the German by Douglas Martin – English ed.
Originally published in German under the title: Gutenberg und seine Wirkung.
Frankfurt am Main: Insel 1999.
Includes bibliographical references and index.
ISBN 0-7546-3537-6 (alk. paper)
1. Gutenberg, Johann, 1397?–1468. 2. Printers – Germany – Biography.
3. Printing – History – Origin and antecedents.
I. Title
Z126.Z7F9613 2005   686.2'092–dc22
2004001759

Contents

Foreword

Johann Gutenberg was voted "man of the millennium" by an American team of journalists (see Agnes Hooper Gottlieb, Henry Gottlieb, Barbara Bowers, Brent Bowers: 1000 Years, 1000 People: Ranking the men and women who shaped the millennium. New York, Tokyo, London, 1999). In their reasoning it was stressed that Gutenberg had created, by means of his invention, the conditions for all other intellectual, political or religious changes in the centuries ahead. The exceptional story of Gutenberg's influence lay at the heart of their final decision, based not on a single timely invention, but rather on his fundamental significance for the global history of human communication.

We know that methods also existed in the Far East from as early as the eighth century for the multiplication of texts from woodcuts, from 1100 using clay letters, and after 1377 by means of the sand-casting process; but it was Gutenberg's related sequence of inventions involving casting and setting single metal types and printing from them in a press, that first created texts which were comparable in beauty to the finest manuscripts, and at the same time distributed them in unprecedented quantities. The possibilities opened up by printing supported the educational trends of the late Middle Ages that had launched the aspiring European universities of the fourteenth and fifteenth centuries, promoted the spread of the ideas of the Italian humanists with their belief in a universal human capacity for education, whilst at the same time bringing about the preconditions for the Reformation of the Church and the popularisation of the contents of faith in the vernacular languages. Printing also heralded the birth of public opinion mediated through newspapers and the press, and prepared the way by circulating factual information as well as agitation and propaganda through pamphlets and broadsides.

It is the interaction between technological history and intellectual history which makes the study of early printing history so fascinating. This shows that the new medium did not take over from what had gone before with a bang, but rather that for quite some time the old contents continued to be handed down in their familiar external forms.

Thus the page layout, choice of letter-form and format for early printed books followed directly from that of similar manuscripts, and it was
those same grammars and textbooks that had proved themselves over
the centuries that were selected for wider distribution in print. The true
nature and potential of the new medium came to light at first little by
little: a title page was grafted on at the front, more convenient formats
were developed, the vernacular gained ground alongside the learned
Latin tongue, and all this encouraged the habit of personal reading.

Epics in verse form – an outward indicator of public reading – were
no longer published, their place being taken by pocket editions of prose
romances for private reading; and the first factual books on medicine
and natural history, printed maps of Europe and the world, calendars
and almanacks were circulated. Only fifty years after the invention,
more than a thousand printing offices using the new technology were
at work in some 350 towns right across Europe, and between 1450 and
1500 about 30,000 titles were published with a total estimated output
of 9 million volumes. Contemporaries rejoiced that it was now possible
for "everyone of moderate means to acquire a higher education."

The technical essentials of Gutenberg's invention remained unchanged
for 350 years. The first modifications came in the nineteenth century
with steam-driven cylinder presses, mechanical composition and manufacture of paper in continuous reels, but metal composition and the
letterpress process held out until the middle of the twentieth century.
Filmsetting and the offset process took over from that point until the
scope of present-day electronic publication created a new technological
environment. The communication revolution associated with Gutenberg's name, however, continues on its way.

Gutenberg – his life and work

In May 1451 the papal legate Nicholas of Cues, known as Cusanus, took part in the fourteenth general chapter of the Benedictines in Mainz, which dealt with the adoption of monastic reforms, and which also looked into the resources of monastic libraries and their central importance for the monastic community. In an earlier work De concordantia catholica (1434), written during his visits to the Council of Basle (1431–48), he had already spoken out for a correct and reliable edition of the text of the missal for use throughout the Catholic world, for only a standardised text could ensure that mass would be performed in the same fashion everywhere. On the tours of visitation he made after 1450, Cusanus must have seen for himself that the basic prayers of the faith were insufficiently familiar to the parish priests, let alone to the congregation. And so in order to improve popular religious education in the churches he had wooden or stone tablets set up on which the Lord's prayer, the creed, the "Hail Mary" and the ten commandments were inscribed. Whilst Cusanus was still hoping that the reforms so urgently needed in the Church could be brought about – as in former centuries – through religious knowledge put across by stained glass, murals or suchlike one-off inscriptions; Gutenberg was sitting just a few yards away from Mainz's cathedral square in his workshop in the Humbrechthof, cutting punches for the successful casting of metal types.

THE COURSE OF GUTENBERG'S LIFE

The fifteenth century was an age of stagnation in politics and Church affairs; the emperor stood opposed to the imperial hierarchy, of whom the electors formed a particularly factious element. The imperial diet which met at irregular intervals revealed the emperor's dependence on the princes when it came to the Hussite and later the Turkish campaigns. The territorial overlords gained an ever more commanding position, and the free cities frequently invoked their special status under the law. Learning flourished, leading to changes in higher education and the foundation of universities in Cologne and Erfurt in 1389, Würzburg in

1402, Leipzig in 1409 and Louvain in 1425; jurisprudence and mathematical sciences were strongly promoted. The dominant intellectual current of the age was humanism, with its belief in universal educability and a new spiritual openness that tried to bring together Platonism and Christianity. Although only about six per cent of the population lived in towns, these grew in importance with the introduction of simple industries such as cloth and linen production, whilst the agricultural economy was in slow decline. The old Hansa privileges were being lost and new methods of trading were taking their place, which benefited the international trade fair centre of Leipzig and made use of merchant and private banking houses, particularly those of Augsburg and Nuremberg in southern Germany.

At the beginning of the fifteenth century, the city of Mainz had about 6000 inhabitants. At this time of radical upheaval the city council enacted a new constitution, which was more strongly weighted in favour of the right of the guilds to be informed and to participate at the expense of the old patrician class. In the quarrels between patricians and guilds the families of the "ancients" were several times forced to leave the city, and at other times they absented themselves in protest. The financial situation of the city developed so catastrophically during the 1540s that it had to borrow massively from the surrounding towns, and above all from Frankfurt. By 1456 the city was literally bankrupt and more or less in pawn to Frankfurt. At the same time Mainz, however, still retained its legal status as an imperial free city, whereas after the archbishops' war of 1462 it became a dependency of its archbishop and elector. The economic position of Mainz – which had been such a prosperous city in the fourteenth century – became ever more critical until it went into recession around 1450 with a drastic population decline. Immigrants were welcomed because of this underlying problem, and in 1436 new citizens were solicited with the offer of a ten-year break from taxes and levies. The local trades and occupations included woodworking and the timber-trade, river transport, farming and viticulture, and also cloth-weaving, wrought-iron and non-ferrous metal crafts as well as goldsmithing.

No certain date of birth has been handed down for Gutenberg. In connection with the division of his father's estate in 1420, he was considered to have come of age, and – on the basis of different arguments – researchers have settled for various years from the range between 1393 and 1403. Since the turn of the century was accepted as the token year by international consensus in 1900, then this traditional argument allowed his 600th birthday to be celebrated in the year 2000. And as it was not uncommon at the time to name someone after the patron saint of their date of birth, then traditionally 24 June (St John's Day) has been the accepted birthday; but it is very probable – as the name Johann (or Johannes, or in Mainz dialect of the fifteenth century Henchen, or Hengin or Henne) was so popular and widespread – that the name-day connection is tenuous indeed. His father, Friele Gensfleisch zur Laden, born in about 1350 and a Mainz citizen from 1372, married Elsa Wirich in 1386 as his second bride. A Mainz patrician, he was by occupation a merchant, probably in the cloth trade; he belonged to the companionship of the mint and served for a time as one of the masters of accounts for the city. During his lifetime he never used the surname "zum Gutenberg"; this additional family name was only taken up by his relatives in the 1520s. Ever since the early fourteenth century the Hof zum Gutenberg had belonged in the family. This house, which stood at the corner of Schustergasse and Christophstrasse, no longer exists. It was a two-storey Gothic building with room for a number of families and most probably for a composing room and a press room as well.

We can only speculate about Gutenberg's childhood and youth. At best we may suppose from his good grasp of Latin and his technical knowledge that he was well educated in a monastic school, probably followed by a spell at university. It has been suggested, and also disputed, that he may have attended the monastery of St Victor (south of the city near Weisenau) and acquired Latin and the rudiments of learning there, since at an advanced age he can be traced as a member of the brotherhood of St Victor. Whilst still quite young, Gutenberg probably had to leave Mainz with his family as yet another dispute between patricians and guilds came to a head in August 1411, leading to the withdrawal from the city of 117 patricians who were seeking by this strategy to protect their privileged exemption from tax and tolls. In all probability they moved at short notice to Eltville, where Gutenberg's mother had inherited a house on the town walls (in the Burghofstrasse). Once again in 1413 his father had to leave Mainz hurriedly on account of hunger rioting and once more the family members would have accompanied him. An equally good schooling could have been had in Eltville at the "community school" attached to St Peter's church, for grammar was taught there from Aelius Donatus's textbook, and rhetoric through readings from the leading Latin writers. We find one "Johannes de Alta villa" enrolled for the summer semester of 1418 and winter semester of 1419 at the University of Erfurt (which fell within the diocese of Mainz), which provides a clue that might encourage us to identify this "John from Eltville" with Johann Gutenberg. But just as we are unable to find more evidence for this theory, so we lack information about possible further training in the 1420s. The few documentary records confine themselves to inheritance settlements and the payment of life annuities. His immediate neighbour in the Gutenberghof was Heinz Reyse, who was a companion of the mint and probably an active coin-maker. Heinz Reyse and "Henchin zu Gudenberg" were among those who once again left the city as its finances were threatened with bankruptcy and the guilds took command. We know for certain from a further document that Gutenberg was no longer resident in Mainz after 16 January 1430.

Four years later, we pick up his trail in the Strasbourg suburb of St Arbogast. He had caused the city clerk of Mainz Niklaus Wörstadt, who was passing through Strasbourg, to be imprisoned for debt, because the city of Mainz had not yet paid him 310 Rhenish gulden due on an annuity from the division of his late mother's estate. More important for us than sketchy personal suggestions of an engagement and the breaking off of an engagement in Strasbourg, are those sources which reveal Gutenberg as an entrepreneurial businessman, as an experienced inventor, and as a master-craftsman. Since 1437 he had taught the Strasbourg citizen Andreas Dritzehn the "cutting and polishing of precious stones", that is to say, he had offered a kind of apprenticeship in the coin-maker's or goldsmith's crafts. Now, as on several occasions later in his career, he set up a financing consortium with various associates to put up the capital for a project which involved both a technical process and the production of wares. On the next big pilgrimage to Aachen for the display of the relics, visitors would want to buy mirrors as souvenirs, and because it was deeply rooted in popular devotion that something of the beneficial radiation from the relics could be captured in these mirrors and carried home. These much-loved mirrors were made from an alloy of lead and tin, and – although we can only speculate about the exact production method – were turned out in great numbers by a casting process. The consortium threatened to fall apart on discovering that it was mistakenly producing for 1439, whereas the Aachen pilgrimage with its marketing opportunity would not in fact take place until the following year, 1440. We know about this through an action brought by one of the brothers of the deceased associate and former apprentice Andreas Dritzehn. From this lawsuit it emerged that Gutenberg acted as master in teaching goldsmithing, that they worked together in manufacturing the mirrors, and that a further, third project was planned.

A great deal of speculation has been caused by the secretive sounding phrase "Aventur und Kunst" which occurs several times in the documentation. A glance at the contemporary contexts in which the word is used, however, will show that "Aventur" does not indicate some colourful adventure from knightly romance, but rather a risky business "venture" in the modern sense. And similarly the term "Kunst" stood for skilful knowledge of handicrafts. Gutenberg is revealed here and in the following years as an inventive entrepreneur and technologist.

Other intriguing terms from the documents of the Strasbourg period that are hard to pin down include the "Pressen" (presses), the "Form" (forme), and the "Gezeug" (tool, instrument). These could be used to describe either coin stamping or perhaps an experiment in letterpress printing, the latter more likely as one of the associates was the co-owner of a papermill. Strasbourg was a world trading city, with connections to the south of France and Italy, but also via Nuremberg and Prague to the Orient. In Strasbourg, the use of high relief stamps for bookbinding had been developed, for example, and it was the leading city for bellfounding. It is interesting that paper currency notes, which had been produced by a printing process in the Far East, were known about there in Gutenberg's day. Since the early seventh century in China and Korea, and somewhat later in Japan, Confucian and Buddhist texts had been written on wood and circulated. These written *Sutras* (doctrines) were cut into the woodblock to prevent changes or wear, so reproducing them by inking and rubbing onto paper was at first an incidental use. In many instances only two to five copies would be taken, but in contrast the original woodblocks were kept safely and many Korean examples still survive. Experimentation with ceramic types took place in China from the eleventh century, and with types cast in various metal alloys in Korea from the fourteenth century. If at first the huge number of over 10,000 signs required was an obstacle to casting and printing from moveable types, then the introduction of the Hangul-alphabet in about 1444 should have given the Koreans an opportunity to develop more practical casting methods. Castings were made from sand-moulds, which could not give a sharp-edged quality to the types to compare with Gutenberg's later developments. Furthermore it was not permissable at the time to use this alphabet for general purposes. Experiments with composition from single types in the Far East are clearly attested, but despite much reflection there are still no routes by which information about them could have reached Strasbourg by 1440.

Paper, which had been developed in China by the second century, did, on the contrary reach Baghdad and Cairo along the Silk Road by the tenth century, and with the expansion of Islam, extended over North Africa, Sicily and Gibraltar to reach Europe in the twelfth century. The first papermill in German lands was set up by Ulman Stromer in Nuremberg in 1390 and with it one of the essential preconditions for Gutenberg's invention fell into place, and an early instance of mass production was created.

Similarly woodcutting, which originated in the Far East, can be shown to have reached central Europe by the early fifteenth century. The earliest woodcuts were used to produce playing cards and devotional images. The latter noted miraculous events or special pilgrimages, and often contained a few woods of text which also had to be cut into the woodblock. So the means of providing large numbers of single-sided sheets of paper by this method was common knowledge by 1440, but it was not very practical since a woodblock could not be re-used once a particular text or image had been cut.

We simply do not know what Gutenberg did between 1444 and 1448; but there is evidence to show that he was back in Mainz by 17 October

1448. On that day he took out a loan of 150 gulden at 5 per cent inter-est from his cousin Arnold Gelthus. Just as in Strasbourg, Gutenberg sought business relationships with bankers and merchants with whose financial support he could put his new technical developments into practice. By 1450 his experiments had reached the stage that he could go ahead with the setting and printing of broadsides and extensive books.

BRINGING THE TECHNICAL INVENTIONS TOGETHER

Gutenberg's invention is as simple as it is ingenious: texts were broken down into their smallest components, i.e. into the 26 letters of the Roman alphabet, and from placing single letters in the right order the new text required would result time and again. Texts had been copied over the centuries by writing them out completely and sequentially, or by cutting them equally completely in wood (text and illustrations were being cut in wood for such contemporary "blockbooks" as prayers, *ars moriendi* or cribs for sermons), but now only the letters of the alphabet had to be cut and supplies cast and they would always be available for setting up whatever text was chosen. His second brain-wave was in effect as simple as it was technologically revolutionary: instead of transferring the ink to the paper by rubbing as had been done for 700 years in Asia, Gutenberg used the physical action of the paper- or wine-press to trans-fer the ink from typematter to dampened paper with one even and force-ful impression (see Plate 2, the first contemporary woodcut to show a press, dating from 1499).

Very many stages were naturally called for in the development of this apparently obvious and straightforward procedure. Punches for indivi-dual letters, skilfully cut by goldsmiths, had been around for some time, and the engraving of sacred artefacts such as chalices and monstrances was a widespread technique. Casting methods were in use whether for bellfounding or coinmaking. It was a question of realising the idea by bringing together individual letters, and casting techniques, and fin-ding the appropriater constituents of the typemetal. At the heart of Gutenberg's discovery stands the development of a casting instrument which allowed the casting void to be precisely adjusted so that identi-cal supplies of each type could be cast. No original instruments have survived from the fifteenth century, and the so-called adjustable hand mould shown in the textbooks only reached that precise form some two centuries later, but the earliest types which do survive and the quality of Gutenberg's impression make it evident that some comparable casting instrument must have been part of the original invention.

To start with a letter was engraved on the top of a tall steel bar or cube. This bar carried a single character in deep relief and in mirror image; it was then struck by a hammer into softer copper so that a right-reading, deeply sunken letter resulted. This was now the matrix, which had to be correctly fitted into the casting instrument. Molten metal was poured in, and a single type cast, with the letter at its head in relief but again in mirror-image. As the casting matrix in harder metal could be used again and again, a theoretically endless supply of identical types of the same letter and shape could be cast. The exact constitution of the first alloys is not known but may be inferred from later discoveries to have been about 83 per cent lead, 9 per cent tin, 6 per cent antimony and 1 per cent each of copper and iron; this compares with an actual find from the mid-seventeenth century in Mainz, where the lead content was markedly lower at 73 per cent and tin and antimony totalled 25 per cent (a composition which would have had the advantage of cooling more rapidly, allowing a higher rate of production).

Supplies of these singly cast types were then placed in compartmented cases where an ergonomic principle operated, in that the most frequently used letters had larger, well-positioned compartments close to the compositor's hand. The individual letters were then assembled in a composing stick, in which the lines could be "justified". For this purpose metal spacing material that was blind (i.e. below printing height) was introduced to equalise the space between the words and bring the lines out to equal length. These composing sticks were at first made of wood and later replaced by metal. Small groups of completed lines were transferred to a galley, a stable wooden tray in which they could be made up into column or page depths. These could be brought out to the correct depth if needed by "leading", or adjusting the space between lines, using further strips of blind spacing material. The finished pages were placed in correct relationship to each other, and locked up into a "forme" or frame to fit the bed of the press.

The typesetting was then inked using mushroom-shaped leather balls (the printing ink developed by Gutenberg was made from soot from lamps, varnish and egg-whites). The paper to be printed had been dampened so that it would take the impression from the type better, and was positioned on a number of pins within a hinged tympan. A frisket, which in turn hinged over that, had a cut-out corresponding to the type area, and otherwise protected the margin of the paper from coming into contact with the forme and possibly being soiled. The frisket was closed and then the tympan with the frisket and paper was folded above the forme which rested on the bed of the press. The bed was drawn in under the platen, which was brought down by a heavy pull on the lever to take an impression. This first impression was "backed-up" on the other side of the sheet, with the pin-holes keeping the registration exact so that the lines of type on both sides of the sheet corresponded. Sheets of various sizes could be printed, in the early days a page at a time, and later two, four or eight pages together, and allowed to dry before the other side could be printed, and later folded into sections. Careful "imposition" ensured that the pages fell in the right order when folded into 16-page sections for sewing.

Early printing was produced in black only as a rule, and all special features such as illuminated initials, coloured page headings, illustrations, as well as rubrication (lit. writing in red) had to be added later by hand. As a result many early printed books can be mistaken for manuscripts at first glance, since their decoration was added individually by hand. None of the 49 surviving copies of the Gutenberg Bible resembles another, for each has its own illumination and finishing touches. At first woodcuts were not printed together with typematter, as it was difficult to get the inking and impression right for printing from wood and metal at the same time. In the earliest instances, text and illustrations were usually printed in two separate operations, although this could bring its own problems when it came to register. This is well illustrated in Der Edelstein, the fable collection printed by Albrecht Pfister in Bamberg in 1461 (see Plates 42/43).

Whereas it would have been theoretically possible to make do with two sets of 26 characters – one each for the capitals and lower case – Gutenberg was evidently concerned to imitate the manuscript as faithfully as possible, in that he reproduced double-column setting and the same marginal proportions and went to great trouble to match the look of the page en masse. To that end he cut and cast a total of 290 different characters: 47 capitals, 63 lower case, 92 abbreviations, 83 ligatures or combined letters and 5 punctuation marks (see Plate 3). The ligatures, such as **ff, fi, ffl, ft**, saved space by being cast on a single body. Abbreviations and contractions taken over from Latin manuscript usage for prefixes (pro, prae, per), case-endings (um, am, as) and doubled letters (mm, nn), were also great space savers. All these, and the width variants available for many lower-case letters, helped the skilled compositor to produce evenly spaced lines and a wonderfully close and evenly spaced page. At the same time it becomes apparent what high demands were placed on the compositor's knowledge of Latin. Some 100,000 types would have had to be cast for the compositors' work on the *Gutenberg Bible*. This allowed every detail of a manuscript text to be followed, whilst surpassing it in accuracy and quality. The first experiments and attempts at printing in this typeface must have related solely to Latin texts, for many of the abbreviations provided were only called for in Latin.

THE "WORK OF THE BOOKS": THE 42-LINE BIBLE

Those early pieces of printing which we can confidently attribute to Gutenberg fall into two main groups, on the one hand jobbing printing such as indulgences, calendars and vocabularies, and on the other hand that great masterpiece of 1282 printed pages, the Latin *Bible*. Gutenberg chose for this the *Vulgate* of St Jerome, the definitive textual basis for all theological work and religious instruction during the Middle Ages. It is most probable that he would have taken a handwritten *Bible* available in Mainz as his example from which to set the text. That same copy has never been rediscovered, but then it is likely to have been little short of worn out by the treatment it would have received. However, there is a manuscript *Bible* preserved in the Library of Congress that was written in Mainz in 1450 and which must come close to the model Gutenberg in fact used (see Plate 4). It is striking to note that it contains illuminated pages by the same artist who decorated the printed copy of a *Gutenberg Bible* to be found today in Göttingen University Library.

Gutenberg imitated the manuscript in all its aspects, so he adopted the division into columns, and the massed look of the text panel – which he was able to improve upon through typesetting – and that placing of the columns on the page which yielded ideal margin proportions. The missal type he used was a textura, that gave a very dense type area, in which individual letters had a perpendicular emphasis and produced a latticed effect so that the finished page resembled a woven textile (Lat. *textura*).

In his *Chronik der Stadt Köln* of 1499, Johann Koelhoff has this to say about our *Bible*: "In the year of our Lord which one wrote as MCCCCL (1450) – that was a golden year – printing began. And the first book to be printed was the *Bible* in Latin which was printed in a large type of the kind only used nowadays for printing missals." The chronicler not only places the beginning of printing in elevated conjunction with a holy year, but also sets it in the right liturgical context. These missal letter-forms were relatively large on the manuscript page – and consequently on the printed one – so that they would be readable from the lectern in dark church or refectory interiors. The *Gutenberg Bible* is set in a choral type of 4.2 mm (x-height), and it followed that in this fairly large size the extensive text would occupy 1282 printed pages in large folio format. In order to use paper economically, Gutenberg experimented with the number of lines per column. For the initial setting trial he started with 40 lines to the column (fols. 1–5r and fols. 129–132r), increased to 41 lines (fol. 5v only), and then to the 42 lines with which he decided to stay (from fol. 6 and throughout). He evidently had the faulty pages set again at 42 lines per column depth. Examples of both setting variants are to be found among the surviving copies.

For the first pages to come off the press, Gutenberg had also made the experiment of taking over the work of the rubricator, so on leaves 1, 4, 5, and 129 and 130 the headings of the chapters are printed in red. Thereafter he gave up on this red printing, and it was omitted when it came to reprinting sheets from the second typesetting. It is obvious that two-fold inking and problems with impression were holding up the work-rate and giving unsatisfactory visual results, so he left further rubrication in the hands of the professional scribes as hitherto in the manuscript era. The Vienna and Munich copies of B42 still contain their complete *Tabula Rubricarum*, or printed list of headings to be inserted in red with instructions on where they are to appear.

On the final folios of both volumes of the copy on paper at the Bibliothèque Nationale in Paris, there is a handwritten note from Heinrich Cremer, vicar of St Stephan's in Mainz, stating that he completed the work of rubricating, illuminating and binding these volumes by 24 August 1456. This gives us a useful guide as to when the finished printed books must have been available.

Close textual analysis and the study of individual habits in handling abbreviations let us conclude that there were four different compositors at work when typesetting began, and six as production reached a more advanced stage. Examination of inks through electron spectrography has confirmed these numbers. At least half a year has to be allowed for the casting of a supply of 100,000 types, and the typesetting would have extended over about two years. At the height of production at least twelve printers would have been teamed with the compositors to keep six presses busy, and other helpers would have been needed for inkmaking and paper handling. To print 180 copies of 1282 pages would have involved 230,760 passes through the press, which in turn would require at least 330 working days. Allowing for the fact that the medieval working year had only about 200 days (because of the large number of religious festivals) and that only four presses were operated to start with and that there were bound to have been teething troubles, it is certain that typesetting and printing would have taken more than two years. Whereas a scribe would have worked a whole three years on a single copy of the Bible, it was now possible to produce 180 copies in the same time, 40 on vellum and 140 on paper. The paper imported from Italy would have cost about 600 gulden, the vellum (i.e. the skins of 3,200 animals) perhaps 400 gulden.

Such high charges, not to speak of the development costs, were beyond Gutenberg's personal means. As we have already seen him do in Strasbourg, he set about finding partners with capital to invest in his technically innovative and commercially bold enterprise as soon as he was back in Mainz in 1448. He borrowed 150 gulden from his cousin Arnold Gelthus straight away and took out a loan from Johann Fust (c.1400–66) in each of the years 1449 and 1452. Fust placed the initial loan of 800 gulden at Gutenberg's free disposal against the security of the equipment to be produced with the money. The second advance was specifically intended as working capital for their joint "work of the books". These arrangements show both of them as financial partners in the process of developing their business collaboration. From their legal dispute of 1455, for which only part of the proceedings has come down to us (in the legal instrument named after the lawyer Helmasperger, see Plate 10), we learn that Fust accused Gutenberg of having paid no interest (Gutenberg's counter-argument was that Fust had told him that no interest would be due), and of Fust's further charge of embezzlement, namely that the money had not been applied to their joint project.

After simple and compound interest had been added, Gutenberg was faced with paying back 2026 gulden, the equivalent in purchasing power to about four houses. A valuable letter of 1455 from Enea Silvio Piccolomini, who later became Pope Pius II but was still at that time secretary to emperor Friedrich III, tells us that the *Bible* was already finished by autumn 1454 and had already found buyers. Piccolomini wrote from Wiener Neustadt to the Spanish cardinal Juan de Carvajal in Rome on 12 March 1455, reporting an interesting encounter when in Frankfurt (probably for the Reichstag held there in October 1454). There he had met a "remarkable man" (*vir mirabilis*) who had shown him quinternions (sections of five folded sheets) of a Latin *Bible* that could be read without difficulty and "without spectacles". What is more some sheets had already been sent to the emperor in Vienna. Piccolomini was able to ascertain that the edition (and this consisted either or 158 or of 180 copies) had sold out before printing had been completed. This would suggest that the business had run its profitable course, if we had not heard arguments to the contrary in the Helmasperger legal instrument. We can only suppose that, because of the customary trading practice whereby payment only became due when the next fair was held, or perhaps as a result of further delays in finishing the work, Gutenberg was in no position to pay Fust back in the autumn of 1454. Another possibility is that Gutenberg had proceeded to tie up the incoming funds in new projects.

Forty-nine copies have survived to the present day, of which a few were apparently placed with rubricators, illuminators and binders through the agency of Fust and Schoeffer. Each of these copies is unique, as has been said, on account of its individual rubrication and illumination. The rubricator's main job entailed underlining Nomina Sacra with fine red strokes or bringing out individual capitals at the start of sentences to ease the reader's task. The illuminator provided the printed text with decorated initials, and in certain cases, with further marginal scroll-work. According to the importance of the context, blank spaces of two, three, four or even as many as ten lines' depth were left for these initials. This left the purchasers free to determine what decoration should be added to their copies according to personal, regional or contemporary taste. As with high and late medieval manuscript illumi-nation, so in the practice of illuminating printed books that persisted for at least thirty or forty years we can recognise schools with distinct characteristics of region and period. Two outstanding illuminated Bibles that are to be found in Göttingen University Library and in the Biblioteca Pública Provincial in Burgos, Spain, will repay closer scrutiny.

The Burgos copy of the Bible

The first page of the second volume of the Burgos copy (see Plate 5) has three lines handwritten in red: two lines preceding the initial "I" which occupies the left-hand margin, and a single-line heading in the right column above the ornamented six-line initial "P" for the opening word Parabolae of the Wisdom of Solomon. This distinguished letter "P" with its slender tendrils fits compactly into the space between the columns, whereas the initial "I" extends into the outer margins where it links up with more fanciful scrollwork richly embellished with gold leaf. These floral elements are not taken from nature but spring from the illumi-nator's creative imagination and twine playfully around both columns.

The colours, as in the volume as a whole, are well attuned to each other; light pastel shades, often mixed with white, which go together admir-ably. Light greens, pale blues, and a variety of reds and ochres make up a harmonious whole. The eye is caught by the two crossed knotty bran-ches in the centre of the lower margin, from which fresh foliage appears to grow. These remarkable crossed branches are to be found in other books as well, amongst them an incomplete Gutenberg Bible belonging to the Pierpont Morgan Library in New York. It is true that the foliage in this New York copy is differently intertwined and the colouring also differs, nevertheless the same painter's hand is unmistakable, particularly in this central motif of the crossed branches. We encounter this same hand again in a copy of the 48-line Bible (1462) of Fust and Schoeffer, in a Cicero edition of 1465, a Constitutiones of Clement V (1460), and in all illuminated copies of the Rationale divinorum officiorum by Guillelmus Durandus (1459) and the Liber sextus Decretalium of Boniface VIII (1465). Since all these works came from the Mainz printing office of Fust and Schoeffer, and as the Latin surname fustis means "Knotenstock" (knotty stick), it was soon conjectured that these branches symbolised Fust's name. The conclusive evidence is provided by the familiar partnership mark of Fust and Schoeffer which shows their arms hanging from such a branch (see Plate 18). The Berlin art historian Eberhard König has shown that this illuminator was already at work in Upper Austria during the manuscript era; and that he was based in Mainz from the mid-1450s to the mid-1460s, where he decorated numerous works for the Fust and Schoeffer workshop, probably on a commission basis. This workshop had added to Gutenberg's purely black and white process that intricate technique for printing two-colour decoration from metalcuts to be seen in the Mainz Psalter, and, on the publishing side, had apparently specialised in the sale of ready-illuminated printed books.

The Göttingen copy of the Bible

The illumination of one of the rare complete examples on vellum, belonging to Göttingen University Library, leads us to another school of Mainz book decoration and reveals how the artist adhered strictly to the rules to be found in a copy book. Once again further examples of this illuminator's work are to be found in manuscripts at Frankfurt University Library, in the Giant Bible at the Library of Congress in Washington (see Plate 4), and also in the Gutenberg Bible from Cardinal Mazarin's Library that is to be found today in the Bibliothèque Nationale in Paris.

The Göttingen copy is one of only four complete vellum copies in the world and is uniformly rubricated throughout its 1282 pages and illuminated to a high standard. The remaining complete copies printed on vellum are to be found in the British Library (probably from the Charter-house in Mainz), the Library of Congress (from the Benedictine monas-tery of St Blasius in the Black Forest) and in the Bibliothéque Nationale (from the Benedictine monastery of St James in Mainz).

The Göttingen example has running titles writtten in red in a missal hand (matching the text face), the chapter numbering is in red, but the opening initials alternate between red and blue, giving the pages a state-ly look. All the required initials have been inserted, some with finely drawn flourishes, the larger ones rich with gold, colour and ensuing scrollwork. The opening page of the Bible and those of the individual books are framed with colorfully designed scrollwork of acanthus, fern or thorn. (see Plates 6 and 7).

The design is the outcome of following a mid-fifteenth-century pat-tern book which has survived by pure chance and is housed today in the same Göttingen library. This copy book is of exceptional interest for us in that it provides not merely the range of colours to be used and the painting method, but shows the juxtaposition of the colours in detail. It starts with colour samples for scrollwork, and then for the square or lozenge-shaped backgrounds or "fields", and finally for a few ornamen-tal initials and flowers. The successive stages in painting foliage and these various chequered fields in paint are comprehensively explained. It pro-vides guidance – using in each case a standard outline for the foliage – on how different colourways may be used: a soft raspberry red on one side of the leaf and a complementary slate green on what the writer calls the "turnover" side; alternatively a light blue may be paired with a deep minium red or a rather powdery-looking gold colour (see Plate 8). The dark red was obtained from ground brazilwood to which lye, chalk and alum were added. This is brighter than the carmine in use in the high Middle Ages which had a heavier consistency. The green hues such as mountain green or slate green were derived from malachite, and shaded down to a sap green with a vegetable varnish of uncertain con-stituency. The gold coloured tint was achieved through a mixture of mercury, tin, sal-ammoniac and sulphur. This gold colour is more reserved in effect than the genuine gold leaf or powder used where boldness and contrast were required instead. Fine brush shadings and accents in lead white conveyed modelling and surface detail.

Besides the manufacture of colours, the copy book describes how to use them and build up the painting in layers. To produce the "third chequered background" (see Plate 9, folio 8v), one is shown how to draw the outlines of the field, plan the gold and red squares with a brush, cross through with the black lines and add the gold, then build up the blue, red and green squares. One heightens the florets in the blue squares with lead white, and then the green and red squares are finished with white and yellow dots. A comparison of these colours and painting methods demonstrates conclusively that this pattern book served as the actual model for the illumination of the Göttingen B42. A micro-photographical analysis confirms that the assembly of the colours and their layer by layer application follows the instructions to the letter.

This outstanding copy originally belonged to a monastery, as the hand-written marginal notes reveal. It entered the Wolfenbüttel Library in 1587, which placed it at the disposal of Helmstedt University Library in 1614. After the dissolution of Helmstedt University in 1812, it found its way to Göttingen.

Since we have already found a comparable painting technique and approach in the manuscript *Giant Bible* of Mainz (1450), it may at the very least be suggested that both could have been illuminated in Mainz. It must be borne in mind, however, that it was still rather the exception in the incunabula period for a publisher to burden himself with the final decoration. And so it became possible, as far afield as Scandinavia and Britain, Italy and Poland, for regional and local traditions to come into play to create unique works of art.

JOBBING PRINTING IN LONG RUNS
Indulgences and propaganda against the Turks

Fust alleged in 1455 that Gutenberg had not put the loans made to him exclusively into their joint "work of the books" but had also used them to finance other projects. And there are a whole series of minor publications such as broadsides, indulgences, short grammars and calendars that can be dated to the very years which saw the emergence of the *Gutenberg Bible*. It is interesting that these texts are set in a different type to that reserved for the *Bible*, in fact in Gutenberg's original typeface, known for the uses to which it was put as the Donatus and *Kalender* or DK-type. This is similarly a textura, although cruder in cut and larger in point size than the B42-type. Again a multitude of abbreviations, ligatures and variants were cut for it, so that the reconstructed fount consists of 202 individual characters. After several stages of improvement it served for printing the 36-*line Bible* (probably in Bamberg, c.1458–60, see Plate 14).

Unquestionably one of the most lucrative commissions for early jobbing printing was to print massive numbers of indulgences for the Church. These indulgences, which became such a bone of contention for the Reformers, played a material role in fifteenth-century religious practice and were extensively circulated in manuscript. Such certificates of indulgence were issued against an individually assessed contribution, and could be presented at the next confession in order to obtain a full remission of the temporal penalities for sin. The text was formally laid down, and wanted only for a name, date and signature to be added to the single-sided printed sheet. The new printing process was ideally matched to such an opportunity for mass production, for once a single page had been set in type it could be run off in a massive edition. Both of the earliest printed indulgences survive in several editions. In the years which followed we learn of print-runs ranging from several thousands to – in one exceptional case – 190,000 copies. The significance the recipients attached to these indulgences is to be measured by the fact that all early surviving letters of indulgence are printed on vellum.

The grounds for issuing these indulgences lay in the very real fear of further advances by the Ottoman empire which coloured the fifteenth century. When Constantinople fell to Sultan Mahommed II on 29 May 1453, a hitherto unfocussed danger drew menacingly closer. This dread of the "Turks", everywhere understood to mean Ottoman invasion and the expansion of Islam, was widespread. Pope Nicholas V had earlier granted the King of Cyprus the right to issue a plenary indulgence to run from 1 May 1452 to 30 April 1455. The Cypriot agent Paulinus Chappe arranged for such indulgences to be printed in Mainz from the late summer of 1454 onwards. The earliest surviving example carries the handwritten date 22 October 1454.

It is however possible that indulgences had been printed in Mainz two years earlier than that, as on 2 May 1452 Nicholas of Cues had authorised the prior of St James on to sell two thousand indulgences to Frankfurt citizens. Since Cues, in his licence to produce these forms, uses the un-usual word *expressio*, it is reasonable to conjecture that this word had been pressed into service to refer to the new printing process (otherwise we find *imprimere* rather than *exprimere* used at the time for "to print"). But as no example of this edition has so far been found, we must return to the above-mentioned letters of indulgence of 1454–55. The example in the possession of Göttingen University Library (see Plate 11) uses for its text face a printed bastarda, a letter form which copies a hand in which legal documents were written. The DK-type is used for the two headings. The copy reproduced comes from the fourth edition of this item in 1455, is printed on vellum and has the date 26 February 1455 inserted by hand.

There is a parallel 30-line setting of this indulgence which uses the B42-type for the displayed headings. This leads us to conclude that it appeared from the same printing office as the B42, whereas the 31-line version came from the jobbing printing works.

One of the most active champions of a Turkish crusade was the imperial secretary Eneo Silvio Piccolomini, who addressed the imperial assembly in Frankfurt am Main on 15 October 1454 (when he was apparently able to examine printed sections from the *Gutenberg Bible*). On that occasion the crusading preacher Johann Capistrano, one of the most eloquent of anti-Turkish agitators, also spoke. Therefore it is not surprising, given these proximities of time and place, that the first surviving pamphlet from Gutenberg's office should deal with the Turkish crisis. It took the form of a calendar for the year 1455 entitled *Eine Mahnung der Christenheit wider die Türken* (A warning to Christendom against the Turks). A unique but complete copy of this six-leaved publication set in the DK-type survives in the Bavarian National Library in Munich (see Plate 12). The types in evidence from the setting include 93 lower case characters, abbreviations and punctuation marks, and 15 capitals. We may assume that these type were originally produced for setting Latin texts, because the capitals K, W, X, Y and Z are missing. In the German-language *Türkenkalender* there is a makeshift use of lower case in place of these missing capitals. This fount already appears to have been in use for some time as signs of wear are evident. Under the guise of a calendar for the year 1455 – which offers the dates of twelve new moons as its sole concession to the kind of information expected of a calendar – a rhetorically impressive piece of propaganda has found its way into print:

> Almighty king on heaven's throne [. . .]
> help us prevail in parlous times
> against our foes the Turks and heathen,
> let them suffer for their evil acts of violence,
> committed against many a Christian mortal
> at Constantinople on Grecian soil . . .

In the twelve "months" which follow at first the pope, then the emperor, the European monarchs, the German nation, the free imperial cities, and eventually the whole of Christendom are exhorted to rise up against the Turks:

> Germania, proud teutonic nation,
> who chooses through the seven electors,
> the king who wears the Roman crown by right;
> so shall your admirable and cheerful might
> willingly help combat the armed aggressor
> with all your lordships, counts and knights,
> for Christian faith and lasting salvation.

We may conclude that printing took place in Mainz during the second half of December 1454; that is to say between receiving news of the Turkish war which was made known in Frankfurt on 6 December 1454 and the calendar coming into operation on 1 January 1455.

The lines are run-on although the piece is written in rhymed couplets, and so at first glance it looks as though one is dealing with a text in prose. Apparently this was done to save space, but at the same time the lines have not been justified and retain a ragged right hand edge. The author of the *Türkenkalender* is unknown, but its language is a mixture of Middle Rhenish and Alemannic dialects. It is therefore quite possible that the manuscript originally came from Strasbourg or Alsace before being set up by a Mainz compositor. Attempts to attribute this text have so far remained unconvincing.

In a solemnly promulgated bull of 29 June 1455, pope Calixtus III (successor to Nicholas V) exhorted the whole of Christendom to join in a crusade against the Turks. Everyone was called upon either to take part personally in this crusade, which was set to begin on 1 May 1456, or to support it through prayers and cash donations. The printing of the German translation of this bull must accordingly have taken place between June 1455 and April 1456. The Koblenz-born bishop of Trondheim, Heinrich Kalteisen, who was responsible for propaganda within the German empire, translated the bull himself: "This is the bull and indulgence which our holy father and ruler pope Calixtus has sent and given us against the evil and accursed Turks, anno MCCCCLVI . . ." This pamphlet of 14 leaves with 25 printed pages survives in a complete and unique copy at the Berlin State Library, and was facsimilied at the beginning of the twentieth century. An edition of the same date in Latin is to be found in the Scheide Library, Princeton, USA.

To judge from the condition of the types, the Provinciale Romanum – a listing in Latin of all the bishoprics and archiepiscopal sees – must date from 1457. A substantial fragment, comprising leaves 2 to 9 of what would originally have been ten printed leaves, is housed in the Library of the Academy of Sciences, Kiev.

Once again, in the case of another piece of early printing, the Aderlass- und Laxierkalender for the year 1457 (GW 1286), only a fragment (January to June) survives in Paris. Its none-too-accurate dates for new moons were apparently calculated by the same author as those for the Türken- kalender. Typical of the popular medical literature of the period (as evidenced in manuscripts after 1439), advice was given on the days best for bloodletting and those most propitious for taking laxatives.

A fragment of a further broadsheet from the same period is preserved in Cambridge University Library, the so-called German Cisianus (GW 7054), from which the calendar of feast days could be learned by heart and which was named after the opening words of the (Latin) edition:

"Cisio-Janus" (*circumcisio Januarius* = 1 January). As German versions of these mnemonic rhymes, known since the fourteenth century, were not linked to any specific year, this fragment is difficult to date precisely. The types in use point to the second half of the 1450s.

School books

Alongside those writings needed for use in religious connections – the Bible, indulgences, and the Turkish ephemera with their dual spiritual and worldly propaganda appeal – educational books offered by far the most rewarding texts for the early printers to call upon. The Latin grammars of the late Roman writer Aelius Donatus (c.310–380), the teacher of St Jerome, were particularly widely distributed both in manuscript and in print. His Ars *minor* for beginners served throughout the Middle Ages as the most important introductory textbook, and was printed over 350 times during the fifteenth century, including several editions by the blockbook process; i.e. where the entire text had to be cut letter-by-letter in wood and impressions taken from the woodblock by rubbing. This universally popular textbook quickly established itself as a bread-and-butter item for Gutenberg's earliest workshop. In Mainz during Gutenberg's lifetime at least 24 different editions have been identified, most of them set in his proto-typeface, which has been named after this text as the Donatus and *Kalender* or DK-type. Despite this high number of editions for which there is evidence, not a single complete example has survived from the printing office of Gutenberg or his immediate successors, merely such fragments as have been found in bookbindings, etc. Apparently such schoolbooks were little short of worn to death, but with their relatively small compass of 28 pages they were quick to set up and print.

In order to teach the pupils their five declensions and four conjugations, these were not set out in tabular form to give a schoolmasterly overview, but simply given through run-on examples. The only organisational feature was that a space was left at each section opening for a two-line initial to be added by hand. The verbs chosen as examples for conjugation were – then as nowadays – *legere* and *docere*. Our specimen page (a fragment belonging to the Gutenberg Museum and set in the

B36 state of the typeface, see Plate 13) teaches the participles of *docere*. All the fragments which have been recovered are printed on vellum, indicating that they were destined to pass through many hands in the classroom. The 24 distinct editions in the DK-type can be divided into 26-, 27-, 28- or 30-line Donatuses. The 27-line Donatus fragments are considered to be the earliest and to date from the early 1450s. The 26-line versions were printed in the 1460s. There are also editions set in the polished form of the DK-type – as it was used for the 36-line Bible – and thus likely to have been printed in Bamberg at the beginning of the 1460s.

The Donatus had served as an instructional work throughout the Middle Ages, but it was printing, together with the revival of the linguistic sciences and the cultivation of classical Ciceronian Latin by the humanists, that put paid to it in the sixteenth century; it was supplanted by more sophisticated and voluminous grammars.

Further ephemera

In 1909 a fragment of an *Astronomical Calendar* was discovered in Wiesbaden, that showed the position of the planets for the year 1448 and then again for 1467, etc. The state of the DK-type clearly indicated that printing must have taken place after that of the *Turkish Bull* of 1456. A proof sheet later found in the Jagiellonian Library in Kraków confirmed this typographic discovery, especially since the reverse of this proof contained a trial page for a 40-line Bible in the type later used for the B36. This appears to be a trial proof relating to the pre-history of that Bible, which was probably printed in about 1458. It is possible to conclude from both these fragments that the astronomical data would have occupied six pages which would have been pasted together to give an imposing broadside of 65 x 75 cm. This evidently constituted an early poster for casting and interpreting horoscopes.

There is a single-sided print using the same typographic material which contains a Latin prayer: *Respice, domine sancte pater* from the pen of Ekbert von Schönau in the twelfth century. This broadside measures 20.5 x 29.5 cm, and survives in a unique copy belonging to the University Library in Munich.

Controversy surrounds the dating of a small fragment from the *Sibyllen-Buch*. This scrap of paper is printed on both sides with 'dancing' lines of unevenly impressed types, and little attempt at justification. The fact that the edges of the types are so unclear has to be put down to inadequate casting or even to the suggestion that the casting instrument was still at an experimental stage. But the fact that the fragment is printed on both sides with consecutive texts rather rules out the suggestion that it is just a proof. Far-reaching speculations falter when confronted by the slight extent of a mere 11 lines on each side of the fragment. The text goes back to the corpus of *Sibylline Prophesies* from the fifth century AD, which had been translated into German in Thuringia in 1361. It was repeatedly republished towards the end of the fifteenth and beginning of the sixteenth centuries, and enjoyed great popularity. Since, as we have seen, the DK-type was initially cut and cast with the characters necessary for setting Latin texts, in the *Sibyllen-Buch* (also known as the *Fragment vom Weltgericht* or Fragment of the World Judgment) we are unlikely to be dealing with the earliest surviving piece of printing, as has been variously claimed. Insofar as the wretched condition of the fragment permits an overall assessment, it belongs to the second half of the 1450s.

Alongside the central enterprise of the "work of the books", numerous bread-and-butter titles were set and printed – such as school books, calendars and indulgences – that found a ready market and led to a dependable cashflow during the long drawn-out production of the *Bible*. Simultaneously, alongside the qualitative aspect – the intention to surpass the manuscript book with the *Gutenberg Bible* – the quantitative aspect of the new invention also became apparent; it was those very school books or indulgences in greatest demand which, by virtue of the minimal amount of typesetting involved, could be produced in the hugest editions and against the clock.

THE 36-LINE BIBLE

On the back of the proof sheet containing the Kraków fragment of the *Astronomical Calendar* we find an impression of a *40-line Bible* page set in a developed form of the DK-type. As a larger body was eventually used,

Plate 1: Fictional portrait of Gutenberg. After the copper engraving by André Thevet (1584), this version by Nicolas de l'Armesin, c. 1660. Mainz, Gutenberg Museum.

Plate 2: *Danse macabre* (The Lyons dance of death), Lyons, Matthias Hus, 1499.
The first representation of a printing press (showing setting cases, inking balls,
and adjacent bookbindery).

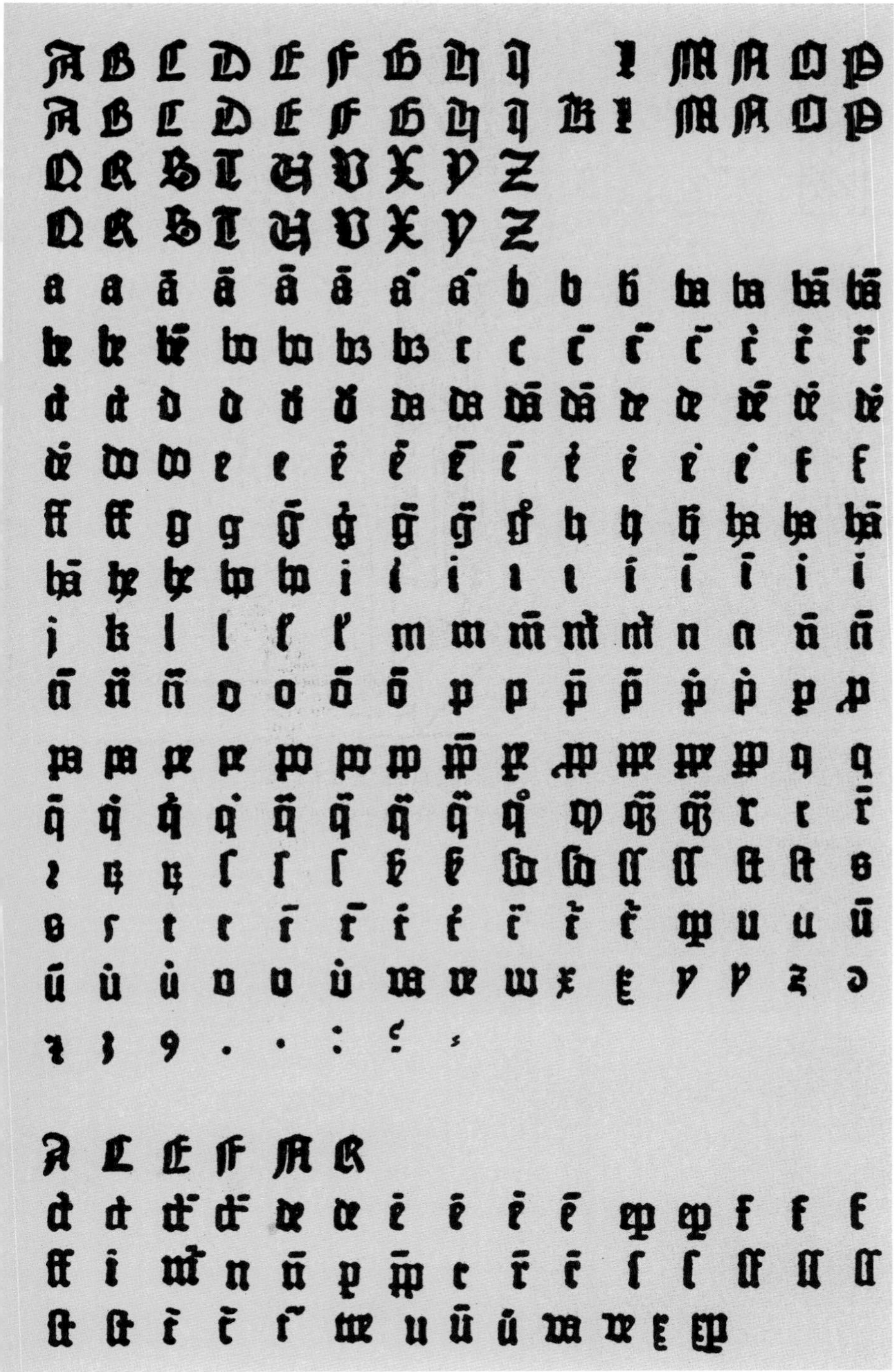

Plate 3: Synopsis of the B42-types.
The bottom 4 lines show characters added later.

Plate 4: Latin Bible, the so-called "Giant Bible of Mainz", fol 2v.
Mainz manuscript of about 1500. Washington, Library of Congress.

Plate 5: The 42-line or Gutenberg Bible, c.1454.
Example belonging to the Biblioteca Pública in Burgos, Spain.

Plate 6: The 42-line or Gutenberg Bible, c. 1454, vol I, fol 1r.
Complete example on vellum at Göttingen State and University Library.

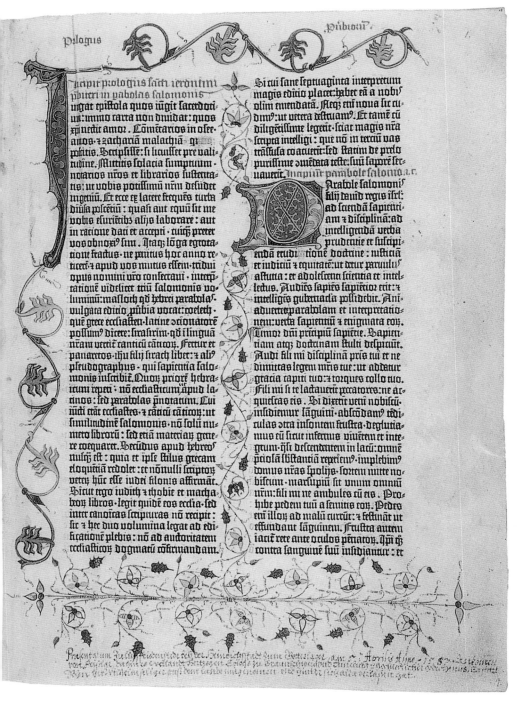

Plate 7: The 42-line or Gutenberg Bible, Göttingen copy, vol 2, fol 1r.
Handwritten ownership entry in lower margin.

Plate 8: The Göttingen Pattern Book. Manuscript on vellum of about 1450, fol 3r.
Göttingen State and University Library.

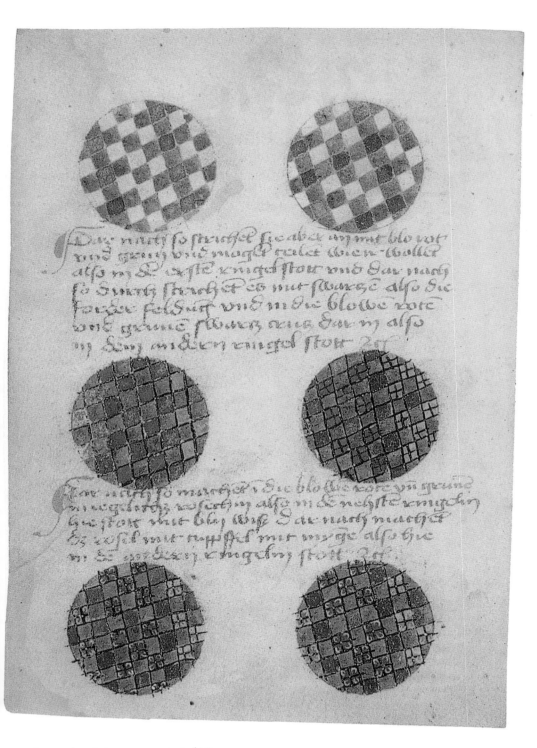

Plate 9: The Göttingen Pattern Book. fol 8v.

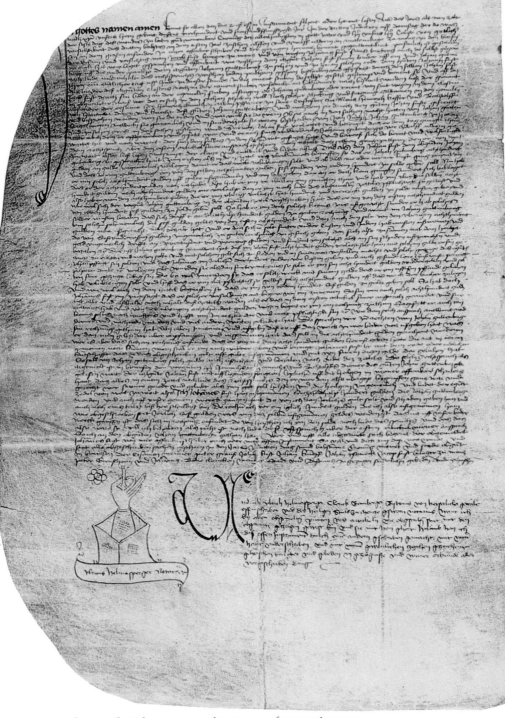

Plate 10: The Helmasperger Legal Instrument of 5 November 1455.
Göttingen State and University Library.

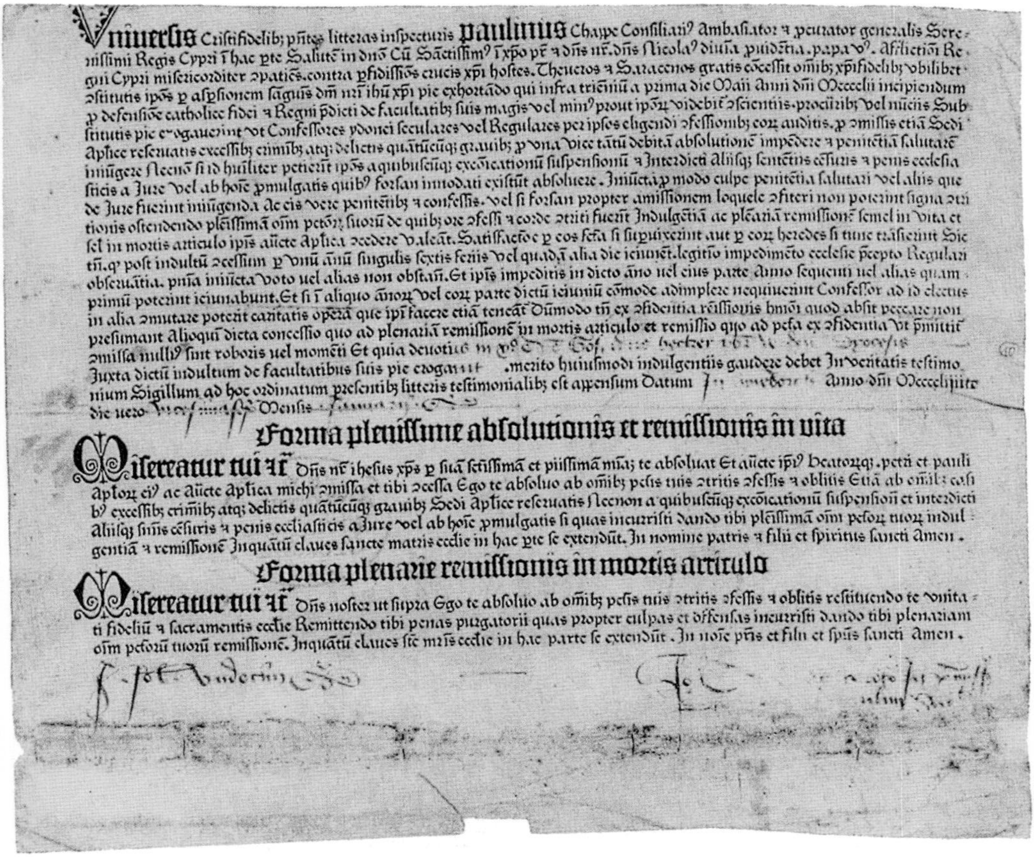

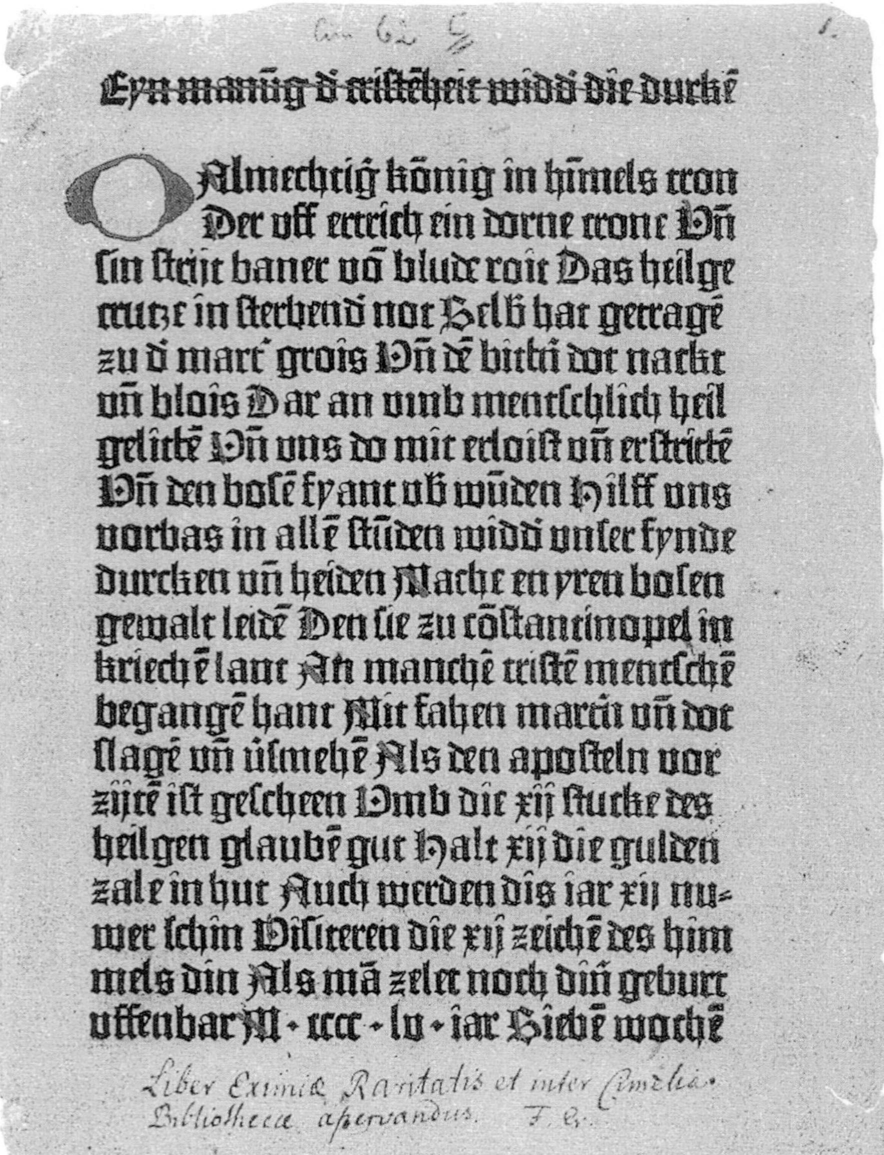

Eyn manüg d' cristenheit widd' die durcke

Almechtig konig in himels tron
Der uff ertrich ein dorne crone Vn
sin streit baner vo blude roit Das heilge
cruce in sterbend not Selb hat getrage
zu d' mart' grois Vn d' bitbi dot nacke
vn blois Dar an vmb mentschlich heil
geliebe Vn vns do mit erloist vn erstricte
Vn den bose fyant ob wuden Hilff vns
vorbas in alle studen widd vnser fynde
durcken vn heiden Mache en yren bosen
gewalt leide Den sie zu costantinopel in
krieche lant An manche criste mentsche
begange hant Mit cahen marcu vn dot
slage vn usmehe Als den aposteln vor
zijte ist gescheen Vmb die xij stucke des
heilgen glaube gut Halt xij die gulden
zale in hut Auch werden dis iar xij nu-
wer schin Visieren die xij zeiche des him
mels din Als ma zelet noch diis geburt
uffenbar M · cccc · lv · iar Siebe woche

Liber Eximie Raritatis et inter Cimelia.
Bibliotheca asservandus. F. E.

Plate 12: Eine Mahnung der Christenheit wider die Türken
(A warning to Christendom against the Turks), Mainz 1454 (H 10741).
Bavarian State Library, Munich. Reproduced from the facsimile with
commentary by Ferdinand Geldner, Wiesbaden, Reichert 1975.

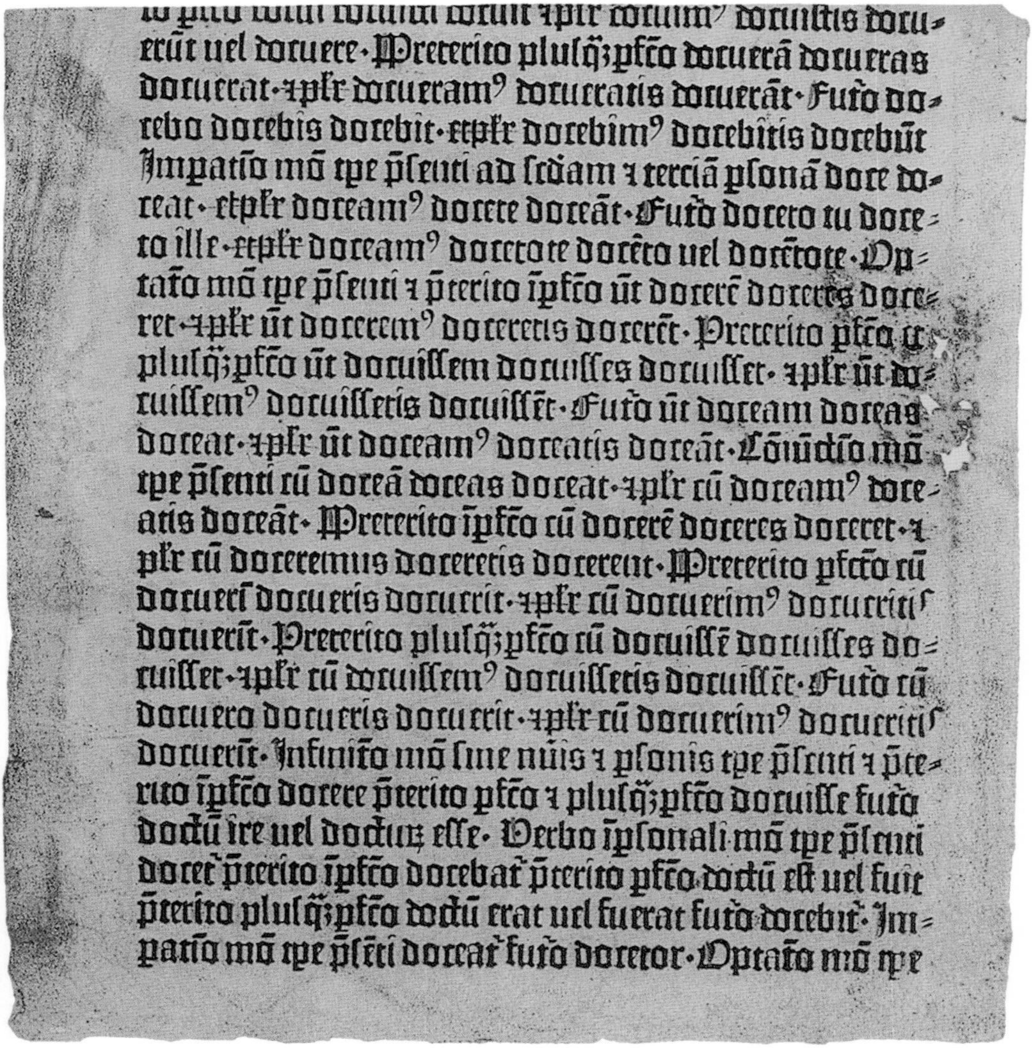

...pito totint tottntat tottnt ꝓptr tottum̄ totuiſtis tott=
erūt uel tottere · Preterito pluſꝗͥ ꝓfēo tottuerā tottteras
tottterat · ꝓ͛ptr tottteram⁹ tottteatis totttrāt · Futō do=
rebo doreebis doreebit · eꝓ͛ptr doreebim⁹ doreebitis doreebūt
Jmpatīo mō tpe p̄ſenti ad ſcdam ⁊ tertiā p̄ſonā dore do=
reat · eꝓ͛ptr doreeam⁹ doreete doreeāt · Futō doreeto tu dore=
to ille · eꝓ͛ptr doreeam⁹ doreetote doreeto uel doreetote · Op=
tatīo mō tpe p̄ſenti ⁊ p̄terito īpfēo ūt doreere doreeres dore=
ret · ꝓ͛ptr ūt doreeream⁹ doreeretis doreeret · Preterito pfēo ⁊
pluſꝗͥ ꝓfēo ūt docuiſſem docuiſſes docuiſſet · ꝓ͛ptr ūt do=
cuiſſem⁹ docuiſſetis docuiſſet · Futō ūt doreeam doreeas
doreeat · ꝓ͛ptr ūt doreeam⁹ doreeatis doreeāt · Cōiūctīo mō
tpe p̄ſenti cū doreeā doreeas doreeat · ꝓ͛ptr cū doreeam⁹ dore=
atis doreeāt · Preterito īpfēo cū doreere doreeres doreeret · ⁊
ptr cū doreeremus doreeretis doreerent · Preterito pfēo cū
docueri docueris docuerit · ꝓ͛ptr cū docuerim⁹ docueritis
docuerit · Preterito pluſꝗͥ ꝓfēo cū docuiſſe docuiſſes do=
cuiſſet · ꝓ͛ptr cū docuiſſem⁹ docuiſſetis docuiſſet · Futō cū
docuero docueris docuerit · ꝓ͛ptr cū docuerim⁹ docueritis
docuerit · Infinito mō ſine nūis ⁊ p̄ſonis tpe p̄ſenti ⁊ p̄te=
rito īpfēo doreere p̄terito pfēo ⁊ pluſꝗͥ ꝓfēo docuiſſe futō
docū ire uel doctuꝫ eſſe · Verbo iꝑſonali mō tpe p̄ſenti
doreē p̄terito īpfēo doreebat p̄terito pfēo doctū eſt uel fuit
p̄terito pluſꝗͥ ꝓfēo doctū erat uel fuerat futō doreebit · Jm=
patīo mō tpe p̄ſēti doreeat futō doreetor · Optatīo mō tpe

Plate 13: Aelius Donatus: Ars minor, fragment, B36-type, c. 1460–62.
Mainz, Gutenberg Museum. Reproduced from facsimile print
of the Gutenberg-Gesellschaft no. 1.

Incipit epla sancti Jeronimi pbri
ad paulinu
pbim. de oib
diuine histo
rie libris.

Rater am
brosius mi
chi tua munuscula perferens de
tulit simul et suauissimas litte
ras: que a principio amicicias
fidem iam pbate fidei et veteris
amicicie noua preferebant: Ve
ra eni illa necessitudo est et xpi
glutino copulata. qua no vti
litas rei familiaris non presen
tia tantu corpoz non subdola
et palpas adulacio: sz dei timor
et diuinaz scripturaz studia co
ciliat. legim9 i veterib; histori
is quosda lustrasse. puincias
nouas adisse. ppos maria tra
sisse: ut eos quos ex libris no
uerant coza q uideret. Sic pita
goras memphiticos uates. sic
plato egiptu et architam tarenti
num eamq oza ytalie que quo
dam magna grecia dicebat la
boriosissime pagrauit. ut qui
athenis mgr erat et potens. cu
iusq doctrinas achademie gig
nasia psonabat. fieret pegrin9
atq discipulus malens aliena
verecude discere qua sua impu
denter ingere. Deniq cu litteras
quasi toto orbe fugietes psequi
tur. captus apiratis et uenunda

tus. etia tyrano crudelissio pa
ruit ductus captiuus uinctus
z seru9: Tame qa philosoph9:
maior emete se fuit. Ad tytu li
uiu lacteo eloquentie fonte ma
nantem. de ultimis hispanie gal
liaruq finibus quosda uenisse
nobiles legim9. et quos ad co
templacionem sui roma non
traxerat. unius hominis fama p
duxit. Habuit illa etas in audi
tum omnibus sclis celebraduq
miraclm: ut urbem tanta ingres
si. aliud extra urbem quererent
Appollonius siue ille magus
ut uulgus loquitur siue philo
sophus ut pytagorici tradut: i
trauit psas. ptransiuit caucasu
albanos. scitas. massagetas.
opulentissima regna indie pene
fuit: z ad extremu latissio philo
amne transmisso puenit ad brag
manas: ut hyarcas in throno
sedente aureo et de tantali fote
potante: inter paucos discipu
los de natura de moribz de die
ru ac sydeu cursu audiret doce
tem. Inde p elamitas. babiloni
os. chaldeos. medos. assirios.
parthos. syros. phenices. ara
bes. palestinos. reuersus alexan
dria: p rexit ethiopiam: ut gig
nosophistas et famosissimam
solis mensa uideret in sabulo:
Inuenit ille uir ubiq qd disce
ret: z semper pficiens. semp se me

Plate 14: The 36-line Bible, Bamberg (?), Albrecht Pfister (?), c. 1460, fol 1r.
Wolfenbüttel, Herzog August Library.

Plate 15: Johann Balbus: Catholicon, Mainz, c. 1460 (GW 3182).
Göttingen State and University Library.

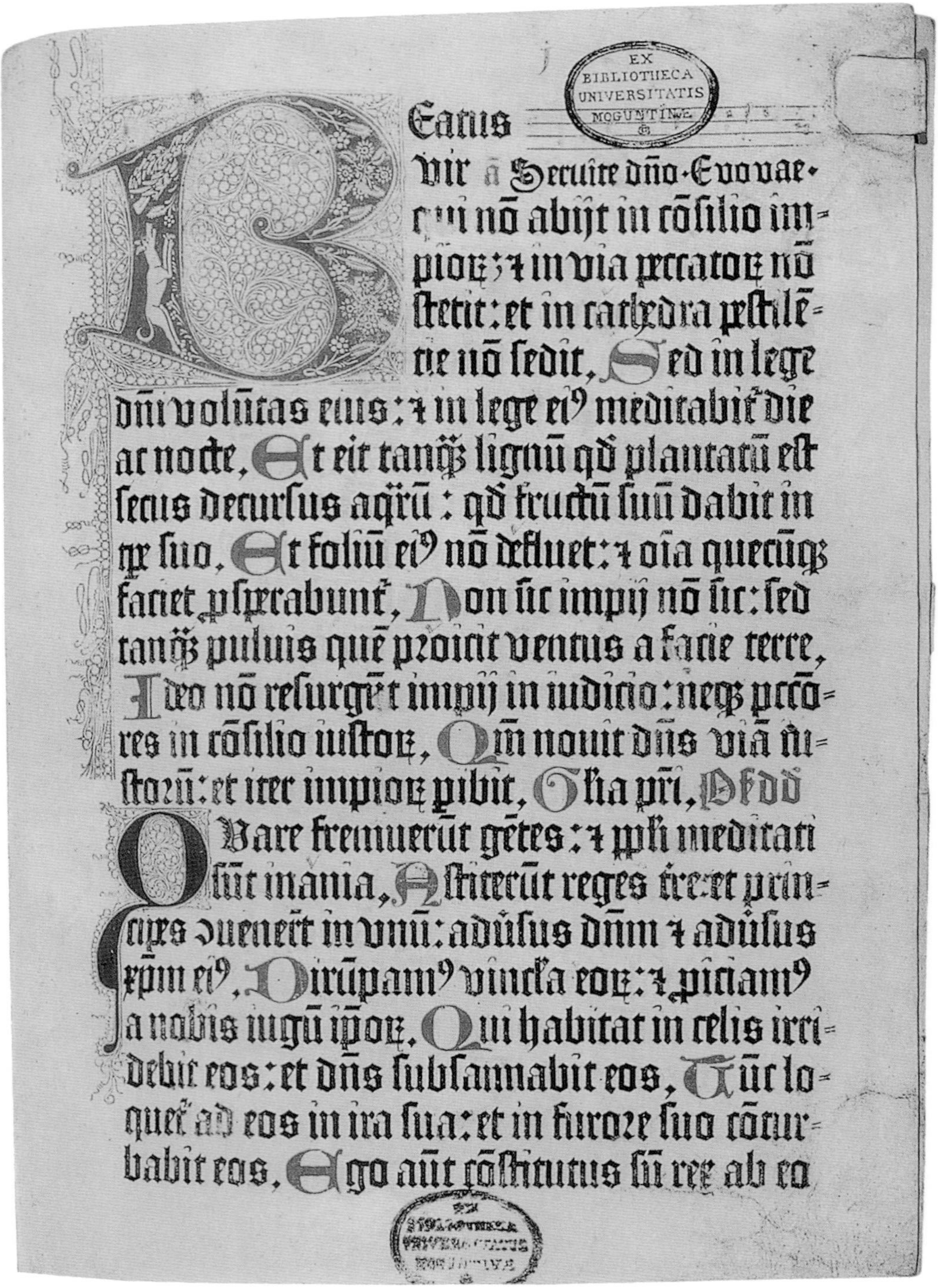

Eatus

vir á Seruite dño·Euouae·
qui nõ abijt in cõsilio impioꝝ: ꞇ in via peccatoꝝ nõ
stetit: et in cathedra pestilē-
tie nõ sedit, Sed in lege
dñi voluntas eius: ꞇ in lege ei⁹ meditabit die
ac nocte, Et erit tãꝗ lignũ qð plantatũ est
secus decursus aꝗrũ: qð fructũ suũ dabit in
tꝛe suo, Et foliũ ei⁹ nõ defluet: ꞇ oĩa quecũꝗ
faciet ꝓsꝑabunt, Non sic impij nõ sic: sed
tãꝗ puluis quē proicit ventus a facie terre,
Ideo nõ resurgēt impij in iudicio: neꝗ ꝑcõ-
res in cõsilio iustoꝝ, Qm nouit dñs via iustoꝝ: et iter impioꝝ pibit, Gła pʼi, Et do

Vare fremuerũt gētes: ꞇ ꝓpli meditati
sũt inania, Astiterũt reges tꝛe: et prin-
cipes conuenerũt in vnũ: aduʼsus dñm ꞇ aduʼsus
xpm ei⁹, Dirũpam⁹ vincla eoꝝ: ꞇ ꝓiciam⁹
a nobis iugũ iꝓoꝝ, Qui habitat in celis irri-
debit eos: et dñs subsannabit eos, Tũc lo-
quet ad eos in ira sua: et in furore suo cõtur-
babit eos, Ego aũt cõstitutus sũ rex ab eo

Plate 16: *Psalterium Moguntinum* (Mainz Psalter), Mainz, Johann Fust
and Peter Schoeffer, 1457. Mainz, Gutenberg Museum.

the decision came down in favour of having 36 lines to the column. (see Plate 14). This increased the extent of the *Bible* appreciably so that, at 1768 pages, it made almost 500 pages more than the B42. Through a rubricator's entry on a single leaf held by the Bibliothèque Nationale we learn that the work of rubrication was finished in 1461. Accordingly printing would probably have taken place between 1458 and 1460. Careful textual examination has shown that the opening 12 pages follow an unknown manuscript source, but thereafter it is continuously set up from a copy of the B42. The B36 is considerably rarer than the B42, only 13 copies and a few fragments have survived. There is no information whatever concerning the size of edition. The *Bible* also lacks any printer's imprint, leaving both printer and place of printing wide open to speculation. Since once again we are confronted by a masterpiece in the setting and printing of the B36, we must assume experienced compositors and pressmen.

The Bamberg printer Albrecht Pfister was printing with these same B36-types by no later than 1461, so he has often been proposed as the actual printer of the B36. But as Pfister's first dated piece, Boner's *Der Edelstein* of 1461, fails to exhibit the same mastery of typesetting, this suggestion does not altogether hold water. More compelling is the evidence that all ten of the sorts of paper used are drawn from mills in the vicinity of Bamberg and that most of the surviving copies were once owned by monasteries close to Bamberg. This raises the question of whether around 1458 it may have been possible for some of Gutenberg's fellow craftsmen to have taken this typographic repertoire with them on their travels and to have set up a new works in Bamberg, with which Albrecht Pfister became associated from about 1460. As Heinrich Keffer, who is named in the Helmasperger legal instrument as Gutenberg's co-worker, set up in business in Nuremberg a decade afterwards, it has often been asked whether Keffer may not have been the B36 printer, very possibly in Bamberg. Albrecht Pfister was formerly secretary to Georg I von Schaumberg, who was chosen as prince-bishop of Bamberg in 1459. Pfister can be shown to have published mostly popular vernacular texts over the next decade, such as the fable collection *Der Edelstein* which has already been mentioned, or the early humanistic tract *Der Ackermann aus Böhmen* by Johann von Tepl.

An electron-spectrographic examination and comparison of the ink of the unique surviving copy of Der Edelstein with that of the B36 could shed light here, but the library concerned has up to now refused permission.

THE CATHOLICON

Whereas all the books so far considered have been set either in the B42-type or the DK-type (forerunner of the B36-type), a new typeface in a much smaller size is found in the Catholicon of 1460 (see Plate 15). This belongs to the Gothic-roman (or fere-humanistica) class of typefaces, since it looks back to humanistically influenced Italian models whilst at the same time combining with them features from the Germanic tradition. Roman type with its excellent legibility evolved swiftly – and primarily in Italy – from the current humanist writing hand, which was in turn a revival of the Carolingian minuscule hand of the eighth century. Most of the writings of classical antiquity had been transmitted in this script, so imitation of the spirit and ideas of the ancients in the content of humanist writings found an external parallel in this attachment to humanist handwriting. (For Italian examples of typefaces see Plates 22 and 23.) But a different Gothic-roman was in use in the Fust and Schoeffer workshop, to be seen in the Rationale of Durandus (1459) and the 48-line Bible of 1462. The fact that Fust and Schoeffer were in possession of this other Gothic-roman typeface makes the theory that only Gutenberg could have printed the Catholicon in about 1460 all the stronger. And Gutenberg had entered into a new business partnership, this time with the Mainz patrician and scholar Konrad Humery.

The Catholicon had been compiled in 1286 by the Dominican, Johann Balbus de Janua (of Genoa) as an aid to clerics studying the Latin Bible, and it had already enjoyed wide circulation during the manuscript era. It contained a Latin grammar, and a dictionary which offered encyclopaedic information throughout with a full explanation of terms. The title Catholicon indicates the comprehensive scope of the work. Despite its small typesize and double-column setting the work calls for no less than 726 printed pages. In consequence, it placed considerable demands on the learning and skill of the compositors and the astuteness of its printer-publisher. The colophon presents a self-confident appraisal of the art of printing and of the city of Mainz, which in English translation reads as follows:

> By the help of the most high, at whose bidding the tongues of children become eloquent, and who often reveals to the lowly what he conceals from the wise; the noble book, *Catholicon*, in the year of our Lord's incarnation, 1460, in the mother city of Mainz of the renowned German nation (which the clemency of God has deigned with so lofty a light of genius and free gift to prefer and render illustrious above all other nations of the earth), without help of reed, stylus or quill, but by a wonderful concord, proportion and measure of punches and formes has been printed and finished. Hence to thee, holy Father, thyself, the Son together with the Holy Spirit, praise and glory be rendered, the triune Lord and one; and thou, devout believer in the universe, who never ceasest to praise the blessed Mary; join your approval with tribute to the Church for this book. Thanks be to God.

Unfortunately this colophon does not divulge the name of the printer, but only the place of printing. Its theologically well-versed author may well have been the actual publisher or supervisor of the enterprise, who allowed the quotations from the Book of Wisdom and the Gospels of Matthew and Luke to find their own resonances. The printing history of the *Catholicon* is still the subject of debate, as three distinct variants on different paper sorts have been identified. Although watermark research may argue for a later dating, the year 1460 (in roman numerals) is plainly given in the colophon. According to an ownership entry, a *Catholicon* was in any case sold to the Marienkloster in Altenburg in 1465.

GUTENBERG'S FINAL YEARS

Traces of Gutenberg's existence after he had handed over his share in the partnership to Fust are slight indeed; in 1458 his name appears as a debtor in the account books of the St Thomas Chapter in Strasbourg. He never repaid the principal sum he had borrowed there in 1442, and the debt was only written off in 1474, some years after his death.

The archbishops' war of 1462 between Adolf von Nassau and Diether von Isenburg which weighed so heavily on the history of Mainz was not without its consequences for Gutenberg. After the sack of the city on 28 October, Adolf von Nassau expelled many Mainz citizens, among them bakers, butchers and the majority of craft workers. In all probability Gutenberg was among this number. It is possible that at this time he retreated to Eltville for a while. But in any case, by 1465 he was back in favour and appointed a courtier by Adolf von Nassau, receiving each year clothing and a generous fixed allowance of grain and wine to be delivered to him at his Mainz residence. He was further released from taxation and other obligations, and the archbishop expressly thanked him for "the agreeable and willing service he had rendered and may or shall render in future time". The delivery of basic commodities tells us that Gutenberg was not at court in Eltville but living and working once more in Mainz. Provision of foodstuffs on this scale was intended in compensation for the "free table" that would otherwise have been open to him at Eltville. The extent to which Gutenberg may have been at the service of Adolf von Nassau in matters to do with print either in Mainz or Eltville may never be known. The fact some of his own typographic material shows up in the first printing works of the brothers Heinrich and Nikolaus Bechtermünze in 1467 in Eltville has led to the suggestion of a communal workshop. And in Mainz too it is apparent that Gutenberg may not have been financing his own activities independently, for after his death Konrad Humery retrieved from the workshop certain equipment that he had loaned to Gutenberg.

Gutenberg died in Mainz on 3 February 1468 and was buried in the church of St Francis. Two subsequent remodellings of the church amounted to its destruction in the sixteenth century and again in the eighteenth, and no kind of inscription or direct evidence of his resting place survives.

THE SUCCESSOR WORKSHOP OF FUST AND SCHOEFFER

A verse colophon to an edition of Justinian's *Institutiones* printed in 1468 by Peter Schoeffer states that he, Peter, had excelled both the Johanns as an expert in metal cutting (*sculpendi lege sagetius*). Thus Schoeffer embarks on his distinguished career as master printer, whilst paying tribute to his predecessors Johann Fust (d. 1466) and Johann Gutenberg (d. 1468). The same point is made in the colophon to the *Annales Hirsaugiensis* (1515) of Abbot Johann Trithemius, namely that Schoeffer had been the one who improved typefounding. Peter Schoeffer from Gernsheim on the Rhine is known to have been a cleric and a calligrapher at the University of Paris in 1449. The Helmasperger Legal Instrument has him as "Peter Girnssheim, cleric of the city and bishopric of Mainz." Only Trithemius records him as the "adoptive son" of Johann Fust, but it is well established that Schoeffer later married Fust's daughter Christine.

Because the partners Fust and Schoeffer furnished their editions with a printer's imprint and mark, their work is plainly identifiable; consisting for the most part of masterpieces of the printer's art, which extend and excel Gutenberg's work in the areas of typographic repertoire, metalcut embellishment and colour printing. On 14 August 1457 their first magnificent folio appeared: the *Psalterium Moguntinum* (Mainz Psalter) on vellum. It contained, for the first time in printing history, a colophon and a printer's device. The imprint reads: " The present book of psalms . . . is achieved through the ingenious invention of printing and letter forms without any use of the pen, and to the worship of God has been diligently brought to completion by Johann Fust, a citizen of Mainz, and Peter Schoeffer of Gernsheim in the year of the Lord 1457, on the vigil of the Feast of the Assumption."

The new art was described in Latin terms as *Ars imprimendi ac caractericandi*. In classical usage *imprimere* denoted an impressing process, thus Suetonius speaks of a coin or a ring with a stamped out image using this verb. Virgil also speaks in the *Aeneid* of a jug with impressed pictures, and Tacitus of wooden rods into which signs had been impressed or cut. This term for the new printing process was reinforced by a second: *caractericare*. Of Greek derivation this time, it meant to incise, to engrave, to sink (a hole) in, or to imprint. A die used in striking coins was called a "character", so in time this notion was transferred to the product so impressed. Whereas *imprimere* denoted the printing process itself, *caractericare* described the types themselves or the typefounding method. *Imprimere* has survived as *imprimerie*, the French word for printing office, and in the English word "print"; we still use the *Impressum* (Ger.) or imprint for the legally required printer's details, or

Imprimatur "Let it be printed" for a (mainly) religious printing permit.

With the *Psalter*, Fust and Schoeffer elevated the basic idea of reproducing the manuscript as closely as possible to a new level of quality. Whilst a mere handful of trial lines of red printing are to be found in the sheets of the *Gutenberg Bible* to be printed first, Fust and Schoeffer used red printing throughout the *Psalter*; supplying the red uncial initials that would normally have been added by a rubricator, and eliminating the illuminator's work as well by means of large metal-cut initials printed in both red and blue. These initials came in three sizes, our illustration (see Plate 16) shows the largest, the magnificent "B", designed on an 8.8 x 8.8 cm square corresponding to the depth occupied by six lines of the large Psalter-type. Then there are 4-line initials for C, D, E and S to be found, and numerous 2-line initials (see the letter "Q" in our illustration). Each of these was produced from metal printing plates; it seems that each initial with its surrounding scrollwork was supported on a type-high wooden block – just as a woodcut would have shared the same standard height from the bed of the press to paper as its surrounding text. The printing sequence would have been as follows: first a page with all its type and ornamental blocks would have been composed, locked up, and inked in black; then the printer would remove those units to be printed in colour, clean and re-ink them in red or blue respectively (the shallow initial plate fitted into a recess in the deeper ornamental block) and replace everything in position to take a three-colour print with a single pull of the press. This was certainly a very tedious process, yet it offered the best guarantee of maintaining register and preventing erroneous overprintings. A few smeared Lombardic initials show that these were transposed or reinserted into the final forme with difficulty. This first example of multi-colour printing in the history of the craft does, however, merit further superlatives: the type repertoire included a large Psalter-type (c. 39 pt) of 210 individual characters and a smaller Psalter-type (c. 32 pt) of 185 characters to which must be added totals of 53 related uncial initials and 228 initials for colour printing in three different sizes. The design of the type and ornamental elements, casting and typesetting must have taken a considerable time, so that preparations would certainly date back to 1453 or 1444, that is to say, to a time when Gutenberg was still in charge of the printing office.

All of the ten surviving copies, each of 340 folio pages, are printed on vellum, testifying once again to their predominant use in liturgical service. The psalms, canticles, hymns, antiphons and responses included are arranged in the order needed by a breviary. Since this *Psalter* was prepared according to the usage of Mainz – the hymns for religious festivals had a special Mainz flavour, for example – it was only valid within that diocese. In the same year a second edition of only 246 pages appeared which was suitable for sale outside the diocese. Another issue appeared in 1459, the *Psalterium Benedictinum* (H 13480), this time revised to suit the requirements of the Bursfeld Congregation of Benedictines. As a larger, paper format was adopted this time, the generous margins gave its pages a more harmonious effect. It is likely that this edition was produced in response to a direct commisssion from the Benedictine order.

Several of the ten surviving *Mainz Psalters* were originally owned by Mainz monasteries, by that of St Victor – with its close Gutenberg connections – for example, or that of St John. A copy from the Ursuline Convent in Hildesheim belonged for a time in the library of Göttingen University, from whence it was presented to George III. It is now in the Royal Library at Windsor Castle.

Besides these Psalter-types, the Fust and Schoeffer workshop made use of a really small but quite legible Gothic-roman for Latin texts. It was first used for a *Rationale divinorum officiorum* of Guillelmus Durandus (6 October 1459, GW 9101), and works of canon law were also set in these same types: such as the *Constitutiones* of Pope Clement V (GW 7077) in 1460 and the *Liber sextus decretalium* of Pope Boniface VIII in 1465 (GW 4848). The outstanding 48-line *Bible* followed from the same workshop, and this was set in a newly-cut Gothic-roman. The use of a smaller size of type may be taken as an indication that these *Bibles* were intended more for personal reading than for use during services, for reading the lessons or teaching. Fust and Schoeffer were able to draw on their experience of red printing for the *Psalter* and as a rule to print display lines such as chapter openings in red. But one can tell from a copy in the Göttingen University Library what problems printing in red could present even to such experienced printers in these early days. It is evident from the page reproduced (Plate 17) that the incipit of the Letter to the

Hebrews has been set in red, but that the incipit for the Letter to Philemon and other copy was left off and had to be inserted by a scribe. The scribe went to pains to imitate the typeface, but lacked finesse when it came to the spacing and contractions. The running headlines have been added by hand in red throughout, but even here the flowing script follows the printed letter forms closely. In the colophon to this volume as well (see Plate 18), Fust and Schoeffer relate, in what is rapidly becoming a formula, that this book has been produced "by the new art of printing and without help of the pen" in the city of Mainz by Johann Fust and Peter Schoeffer in 1462. This 48-line Bible belongs to those masterpieces of early printing that were already finding their way to a growing educated public, regardless of the directives of the Church.

After the death of Johann Fust in Paris in 1466, Peter Schoeffer, married to Fust's daughter Christine, became sole heir to the printing and publishing house. From the 1470s onwards he took an interest in book illustration, and in 1484 and 1485 respectively brought to the market a Latin *Herbarius* and his *Gart der Gesundheit* (Garden of Health), two important and richly illustrated plant books and guides to herbal medicine. Herbalism can be traced back to the philological work of the humanists, who edited the Latin texts of classical antiquity which contained many translations from Greek. The writings of Theophrastus – pupil of Aristotle and founder of botany – had been re-discovered and debated in this way. Theological, philosophical, medical, folkloric and natural scientific treatises and interpretations found their way into these books that conveyed the sum of medical knowledge in the classical age. When Peter Schoeffer issued his Latin *Herbal* in 1484, using his Psalter-types for the headings, no author's name was mentioned – but then there was nothing unusual in that. It set out to be a compilation of basic instruction about medicinal herbs, intended for the widest popular audience. A total of 150 plants are depicted, mostly in outline, by woodcuts in its 348 pages (see Plate 19). Hatched shadings are used sparingly, and most of the surviving copies have been fully coloured. Because the plants are represented so stiffly, it has been suggested that most of them may have been drawn from pressed flowers.

This edition caused such a stir that pirated copies appeared in the same year from the brothers Hist in Speyer and a year later from Johann Petri in Passau. As no protection existed for originator's rights, this practice went on for many years to come, and, with all its disadvantages, it contributed massively to the spread of knowledge.

In March 1485 Peter Schoeffer brought out a still more popular version in the vernacular under the title *Gart der Gesundheit*. He prepared 378 new woodcuts to illustrate its 720 large-format pages. Here again the author's name was only to be found hidden away in the text, but it was clearly the work of Johann Wonnecke from Kaub. In contrast to the *Herbal*, this text was not extracted from classical sources but offered a state-of-the-art summary of fifteenth-century knowledge of medicinal herbs. One of the main sections gave an account of the pharmacological properties of plants, and also of animal and inorganic materials. A second section dealt systematically with laxatives, fragrances, gums, fruits, seeds, roots, gemstones and animals. A short section was given over to the urine. A form of index gave catchwords for a total of 313 illnesses, recommending the relevant herbs to use.

The *Cronicken der sassen* by Konrad Bote (or Botho, fl. 1475–1501) is worthy of note as a further important vernacular publication from Schoeffer's office (see Plate 20). This much-read Middle Low German "Saxon Chronicle of the World" dating from 1490 gives an annalistic account from the creation of the world to 1489. With numerous woodcut illustrations, coats of arms and decorative initial types, it was printed in Mainz by Peter Schoeffer in 1492 (GW 4963).

Thus Peter Schoeffer became heir in Mainz to Gutenberg, whose invention he improved upon in many technical details, also transforming the trade structures he had inherited with a true publisher's acumen. In 1479 he obtained citizenship of Frankfurt-am-Main, making it more convenient to have a presence at the book fair there and to participate in the international market in books in Latin which had grown up so rapidly.

Of the few further Mainz printers whose work has lasting significance, mention should be made of Erhard Reuwich, painter and maker of preliminary drawings on woodblocks. He accompanied Bernhard von Breydenbach, dean of Mainz Cathedral, on his travels to the Holy Land in 1483 and sketched the most important cities, islands and landscapes. The completed woodcuts made from his drawings formed large format folding plates to the report of Breydenbach's journey; to this day a key source for geographical history as well as a landmark in the art of the woodcut. In the years which followed, these detail-packed illustrations were frequently recut, and they still form an outstanding source for the contemporary appearance of Venice, the island of Rhodes or Jerusalem. The first Latin and German editions (GW 5075, 5077) appeared in 1486, and a Low German one (GW 5081) in 1488. The printer's imprint in the German edition states that Erhard Reuwich has printed these books "at his house". But as the types used are those of Peter Schoeffer, it is more likely that this exceptional printing task was a joint enterprise between workshops. Further editions were printed using the original woodblocks in Lyons and Speyer in 1490 and by Paul Hurus in Saragossa in 1498.

After Peter Schoeffer's death in 1503 his son took over his office, in which his first concern became printing classical Latin texts to meet university requirements. In 1509 he published the first German translation of Livy, which he decked out with 214 woodcuts and had to reprint seven times in his own workshop. In his first publication of 1505, he paid homage to Gutenberg and to his own father, and evaluated their respective contributions: "In Mainz the sagacious Johann Gutenberg discovered the wonderful art of printing, thereafter it was improved and perfected thanks to the industry, outlay and efforts of Johann Fust and Peter Schoeffer in Mainz."

The spread of printing

Part and parcel of the phenomenon of Gutenberg's invention was the incredible speed with which it spread throughout Europe, whilst achieving astonishing quality in the earliest printing to come from each and every centre. At first the new technology was free to develop without regulation by governments, princely houses or the Church, nor is there any evidence that any restrictions were imposed by the guilds or others. A Bible with 36 lines (B36, see Plate 14) had been printed before the close of the 1450s in Bamberg, from which city Ulrich Boner's *Der Edelstein* carries a firm completion date of 14 February 1461. Its printer Albrecht Pfister issued the most significant document of early humanism in Germany, Johann von Tepl's *Der Ackermann aus Böhmen* (see Plate 21), from the same workshop. Johann Sensenschmidt was at work in Bamberg by no later than 1481, printing a *Missale Benedictum* (31 July 1481) and further liturgica.

Printing was already taking place in Strasbourg at roughly the same time as in Bamberg; a copy of a 49-*line* Bible printed there by Johann Mentelin is undated, but was rubricated in 1460. Mentelin (*c*.1410–78) used his own typefaces, a Gothic-roman and further purely roman founts. In general he dispensed with fitted initials or woodcuts and concentrated on textually accurate editions of the fathers of the Church, of Augustine, Aquinas, Jerome and Albertus Magnus, in parallel to the *Opera* of Virgil and the *Comoediae* of Terence. He was responsible for printing the *First German Bible* (GW 4295, see Plate 54), which, despite its antiquated language, formed a not insignificant basis for further biblical versions in the vernacular until Luther's translation appeared. He picked up a few tips from the experienced manuscript manufacturer and distributor Diebold Lauber of Hagenau in Alsace and printed medieval court poetry, including Wolfram von Eschenbach's *Parzifal* (H 684) and the *Jüngeren Titurel* (H 6683) in 1477. He was also engaged in bookselling, as a list of his – one of the earliest sales advertisements of its kind – testifies.

But the first journeymen printers of all were active not only in Bamberg and Strasbourg, but also in the commercial metropolis of Cologne. The first printer there, Ulrich Zell from Hanau (c.1435–1503), could claim direct links with the birthplace of printing, having learned his craft from Fust and Schoeffer in Mainz before setting up at Cologne in 1464. It is probable that his edition of Cicero's *De officiis* was ready for publication by 1465; the start of an extensive output of some 140 titles, 95 per cent of which were in Latin (theological works for the most part, but also humanistic texts). In terms of the number of titles printed, Cologne soon outranked the other German printing centres. It demonstrated that commercial centres offered the best conditions for the new trade to flourish. Whilst Mainz and Bamberg could only muster small production totals for the decades which followed, those for printing offices situated in major trading centres such as Augsburg (1468), Nuremberg (1470) and Lübeck (1475) continued to soar.

ROME

The route over the Alps to the south was crucial in the spread of printing, and to the outstanding and artistically independent art of printing in Italy which was soon to stimulate the whole of Europe. The German printers Konrad Sweynheym (d. 1477) and Arnold Pannartz (d. 1477) were working in the Benedictine monastery of Sancta Scholastica at Subiaco in the Sabine hills west of Rome as early as 1465. Their first publication, dated 29 October 1465, was an edition of Lactantius, active at the start of the fourth century (H 9806). This father of the Church played only a marginal role in late antiquity and the Middle Ages, but he was rediscovered by the humanists on account of his Ciceronian style and promoted as the "Christian Cicero". A further 14 editions followed this *editio princeps* in the incunabula period alone.

That same year saw Sweynheym and Pannartz's printed edition of Cicero's *De oratore* (GW 8742), and Augustine's *De civitate* (GW 2874) followed in 1467. This last apparently proved to be big business for the monastery, as the earliest customs document that we possess for the book trade records that the monastery had sent 60 copies of this title to Rome. In the following year as well books to the value of 1400 to 3000 ducats at a time were supplied from Subiaco to Rome.

Sweynheym and Pannartz themselves had moved to Rome in 1467; where Ulrich Han (d. 1479) from Ingolstadt was already at work. He had published the *Meditationes* of Cardinal Juan de Torquemada (H 15722) in 1466 and was to issue classical authors over the next few years, before concentrating on canonical works and papal bulls and addresses. A petition addressed to Sixtus IV in 1472 by Giovanni Andrea Bussi, Bishop of Aleria, requesting support for Sweynheym and Pannartz in view of their unsold stocks, sheds light on their further activities and their close association with the Curia. This letter shows than a typical print run would be 275 copies, and that an extensive backlist had built up. The only item to have sold out was a *Donatus* with which they had launched their publishing activity back in Subiaco. Early printers at a variety of locations found by bitter experience that Latin grammars and school books continued to sell like hot cakes, but that the market for the wealth of Roman classics which had survived in manuscript was soon satisfied and that it was necessary to move on to new outlets with new wares. Sweynheym appears to have used his contacts with the Curia in 1496 to obtain a five-year monopoly to print an indulgence for his home parish of St Michael in Schwanheim in the diocese of Mainz.

We may infer the close relations between the Curia and the German dioceses, or rather between a handful of prominent representatives of the Church, from a dedication from Giovanni Andrea Bussi to Pope Paul II which appears in the *Epistolae* of St Jerome printed by Sweynheym and Pannartz in Rome in 1468. In it Bussi, who later became the Vatican's first librarian, praises the importance of printing and the special significance of the invention for Germany and names Nicholas of Cues above all others as the great patron of the new art: "Germany is in fact worthy, privileged, and to be praised for centuries to come, as the inventor of this beneficial art . . . It is that which the soul, rich in honours and meriting heaven, of Nicholas of Cues, Cardinal of St Peter in Vinculis, so fervently desired; that this holy art, whose shoots became visible at that time in Germany, should be transferred to Roman soil. May this wish . . . find fulfilment during your pontificate."

Nicholas of Cues (d. 1464), who had apparently turned to Mainz in the matter of having an indulgence printed as early as 1452, and who had stood up for the free dissemination of knowledge and religious doctrine during his lifetime, is here openly spoken of as the middleman between printing in Germany and the development of those techniques in Italy. This encourages the speculation that after journeymen printers were forced to leave Mainz in consequence of the archbishops' war of 1462, they may possibly have found a home in Rome – or more specifically in Subiaco – through his intervention. Although there is no supporting evidence for this in detail, the continuity between the theological interests of Nicholas of Cues and his support for printing is striking.

Sweynheym and Pannartz, and Ulrich Han as well, found a further religious patron in the abbot of Subiaco, Cardinal Juan de Torquemada (a relative of the Spanish inquisitor). His *Meditationes* having formed Ulrich Han's first Rome publication of 1466, Han became a papal *familiare* that same year, and was thus able to lobby the pope directly for a chaplaincy of the church of St Ulrich, Vienna.

Among Sweynheym and Pannartz's productions was an edition of Cicero's De *officiis* (GW 6924, see Plate 22) which was completed on 24 January 1469. The handsome, wide-margined copy at Göttingen University Library with its pleasing roman typeface is surrounded by an interlaced border, showing northern Italian influence, incorporating an initial "Q" in gold, a portrait of the author to the right and an empty wreath into which the owner's arms might be set at the foot. This volume contains interesting signs of use in its underlinings and copious marginal annotations. Rome remained the most important centre of Italian printing throughout the incunabula period, with evidence for over forty printing houses, of which about twenty-five were operated by German printers.

VENICE

Italian-German cultural and academic connections increased markedly in the second half of the fifteenth century, and quite a few patricians' sons from Nuremberg or Augsburg studied the humanities or medicine and law in Italy. But we also find numerous craftsmen, architects and master builders on their travels south of the Alps. The rich interchange of scholarly printers between Germany and Italy in these decades simply formed part of a prevailing cultural scene. Venice's first German printer, Johann von Speyer, puts these matters into perspective in the colophon to his edition of Cicero's *Epistolae ad Familiares* (GW 6800) of 1469:

> Each German once brought home a book from Italy
> For which a German would pay as much again today.
> Since Hans von Speyer shows how to write books better,
> Whom none surpasses in these arts with brazen letter.

Johann von Speyer's origins are unknown, but since one "Hans von Spyre" surfaces as witness to a Mainz document, it has repeatedly been suggested that he may have learned typesetting and presswork there in Gutenberg's day. In 1469, he was awarded a monopoly of printing in Venice for five years by the *collegio* (an organ of Venetian government). However, he had died by 1470, and the business was continued by his brother Wendelin. As in other Italian cities it was the classical Latin writers and legal works that were printed most frequently. The Speyer brothers' printing house was responsible for the first *Bible* in Italian (1471, GW 4311), and for an important product of Italian humanism in the vernacular, the *Canzoniere* of Petrarch in 1470 (GW 12753). A clear, robust roman type is typical of Venetian printing in these early years.

Venice's next printer of importance, Nicholas Jenson from Sommevoire near Troyes, had in all probability also learned his craft in Mainz. He was master of the mint to Charles VII of France, and had been sent to Mainz in order to discover the secrets of printing. From 1470 he began to issue the Latin classics and Church fathers in Venice in a particularly well-cut and harmonious roman type (see Plate 34, showing his 1472 edition of the Elder Pliny's *Naturalis historia*). Jenson ran his office as a syndicate with two German merchants at the Fondaco dei Tedeschi. He was made a papal count in Rome in 1480 and was highly honoured at the time of his death.

There was yet a further German printer active in Venice at this time, Erhard Ratdolt from Augsburg. He had earlier spent some time working with the Nuremberg astronomer and printer Johann Regiomontanus, whose *Calendarium* he printed in an elegant Venetian roman with decorated initials and borders in both Latin and Italian editions (H 13776, H 13789). The actual initials used (white-line capitals and scrollwork out of black) had previously only been used by Regiomantanus himself in Nuremberg. Ratdolt refined these in his Venetian office, and added to them with further decorative strips and borders in the Italian style. One of his finest achievements was Euclid's *Elementa geometriae*, finished on 25 May 1482 (GW 9428). Not only are his deeply-cut white-line borders seen here to fine effect, but geometrical diagrams are printed from woodcuts for the first time (see Plate 35).

The next phase of Venetian printing is dominated by the Italian Aldus Manutius (1449–1515), who opened a printing house there with the express intention of publishing editions of the Latin and Greek classics (see pp. 75–6) One of his loveliest and best-known books is the *Hypnerotomachia Poliphili* (The strife of love in a dream of Poliphilo) of 1499; its Italian text illustrated by 172 woodcuts (GW 7223, see Plates 24 and 25). Its author, Fra Francesco Colonna (whose true identity is still hotly debated), guides the reader with his sleep-walking hero Poliphilo through a fantastic world of mythological riddles and allusions. The printing of this at once obscure and fascinating text presented Aldus with formidable challenges. And if it is universally regarded as the "most beautiful printed book of the Renaissance" then this is not on account of its light and regular typeface alone, but for the careful shape given to each individual page, and the way in which the delicate woodcut illustrations with their wealth of iconographical playfulness fall inevitably into place. Illustration and type areas find a perfect harmony here, perhaps for the first time, and on many pages the text terminates in a tapering inverted pyramid that supports the allegorical illustration placed above. For all the lightness of the typography, many lines are set in the capitals of the text with the formality of Roman lapidary inscriptions. The careful composition of the woodcuts is matched by the elegance of their cutting which puts them in a different class from earlier woodcuts, which were still dependent on hand colouring for their effect, or from contemporary work north of the Alps. These illustrations are no mere afterthought or addenda, but a creative component in the presentation of a literary text. In its travels from Germany to Italy, printing had undergone transformation and acquired autonomy in matters of design and typography. Towards the end of the century this flow was reversed, and journeymen and master printers returned from Italy bringing fresh thinking to German book design. Amongst these was Erhard Ratdolt, who, after some ten years of forward-looking work in Venice, returned to set up his press in Augsburg in 1486 and produced a specimen sheet which showed as well as rotunda types, three sizes of roman and a Greek typeface.

Johann Numeister (c.1435–1512) returned to Mainz where in all probability he had learned to print in 1457, from Foligno in Italy where he had been one of the earliest printers of the Italian humanists, incidentally printing the first edition of Dante's *Divina comedia* in 1472. (GW 7958). In 1479 he printed Juan de Torquemada's *Meditationes*, probably after he was back in Mainz (H 15726). This edition contains 34 metalcuts, which copy the woodcuts from Ulrich Han's Rome edition of 1466. Numeister's travels led him further to Albi and Lyons, where he became one of France's earliest printers as well.

PARIS

It is not possible to cover the spread of printing within individual European countries in any detail in this study. A couple of examples from France and England must suffice to show the close links between the German art and its further development in Europe. The advantages of printing for the spread of ideas and instruction were soon grasped by the universities. Accordingly the first printing office in France was set up within the University of Paris in 1470. The prior of the Sorbonne, Johann Heynlin (1435–96) and the rector and university librarian Guillaume Fichet (1433–96) charged Ulrich Gering (d. 1510) from Constance, Martin Cranz (1440–c.1480) from Strasbourg and Michael Friburger (d. after 1477) from Colmar with printing classical and humanist writings, for which they used a fairly large roman type. In 1473 the three printers set up on their own account in the rue Saint-Jacques and began to publish those standard theological works which had already brought the best returns to Mainz's proto-typographers: a *Vulgata* in 1476 (GW 4225) and the *Rationale divinorum officiorum* of

Guillelmus Durandus in 1475 (GW 9108). Lyons followed Paris as a further major French printing city in 1473, Albi in 1475 and Toulouse in 1476.

Within a decade of Gutenberg's death in 1468, his technology had spread right across Christian Europe, attracting resourceful followers and specialists, who made improvements to the process itself as well as reorganising the channels of book distribution. Gutenberg and Schoeffer had begun by closely aligning themselves to the tradition of manuscript production within a framework of learning dominated by the Church, and had printed the Latin *Vulgate* and familiar liturgical books as well as indulgences, linguistic reference works, grammars and the like; all aimed at a Europe-wide, Latin-reading market. In Italy, apart from the Curia, it was the humanists first and foremost who adopted the new technology and printed – in line with their belief in a universal human capacity for education – the venerated Latin texts of Roman antiquity and the neo-Latin output of their contemporary literary successors. In France, besides Latin *bibles*, it was those texts needed for teaching purposes by the University of Paris that found their way into print.

THE BOOK IN BRITAIN

The introduction of printing to England followed an independent course, in that it took place relatively late on and was concerned almost exclusively with English literature in the vernacular produced solely for an internal book market. This situation also reflected the insular nature of England's cultural outlook in the fifteenth century, which was not as receptive towards the new ideas of Renaissance humanism as were more southern lands. Likewise the Pope was far enough away in Rome for independent and national religious usages to be cultivated. So it is not possible to trace the spread of printing to England back to Church or university roots, but rather to the activities of an erudite merchant, who in the second half of his life brought his rich business experiences as a wool trader – and at the same time his predilictions as a translator and promotor of literature in English – to bear on this novel enterprise.

The history of the book, and equally the history of literature and education, in England is crucially determined by William Caxton (c.1422–

1491). This learned cloth merchant moved to the Netherlands whilst young and rose to eminence as a businessman in Bruges; from time to time he undertook diplomatic assignments for the Crown, becoming Head of the Guild of the Merchant Adventurers and Governor of the English Nation at Bruges. He was active in the Netherlands, based in Flanders, Bruges and Ghent, for more than thirty years. His mercantile prominence made him a kind of Minister of Foreign Affairs for Britain and brought him into personal contact with the King and also with the King's sister Margaret of York, Duchess of Burgundy, and other members of the royal entourage.

Margaret of York was herself greatly interested in literature and manuscripts, and Caxton repeatedly procured manuscripts for her and translated Raoul Lefèvre's *Receuils des histoires de Troye* into English at her behest. He completed the work of translation on 19 September 1471 during a stay in Cologne, as he writes himself in the prologue to the printed version (Bruges 1474): "And ended and fynisshid in the holy cyte of Colen the XIX day of septembre the yere of our sayd lord god a thousand four honderd sixty and enleuen." This statement establishes Caxton's residence in Cologne in 1471, and further documents found in the archives of that city confirm his presence in the following year.

His successor as printer at Westminster, Wynkyn de Worde, later asserted that Caxton had first printed the encyclopedia *De proprietatibus rerum* (1472) by the Franciscan friar, Bartholomaeus Anglicus, in Cologne at this time; but it is probable that Caxton merely sponsored the publication of this encyclopaedia by his fellow countryman, also known as Bartholomew de Glanville. But it was apparently then that he learned to print in the workshop of the typefounder and master printer Johann Veldener.

Together with Veldener, he left Cologne at the end of 1472 and they moved to Bruges, where Veldener let Caxton print vernacular titles for the English market, amongst them his own translation of *The Recuyell of the Historyes of Troye* (c.1473, H 7048). This is considered to be the first printed book in the English language, and its idiosyncratic bastarda typeface from Veldener's workshop was to become typical for his subsequent publications.

After he had printed a further four titles, he returned to England in 1475/6 and set up his own workshop in the precincts of Westminster

Abbey. There he began straightaway to print Chaucer's *Canterbury Tales*, dividing the work between two presses. In between he produced indulgences, just as Gutenberg had done, as a profitable side-line bringing rapid returns. He further attuned his publishing programme towards the English-speaking market, leaving liturgical and theological tomes in Latin and the works of classical authors to the continental incunabula printers. Amongst some one hundred volumes, he offered *The Chronicles of England*, *The Mirrour of the World* (the first English book with woodcuts), *The Golden Legend* and *The Dictes and Sayengs of the Philosophers* (c. 1477, see Plate 26). This last leans heavily on a manuscript by Guillaume de Tignoville entitled *Les ditz moraulz des philosophres* which had been translated into English by Anthony Woodville, second Earl Rivers. Caxton writes in an epilogue that for some incomprehensible reason Rivers had omitted to translate Socrates's statements about women, so that he had translated these himself and reinstated them. Twenty of his publications were translated into English by Caxton himself. Amongst these were assorted commissions from the English king, including the *Fayttes of Armes and of Chyualrye* (Westminster 14 July 1489, GW 6648) translated from Christine de Pisan's *Faits d'armes et des chevalerie*. The French writer Christine de Pisan (1365–1430) was born at Venice and became celebrated for her allegorical fiction. Her political and historical record of Charles V and his court (1405) was also translated by Caxton. Henry VII placed his own manuscript of this work, still to be found in the British Library, at Caxton's disposal for the purposes of his translation. Such close connections with the royal house doubtless made the successful marketing of these titles easier to accomplish.

With the *Statutes* of Henry VII of 1490, Caxton published the first work of jurisprudence in English. His numerous prologues and postscripts to his books reveal his close contacts with the highest circles in Westminster and London and his privileged access to the monarchy. That so many of his works evidently went through second and later editions suggests that in all probabilty he achieved considerable financial success as well. After his death in 1491, the workshop "at the sign of the Red Pale" near Westminster Abbey continued to flourish under his colleague Wynkyn de Worde.

With the exception of Caxton the other early printers in England were foreigners who were nevertheless expressly encouraged in their activities through an act of parliament of Richard III in 1484. Not until the very different political climate of 1534 were foreign printers and booksellers prohibited from pursuing their occupations in England. Apart from Caxton, his colleague and successor, the Dutchman Wynkyn de Worde, who relocated the press to London's Fleet Street in 1500, is worthy of mention, as is Richard Pynson (d. 1530). From 1490 onwards Pynson, who came from Normandy, printed in a most agreeable typeface and from skilful woodcuts. Among his successes was the translation of Giovanni Boccaccio's *De casibus virorum illustrium* by John Lydgate (*c.* 1370–1450) entitled *The Fall of Princes* (London 1494, GW 4431).

Smaller printing offices were set up after about 1477 in nearby St Albans and at Oxford, where Theodoric Rood came from Cologne and printed some twenty classical and patristic texts with no great success; or as early as 1480 in the City of London itself, where John Lettou, a Lithuanian who had studied printing at Rome in about 1478/9, and William de Machlinia (i.e. Malines), practised together until 1482.

William Caxton occupies a significant place in the history of printing and literature, but even this is outweighed by his contribution to the emergence of a standard English which overrides the various dialects. So Caxton serves as a significant promoter of a universal English literary language, to be compared in terms of the history of language to Martin Luther and the tremendous impact on the German language of his *Bible* translation. Lutheran writings were at first banned in England, and in the 1520s they were publicly burned. The first translations of the *Bible* into English by William Tyndale (1490–1536) had to be printed in Antwerp, Cologne, Mainz and Worms. and then smuggled into England. The theologian Tyndale visited Luther in Wittenberg in 1524 and resided in the Netherlands after 1529. Closely following Luther's procedure for his German vernacular *Bible*, he translated first the New Testament and then the Old Testament in parts between 1525 and 1534. Arrested and executed under the Inquisition, he was unable to finish the work of translation. His *New Testament*, translated into English with marginal notes by William Tyndale assisted by William Roye, was published in Cologne in 1525, with a second edition appearing from Worms in the following year. The Pentateuch was published in Antwerp in 1530, as *The firste Boke of Moses called Genesis Newly correctyd and amendyd by W.T.*, and a new edition of the New Testament: *The newe Testament, dylygently corrected and compared with the Greke by Willyam Tyndale* appeared there in 1534. Tyndale's translation had a significance for the English language and the course of theology in England which corresponded to the impact of Luther's translation on the German language and continental theology.

After England, printing reached Stockholm in 1483, Istanbul in 1503, Salonika in 1515 and Moscow in 1553. Printing can be shown to have taken place in Goa (India) by 1556 and in Kazusa (Japan) by 1590. Although texts had been multiplied by taking rubbings since the eighth century in the Far East, it was not for a further eight centuries that Gutenberg's method of printing by means of a press became known to the advanced cultures in these parts of the world.

Printing and humanism

It is thanks to a son of the city of Mainz, wrote the German "arch-humanist" Conrad Celtis (1459-1508) at the end of the fifteenth century in an ode, that the Germans may no longer be ridiculed for the intellectual laziness attributed to them by the Italians. For the art of printing had made the great minds of classical antiquity accessible. And, just as Virgil in his *Georgics* had once postulated the migration of the Greek muses to Italy, so Celtis now expressed the desire to transfer the muses, and therewith the gift for true poetry and learning, over the Alps to German lands. Already in 1486, the year of Maximilian's election as German king, Celtis prayed, in another of his odes, to Apollo, patron of poets, that he should come with his lyre from Italy to Germany: "Come then, so we plead, to our coasts, as once you visited Italy's lands; may barbaric tongues then take flight and all darkness be dispersed".

Celtis stressed the difference between uncultivated barbarians, with their awkward speech, and the educated, well-bred Romans. He equated this language deficiency with a cultural one. In doing so he allied himself intellectually with the leading Italian humanists Francesco Petrarch (1304–74) and Lorenzo Valla (1406–57), who insisted on the function of Latin in providing a basis for culture. They valued Latin as the universal language of civilisation and as the language of scholarship and the liberal arts in general. In their view, however, language was not only the medium, but at the same time the source (*semen* = seed) and even the object, of scholarly communication. The Latin tongue became the badge of each true *eruditus* and each *civilitas*, and thus for any social life worthy of mankind. The close identity of Latin with legal parlance and the language of the Church served as proof for crediting Latin with a fundamental character as the defender of a fixed social and spiritual outlook. Through mastering this language one could share in the wisdom it encapsulated. Conversely, the decay of language may be seen in the overall intellectual decadence and the expulsion from Asia and Africa at the end of the Roman empire. Therefore, as the cultivation of Latin became a national task for the Italian humanists – as a stratagem for re-establishing contact with the former greatness of Rome – so Celtis also hoped that it would fall to him to convey the erudition contained within Latin to the German realm, and so equip scholars there to attain proud equality with cultured peoples. In the ode mentioned earlier, Celtis describes how it would be possible to make up for Germany's intellectual backwardness: solely through Gutenberg's technical invention, which allowed, "fixed types to be formed from metal, and the art of writing with reversed letters to be taught" – this is a scant but equally a sensible description of the new technology. It facilitated:

– The issue of classical texts in editions and anthologies which enabled their implicit "wisdom" to be shared.
– The spread of knowledge (as an educational task) through affordable and accurate texts in convenient format.
– A sound basis for university teaching and research.
– The preservation of international and national manuscript treasures.

RENAISSANCE HUMANISM

By Renaissance humanism we understand the deeper engagement with classical and Christian antiquity, a cultural movement aiming at their ideals, shaping religious, political and social life and soon making itself independent as an educative force and embracing the whole wealth of existence. Antiquity came to be seen as a measure of human conduct, and its aesthetic and stylistic categories were taken over as well. A new breed of poets asserted themselves, the *poeta doctus*, or "scholastic poets", taking up a middle position amongst philosophers, scholars and writers and displacing more naturally gifted poets. Their highest aspiration was stylistic mastery after the model of Cicero, whose rhetorical treatises and letters were far more widely received than his philosophical writings. The return to the Greek classics as well was encouraged through the setting up of the first university chair for Greek language and literature at Florence in 1397. Early Christianity, chiefly transmitted through the Church fathers (and above all by Augustine) was naturally equally close to the humanists. Nineteenth-century researchers in the wake of Jacob Burckhardt had left a one-sided picture of a Renaissance humanism with secular, anti-religious and anti-clerical tendencies, in which criteria such as individualism, atheism and immorality were over-emphasised. More recent research has shown, on the contrary, a fruitful alliance between humanism and theology, not only in philosophical questions, but also in forming a view of the human condition. The "humanistic theology" of an Erasmus of Rotterdam (1466–1536) can accordingly be regarded as a connecting link between medieval and reformational theology.

There had already been weighty voices opposed to a stylistic purism devoid of content, notably those of the Florentine politician and humanist Coluccio Salutati (1331–1406) and the Roman rhetorician Lorenzo Valla in Italy. In German-speaking lands it was Erasmus of Rotterdam above all who, in his polemical letters, reprimanded with biting satire a new generation of scholastics who had failed to encounter the classics on creative terms or to understand the enlightened impulse that lay behind *humanitas*. Alongside Cicero, he promoted Horace, Plutarch and Lucian as intellectual models. According to a definition by the authority on humanism Dieter Wuttke, the point at issue for the humanists – in resorting to the priority of ancient classical learning whilst being aware of the dignity and obligation of mankind as the image of God – was to produce new knowledge, new consciousness and new wisdom that would make humanity more ethically mature and bring it closer to God. The unity of the arts and the natural sciences was obvious to the humanists. Beyond the close circle of *studia humanitatis*, which comprised grammar, rhetoric, dialectics, history, poetry and moral philosophy, lay the challenge to engage with the mathematical arts of the *quadrivium*: arithmetic, geometry, astronomy and music. The most evident token of this interplay was the establishment of a "Collegium poetarum et mathematicorum" at the University of Vienna in 1502 by Emperor Maximilian at the suggestion of Conrad Celtis. In his programmatical introductions and illustrated broadsides, Celtis had defined the ideas of Renaissance humanism as an "integrative force" for the whole of thought and action. The woodcut *Philosophia* by Albrecht Dürer which Celtis initiated for his own *Amores* (1502) depicts philosophy as the sum of all spheres of nature and the intellect. The caption within this print summarizes: "What the nature of heaven, earth, air and water stipulates, and what human life comprises, as well as what the fiery God creates throughout the globe: I, philosophy, carry in my breast."

The importance the humanists attached to their own creative task in the educational field led them to ask a lot from the illustration and technical presentation of the printed works they published. These had not only to be textually accurate but also to correspond in outward appearance to their inner worth. This requirement placed great demands on the training of compositors, proof-readers and publishers. A large number of testimonies from printer-publishers have come down to us pointing out how much care has been lavished on the faultless printing of a text. But typography and page layout attracted the attention of the publisher and before long that of the purchaser as well. The selection of the right size of type, or suitable inter-linear spacing, or the use of a fine, smooth paper came to be extensively debated, as did the fundamental preference for roman types as those most appropriate for setting texts of the classics. These types were adapted for printing from the humanistic minuscule, which in turn imitated the Carolingian minuscule in which numerous Roman writers had been handed down. The roman letter was revived from this earlier hand in the course of reproducing classical sources, and was adopted for contemporary humanist writings inspired by the classics. The earliest printing from a true roman typeface on German soil was produced by the mathematician and astronomer Regiomontanus (Johann Müller from Königsberg, 1436–76) at his printing office in Nuremberg from 1474. This type also became the trademark of Johann Amerbach (1443–1513) of Basle, who in 1486 used it to set the Epistolae of Francesco Filelfo (1391–1483).

Erasmus of Rotterdam expressed similar views to Celtis on the prospects printing offered for popular education. In a letter to the Alsatian theologian Johann Botzheim (c.1480–1524) he lamented the intellectual timelag north of the Alps: "Whilst I was a child, the "liberal sciences" began to flourish again in Italy. But whether it was because printing had not yet been invented or because it was still so little known, no books reached us, and everywhere those who wielded the sceptre held forth on the least informed teachings with never a murmer of discontent." After the spread of printing the Italians used the new technology to more appropriate and telling effect in Erasmus's view, and in consequence he appealed – in his Adagia – for public support north of the Alps as well: "Were our princes' [. . .] endeavours on behalf of scholarship as generous-minded as those of the Italians, then the snakes of Froben would not fall behind the dolphin of Aldus in book trade success. Under his motto *Festina lente* ("hasten slowly"), Aldus earned money no less than fame, and both deservedly. But Froben – who always held the staff upright and had no other end in sight than the common good – would not swerve from the innocence of the dove, and displayed the cunning of snakes more in his printer's mark than in his dealing methods, and so became celebrated but not rich."

Erasmus is making a play on the well-known printer's marks of the eminent printers Aldus Manutius (c.1451–1515) in Venice and Johann Froben (1460–1527) of Basle, both of whom did so much to spread his own writings as well as for the diffusion of classical texts in the spirit of Renaissance humanism.

Aldus Manutius produced texts of the Roman and Greek classics set in roman type in swift succession. To this day these "Aldine" editions are regarded as masterpieces of printing. After his studies in Rome and Ferrara and at the recommendation of Pico della Mirandola, Manutius the classical scholar was appointed tutor to the young princes of Carpi (near Modena), Alberto and Lionello Pio. In 1490 he began to set up a printing office in Venice with the support of his pupils and with the express purpose of helping to disseminate the works of Roman and Greek authors. He surrounded himself with linguists and learned editors, took pains to obtain suitable handwritten examplars for printing and provided his own introductory commentaries. His trademarks became the pocket-sized octavo format and the italic text face which Francesco Griffo of Bologna had cut for him by 1501. Aldus also attracted favourable attention with 28 first editions of Greek classical writers, for which he had special types produced that closely followed good calligraphic models (see Plate 36). Aldus corresponded throughout scholarly Europe. Amongst his authors and correspondents was Erasmus, who frequently enthused over his work. In discussing the proverb *Festina lente* in his *Adagia*, for example, Erasmus digresses to praise Aldus Manutius: "Venice is a most illustrious city, but principally it owes its fame to the printing house of Aldus."

This high regard for the productions of his press is clear from a letter making an offer to Aldus dated 1507: "I am sending you two tragedies which I have been bold enough to translate, whether with success you may judge for yourself. Badius [Ascensius, 1461–1535, printer and publisher in Paris from 1503] has already printed them, so he writes, and he thinks with great success since he has evidently sold practically all the copies. But he takes my reputation rather too lightly into account, for everything is crawling with mistakes, and Badius has offered to repair the damage by issuing a second, improved edition. Yet I am afraid of his mending ill with ill, as the Sophoclean saying goes. I should consider my labours to have been immortalised if they could be printed in your smaller types, the most beautiful of all."

Erasmus strove for a typographic handsomeness appropriate to the text, but also for the literal correctness of his works. Like other scholars of his day he maintained a close relationship with his printer-publishers and worked with them not only on questions of which other titles to publish and how many copies to print but also on matters of content and appearance (illustrations, special spacing for schoolbooks, etc.) and correction for the press.

In his collaboration with Johann Froben of Basle, known as the "second Aldus" because he had introduced the use of roman type to that town, Erasmus went so far as to live in the publisher's household whilst his writings were going to press, and to carry out his own proofreading. He supervised there in part the reprinting of his *Adagia*, the Greek New Testament and the *Praise of Folly*. He often mentions this occupation in his letters, full of complaints about his "forced labour in Basle". This symbiosis of author and scholarly publisher also accounts to some extent for the miserly honorariums he was paid. On the one hand a writer's scholarly sense of duty does not lend itself readily to the idea of direct payment for intellectual work, whilst on the other hand authors often received no more than shelter and free copies in settlement for their pains.

Erasmus let his *Moriae encomium* or *Praise of Folly*, which was to become the most brilliant example of satire for the sixteenth century, be printed in Paris in 1511. In it Moria, Dame Folly herself, ascends the pulpit and rebukes the scholars, theologians, judges and high officials. With its dazzling word play, classical allusion and literary genius, this satire, which emulates Lucian, has remained popular to the present day. On a different plane it follows on from *The Ship of Fools* (*Das Narrenschiff*, 1493) of Sebastian Brant (1457–1521). In a sequence of 112 illustrated poems, Brant deals with all kinds of human foolishness including the vices, the absurdities of life, professional peculiarities, fashionable sillinesses and religious aberrations. The image of the ship brings all these frailties of human nature together for a voyage around the human condition. Brant intended the destination of this world of fools to be the recognition of folly and insight into true wisdom. Brant's masterpiece was eagerly taken up by his contemporaries and by the time of his death in 1521, 17 editions had been brought out in the German language and 18 of the Latin version (*Stultifera navis*) by Jakob Locher (1471–1528). This Latin translation, published by Bergmann von Olpe (c.1460–1532) in 1497, secured Europe-wide circulation for *The Ship of Fools* and surely it can not have failed to have influenced Erasmus.

EDITIONS OF CLASSICAL AUTHORS

The most frequently printed classical texts during the incunabula period were the writings of Cicero (GW 6708–7023). Half the 316 known editions come from Italy, from the great printing towns of Rome, Venice, Milan but from Parma as well (see Plates 22, 23 and 27). Predominant among these editions were the letters and rhetorical works, which became celebrated as artistic and stylistic models. Of the Roman writers, more than 80 Ovid editions are to be found, of which more than half are of the *Epistolae heroidum*, which came to be used as a school textbook.

The comedies of Terence were close to these in popularity, and were circulated in Germany after 1470 through Johann Mentelin. Johann Grüninger (1455–1533) brought out a Latin edition in 1496, and in 1499 a richly-illustrated German Terence (H 15431 and 15434). This last was preceded by a Terence with 159 woodcuts printed in Lyons in 1493 by Johann Trechsel (d. 1498), which is a notable achievement in French book art (H 15424). Grüninger's edition is of great importance not only for its critical text and the history of printing, but also in the fields of theatrical and costume history. The woodcut on the titlepage (see Plate 28) shows for the first time a contemporary "Terence stage", and the full-width stage settings at the head of each comedy depict dramatic characters for the first time in the history of book illustration. Text and accompanying commentary are set in double-column and graphically illustrated with 158 woodcuts in the text (see Plate 29).

Jacob Locher's edition of Horace, richly decorated with woodcuts, appeared from Johann Grüninger in 1498 (H 8898). Petrarch numbered the poet of the Odes among his favourite writers. Landino had published a humanistic commentary to Horace in 1482, the first of several. Conrad Celtis discovered Horace for the German humanists when, in 1486, he introduced the Horatian metre in his Ars versificandi.

Virgil's writings occupy a special position quantitatively speaking; at the end of his lifetime they were widely circulated on papyrus rolls – at the express wish of Emperor Augustus – and subsequently transcribed to parchment codices in the fourth century AD. Eight of these codices, more than for any other classical writer, have been preserved from late antiquity. After some fifty generations in which these texts had been copied and recopied by hand, the first printed edition appeared in 1469 in Rome. Hardly a year has gone by since without at least one of Virgil's works appearing, and there were 81 impressions of the Opera omnia alone between 1469 and the end of the incunabula period. Giovanni Andrea Bussi, bishop of Aleria, prepared the editio princeps for the German printers Conrad Sweynheym and Arnold Pannartz in Rome; it contained the additional material that had become customary in medieval manuscript transmission: the Vita of Donatus, the poems of the Appendix Vergiliana and further loosely ascribed Opuscula, and after 1475 the commentary of Servius was generally printed with it. The typographic layout of this commentary took its bearings from manuscript precedents, as so often in these matters. The main text was framed by the commentary, which was set in a smaller size (see Plate 30 which shows a double-page spread with the opening lines of the Aeneid surrounded by Servius's commentary). The modern convention of placing the commentary at the foot of the text page did not come in until the seventeenth century.

The first illustrated edition of Virgil's Opera was printed in 1502 by Johann Grüninger in Strasbourg with 214 large format woodcuts. Grüninger maintained a printing office in Strasbourg from 1482 and put out German prose tales (among them Till Eulenspiegel in 1515), but above all he issued numerous generously illustrated classics in Latin and German. Beside the Terence already mentioned he published the *Carmina* of Horace in 1498, the *Golden Ass* of Apuleius in 1499, *De consolatione philosophiae* of Boethius in 1501, Virgil in 1502 and Livy and Caesar in 1507/8.

Sebastian Brant edited the text for Grüninger's Virgil but he was also at hand to advise on the selection of themes for the illustrations (see Plate 31). These pictures called for a sound knowledge of the Latin text, and of the commentary and classical mythology (the attributes of the Gods, and so forth). The classical settings reflect a German setting of about 1500: timber-framed houses, churches with bells in Troy, Emperor Octavian wearing the German imperial crown, etc. Nor were the draughtsmen and wood cutters – or their advisor in particular – unacquainted with Christian iconography; realism and vividness prevail in the representation. The actual artists are unknown, but we do know that Grüninger's press made use of Hans Baldung Grien, Hans Leonhard Schäufelein and Urs Graf among others.

However it was not only the works of classic authors which appeared, but also works of jurisprudence and the natural sciences. On 24 May 1468 Peter Schoeffer finished printing the *Institutiones Justiniani* (GW 7580); its page layout freshly and sympathetically adapting manuscript models, with the commentary surrounding and set in a smaller size of type than the text (see Plate 32, a later example of this typical arrangement). Of some two hundred editions of the *Corpus iuris civilis* (GW 7581–7777) catalogued in the *Gesamtverzeichnis der Wiegendrucke*, the majority come from Venice, although Heinrich Eggestein (c.1420–88) in Strasbourg and Anton Koberger (d. 1513) in Nuremberg printed editions of Roman law.

The *Historia naturalis* of Gaius Plinius Secundus (23–79 AD), a compendium of classical physics, mathematics, medicine, zoology, geography and astronomy first appeared in 1469 from John of Speier in Venice and was reprinted fifteen times up to 1500 (H 13087–13106); a richly illuminated copy of Nicolas Jenson's 1472 Venetian edition is shown (see Plate 34). This encyclopaedia of natural history was ever present during the Middle Ages and more than 200 manuscripts have come down to us.

The medical writings of the Greek doctor Galen (129–199 AD) found particular favour in Italy: a few works appeared in Latin translation in the collection *Articella* (GW 26783) and a larger selection in 1490 in Venice (GW 10481), as did a Greek edition of the *Therapeutica* (H 74260) in 1500. These publications led to the establishment in the sixteenth century of a classically-based but "humanistic medicine" that took the motto *ad fontes* and sought to turn the medical wisdom of the ancients, in particular that of Greek antiquity, to the advantage of the present.

Euclid's *Elementa geometriae* of 1482 ranks as one of the most important astronomical and astrological incunabula. Euclid (365–300 BC) brought the entire mathematical knowledge of the Greeks into a logical system in his *Elementa*; accordingly it represents the oldest mathematical text-book in the world. Through an Arabic translation it reached Europe in the twelfth century, where it became known once it had been translated into Latin. The basis of Erhard Ratdolt's Venetian first edition of 1482 was a revision made in 1260 by Johannes Campanus (GW 9428). Ratdolt operated one of the leading printing offices in Venice from 1476. The first page of the *Elementa* (see Plate 35) displays the high quality of his workshop, which featured magnificent initials and borders (with letters and scroll-work in white line on a black ground). In addition to these we find here for the first time geometrical diagrams – which up to this point would have been inserted by hand – printed from woodcut with the text.

One of the last celebrated classical men of learning, Ptolemy (active between AD 125 and 151), was chiefly known during the Middle Ages for his astronomical writings. His *Geographia* (or *Cosmographia*) was first translated into Latin at the start of the fifteenth century. The first edition still contained no maps, but instead only his table of over 8000 place entries with indications of latitude and longitude. Six editions with maps appeared from 1477 onwards. The *Geographia* printed in 1482 in Ulm by Lienhart Holl is the first world atlas to be printed north of the Alps. The maps have a trapezoidal projection and were carefully hand-coloured before leaving the publisher. Holl had a special large roman type made for this edition. Plate 37 shows a double-page spread of Italy that comprised one of five modern, that is to say contemporary, maps, together with maps of Spain, France, Palestine and the Northern Lands.

et nos insipietes increduli errātes suientes
desideriꝗ voluptatibꝰ varijs:et maliciaa
inuidia agētes:odibiles.odientes inuicē.
Cū aūt benignitas ⁊ humanitas apparuit
saluatoris nostri dei nō ex operibus iusticie q̄
fecimus nos sed scōm suā misediam saluos
nos fecit p lauacrū regnacois ⁊ renouacois
spūs sancti quē effudit in nos abūde p ihe-
sum xpm saluatorē nrm:vt iustificati gratia ipsius heredes simus scōm spem vite e-
terne. fidelis sm̄o est. Et de hijs volo te cō-
firmare:ut curent bonis operibꝰ pēsse q̄ cre-
dunt deo. Hec sunt bona ⁊ vtilia hominibꝰ.
Stultas aūt questioēs.et genealogias ⁊
cōtentiones ⁊ pugnas legis deuita. Sunt
enim inutiles ⁊ vane. Hereticū hominē p̄?
vnam ⁊ secdam correptionē deuita:sciens q̄
subūsus est qui eiusmodi est:⁊ delinqut cū
sit pprio iudicio ꝺdemnatus. Cū misero ad
te arteman aut thychicū:festina ad me ve-
nire nicopolim. Jbi enim statui hyemare.
Zenam legisperitū et apollo sollicite pmit-
te:ut michil illis desit. Discant aūt et nris bonis operibus preesse ad vsus necessarios:
vt non sint infructuosi. Salutāt te qui mecum sūt omnes. Saluta eos qui nos amāt
in fide. Gratia dei cum omnibꝰ vobis amē.

Explicit epla ad thytū. Jncip argumētū in
epistolam ad philemonē.
Hilemoni familiares lras facit pro onesimo seruo eius:
scribens ei ab vrbe roma de
carcere per suprascriptum o-
nesimū. Explic. argumentū. Jncip epla
Aulus ad philemonē.
vinctus cristi ihesu et
thimotheꝰ frater:phi-
lemoni dilecto adiu-
tori nostro.et appie so-
rori carissime ⁊ arcippo
cōmilitoni nostro:et
ecclesie que in domo tua est. Gratia vobis
et pax a deo patre nostro:et domino ihesu
cristo. Gratias ago deo meo semp memor-
iam tui faciens in orōnibꝰ meis audiens caritatem tuam et fidem quā habes in dño ihesu
et in omes sanctos:ut cōmunicacō fidei tue
euidēs fiat in agnicōne omnis opis boni in

ihu xpo. Gaudiū enim magnum habui et
consolacōnem in caritate tua:q̄ viscera san-
ctorꝝ requieuerūt per te frater. Propter q̄
multa fiduciam habens in cristo ihesu impe-
randi tibi q̄d ad rem ptinet:ppter caritatem
magis obsecro cū sis talis vt paulus senex
nūc aūt ⁊ vinct? ihesu xpi:obsecro te p meo
filio quē genui in vinculis onesimo qui tibi
aliquādo inutilis fuit:nūc aūt ⁊ michi ⁊ tibi
vtilis:quē remisi tibi. Tu aūt illū ut mea viscera suscipe. Quē ego voluerā mecū detine-
re:ut p te michi ministraret in vinculis euan-
gelij. Sine ō silio aūt tuo michil volui face:
vt ne velut ex necessitate bonū tuū esset:s̄
volūtariū. Forsitan eni ideo discessit ad ho-
ra ⁊ te:vt eternū illū reciperes:iā nō vt suū
s̄ p suo carissimū frēz:maxie michi. Quanto aūt magis tibi:et in carne et in dño? Si
ergo habes me socium:suscipe illū sicut me.
Si aūt aliquid nocuit tibi aut debet:hoc michi imputa. Ego paulus scripsi mea manu.
Ego reddam:ut nō dicā tibi q̄ ⁊ teipsum michi debes. Ita frater ego te fruar in dño:re-
fice viscera mea in cristo. Confidens in obe-
dientia tua scripsi tibi:sciens qm et super id
q̄d dico facies. Simul ⁊ para michi hospici-
um:nam spero p orationes vras donari me
vobis. Salutat te epafras in captiuus me?
in xpo ihesu:marcus aristarchus demas et
lucas adiutores mei. Gratia domini nostri
ihesu cristi cum spiritu vestro amen.

Explicit epistola ad philemonem. Jncipit
argumentum in epistolam ad hebreos.
N primis dicendū est cur aplostolus paul?
in hac epistola scribendo nō suauerit more
suū:ut vel vocabulū nominis sui vel ordinis
describeret dignitatē. Hec causa est:q̄ ad e-
os scribens qui ex circūcisione crediderant
quasi gentiū apostolus ⁊ non hebreorꝝ:sci-
ens q̄ eorꝝ supbiaz suamq̄ humilitatē ipe
demōstrans:meritii officij sui noluit antefer-
re. Nam simili modo etiam iohannes aplus
ppter humilitatez in epla sua nomen suū ea-
dem racōne non pretulit. Hanc ergo eplam
fertur apostolus ad hebreos o scriptā hebraica ligua misisse:cuius sensū ordinē retinēs
lucas euangelista post excessum apli pauli
greco sm̄one composuit. Expl. argumentū.

Plate 17: The 48-line Bible, Mainz, Fust and Schoeffer workshop, 1462 (GW 4202), fol 21r.
Göttingen City and University Library.

singulas. Et singule porte erant ex singulis
margaritis: et platea ciuitatis aurum mundum:
tanquam vitrum plucidum. Et templum non vidi in
ea. Dominus enim deus omnipotens templum illius
est: et agnus. Et ciuitas non eget sole neque
luna: ut luceant in ea. Nam claritas dei il=
luminabit eam: et lucerna eius est agnus.
Et ambulabunt gentes in lumine eius: et
reges terre afferent gloriam suam et hono=
rem in illam. Et porte eius non claudentur
per noctem. Nox enim non erit illic. Et affe=
rent gloriam et honorem gentium in illam:
nec intrabit in ea aliquid coinquinatum aut
abominationem faciens et mendacium: nisi
qui scripti sunt in libro vite agni. XXII
Et ostendit michi fluuium aque viue.
splendidum tanquam cristallum: proce=
dentem de sede dei et agni. In medio platee
eius et ex vtraque parte fluminis lignum vite
afferens fructus duodecim: per menses sin=
gulos reddens fructum suum: et folia ligni
ad sanitatem gentium. Et omne maledictum
non erit amplius: sed sedes dei et agni in illa
erunt: et serui eius seruient illi. Et videbunt
faciem eius: et nomen eius in frontibus eorum.
Et nox vltra non erit: et non egebunt lumine lu=
cerne neque lune solis quoniam dominus deus illuminabit
illos: et regnabunt in secula seculorum. Et di=
xit michi. Hec verba fidelissima sunt et vera.
Et dominus deus spirituum prophetarum misit an=
gelum suum: ostendere seruis suis que opor=
tet fieri cito. Et ecce venio velociter. Beatus
qui custodit verba prophetie libri huius. Et
ego iohannes qui audiui et vidi hec. Et post=
quam audissem et vidissem cecidi ut adorare
ante pedes angeli qui michi hec ostende=
bat. Et dixit michi. Vide ne feceris. Con=
seruus enim tuus sum et fratrum tuorum prophe=
tarum: et eorum qui seruant verba prophetie libri
huius. Deum adora. Et dixit michi. Ne si=
gnaueris verba prophetie libri huius. Tem=
pus enim prope est. Qui nocet noceat ad=
huc: et qui in sordibus est sordescat adhuc.
Et qui iustus est iustificetur adhuc: et san=
ctus sanctificetur adhuc. Ecce venio cito: et
merces mea mecum est: reddere vnicuique
secundum opera sua. Ego sum alpha et o:
primus et nouissimus: principium et finis.

Beati qui lauant stolas suas in sanguine a=
gni: ut sit potestas eorum in ligno vite: et per
portas intrent ciuitatem. Foris autem canes
et venefici et impudici et homicide et ydolis
seruientes: et omnis qui amat et facit men=
dacium. Ego ihesus misi angelum meum te=
stificari vobis hec in ecclesijs. Ego sum radix
et genus dauid: stella splendida et matuti=
na. Et spiritus et sponsa dicunt veni. Et qui
audit: dicat veni. Et qui sitit veniat: et qui vult
accipiat aquam vite gratis. Contestor enim
omni audienti verba prophetie libri huius. Si
quis apposuerit ad hec apponet deus super
illum plagas scriptas in libro isto: et si quis
diminuerit de verbis libri prophetie huius. au=
feret deus partem eius de libro vite et de ciui=
tate sancta: et de hijs que scripta sunt in li=
bro isto. Dicit qui testimonium phibet istorum.
Etiam Venio cito amen. Veni domine ihesu.
Gratia domini nostri ihesu cristi cum omnibus vobis amen.
Explicit liber apocalipsis beati iohannis apostoli.

Presens hoc opusculum Artificiosa adinuentione
imprimendi seu caracterizandi: absque calami
exaracione: in ciuitate Moguntij sic effigiatum
et ad eusebiam dei industrie per Johannem Fust ciuem
et Petrum Schoiffher de gernshepm clericum di=
oceseos eiusdem est consummatum. Anno domini M.
cccc.lxij. In vigilia assumpcionis virginis marie.

Plate 18: The 48-line Bible, Mainz, Fust and Schoeffer workshop, 1462, fol 239r,
with the colophon of Fust and Schoeffer and their printer's mark.

Satirion   stendelwortz

Satirion.i.testiculus vulpis est calidus et hui=
dus in primo.habet folia filia folijs lilij albi et
etiã in floribꝰ cõuenit.et qõ ꝺe ipsa administrat
est radix que dulcis est. Et in humiditate ein s
est inflatio supflua gratia cuius incitat ad libi=
dinem.Et vinũ ꝺecoctionis radicis eius incitat
ad libidinem.Et radix eius elixata cum carnibꝰ
recentibus vel affata magis conuenit ad car=
ms libidinem.Et ꝺiascorides ꝺicit ca.orchis.i.

Plate 19: Herbarius (Latin Herbal), Mainz, Peter Schoeffer, 1484 (HC 8444).
Leipzig University Library.

Plate 20: Konrad Bote: *Chroniken der sassen* (*Saxon world chronicle*), Mainz, Peter Schoeffer, 1492 (GW 4963). Leipzig University Library.

Plate 21: Johann von Tepl: Der Ackermann aus Böhmen (The ploughman from Bohemia),
Bamberg, Albrecht Pfister, c. 1470. From a facsimile.

Plate 22: Cicero: De Officiis, Rome, Konrad Sweynheym and Arnold Pannartz, 1469 (GW 6924), fol 2r. Göttingen State and University Library.

MARCI TVLLII CICERONIS TVSCVLANARVM QVAESTIONVM LIBER PRIMVS.

Vm defenſionũ laboribus: ſenatoriiſq;
muneribus aut omnino:aut magna ex
parte eſſe aliquado liberatus:rettuli me
Brute te hortante maxime ad ea ſtudia:
quæ retenta animo: remiſſa téporibus:
longo interuallo intermiſſa reuocaui .
Et cum omnium artium : quæ ad rectam uiuendi uiam.
pertinerent:ratio & diſciplina,ſtudio,ſapientiæ: quæ philoſophia dicitur : contineretur : hoc mihi latius litteris
illuſtrandum putaui:non quia philoſophia græcis & lŕis
& doctoribus percipi non poſſet:Sed meũ iudiciũ ſemper
fuit:omnia noſtros aut iueniſſe per ſe ſapiétius q̃ græcos:
aut accepta ab illis feciſſe meliora : quæ quidem digna
ſtatuiſſent:in quibus elaborarent.Nam mores & iſtituta
uitæ : reſq; domeſticas:ac familiares nos profecto melius
tuemur:& lautius.Rem uero publicã noſtri maiores certe
melioribus temperauerunt:& inſtitutis:& legibus . Quid
loquar de re militari?in qua cum uirtute noſtri multum
ualuerũt:tũ plus etiam diſciplina.Iã illa quæ natura non
litteris aſſecuti ſunt:neq; cum græcia : neq; ulla cũ gente
ſũt conferenda.Quæ.n.tanta grauitas:quæ tãta cõſtãtia:
magnitudo animi:probitas : fides : quæ tam excellens in
omni genere uirtus in ullis fuit : ut ſit cum maioribus
noſtris cõparanda ? Doctrina græcia nos & omni litterarx
genere ſuperabat : ĩ quo erat facile uicere nõ repugnátes.
Nam cum apud græcos antiquiſſimum e doctis ſit genus
poetarum : ſiquidem Homerus fuit : & Heſiodus ante
romam conditam: Archilochus regnante Romulo:ſerius
poeticam nos accepimus. Annis fere.cccc.x.poſt romam
conditam Liuius fabulam dedit Caio Claudio Cæci filio

POLIPHILO QVIVI NARRA,CHE GLI PARVE AN-
CORA DI DORMIRE,ET ALTRONDE IN SOMNO
RITROVARSE IN VNA CONVALLE,LAQVALE NEL
FINE ERA SERATA DE VNA MIRABILE CLAVSVRA
CVM VNA PORTENTOSA PYRAMIDE,DE ADMI-
RATIONE DIGNA,ET VNO EXCELSO OBELISCO DE
SOPRA,LAQVALE CVM DILIGENTIA ET PIACERE
SVBTILMENTE LA CONSIDEROE.

A SPAVENTEVOLE SILVA,ET CONSTI-
pato Nemore euaso,& gli primi altri lochi per el dolce
somno che se hauea per le fesse & prosternate mébre dif-
fuso relicti,me ritrouai di nouo in uno piu delectabile
sito assai piu che el præcedente. El quale non era de mon
ti horridi,& crepidinose rupe intorniato, ne falcato di
strumosi iugi. Ma compositamente de grate montagniole di non tro-
po altecia. Siluose di giouani quercioli, di roburi, fraxini & Carpi-
ni , & di frondosi Esculi, & Ilice , & di teneri Coryli,& di Alni,& di Ti-
lie,& di Opio , & de infructuosi Oleastri , dispositi secondo laspecto de
gli arboriferi Colli. Et giu al piano erano grate siluule di altri siluatici

Plate 24: Francesco Colonna: Hypnerotomachia Poliphili, Venice, Aldus Manutius, 1499
(GW 7223). Göttingen State and University Library.

EL TERTIO cæleste triumpho seguiua cum quatro uertibile rote
di Chrysolitho æthiopico scintule doro flammigiante, Traiecta per el
quale la seta del Asello gli maligni dæmonii fuga, Alla leua mano'gra-
to, cum tutto quello cħ di sopra di rote e dicto. Daposcia le assule sue in
ambito per el modo compacte sopra narrato, erano di uirente Helitro-
pia Cyprico, cum potere negli lumi cælesti, el suo gestate cœla, & il diui-
nare dona, di sanguinee guttule punctulato.

Offeriua tale historiato insculpto la tabella dextra. Vno homo di regia maiestate ísigne, Oraua in uno sacro templo'el diuo simulacro, quel
lo che della formosissima fiola deueua seguire. Sentendo el patre la eie-
ctione sua per ella del regno. Et ne per alcuno fusse pregna, Fece
una munita structura di una excelsa torre, Et in quella cum
soléne custodia la fece inclaustrare. Nella quale ella cessabonda assedédo, cum ex-
cessiuo solatio, nel uirgi
neo sino gutte do
ro stillare
uede
ua.
*

Plate 25: Francesco Colonna: *Hypnerotomachia Poliphili, liber secundus.*

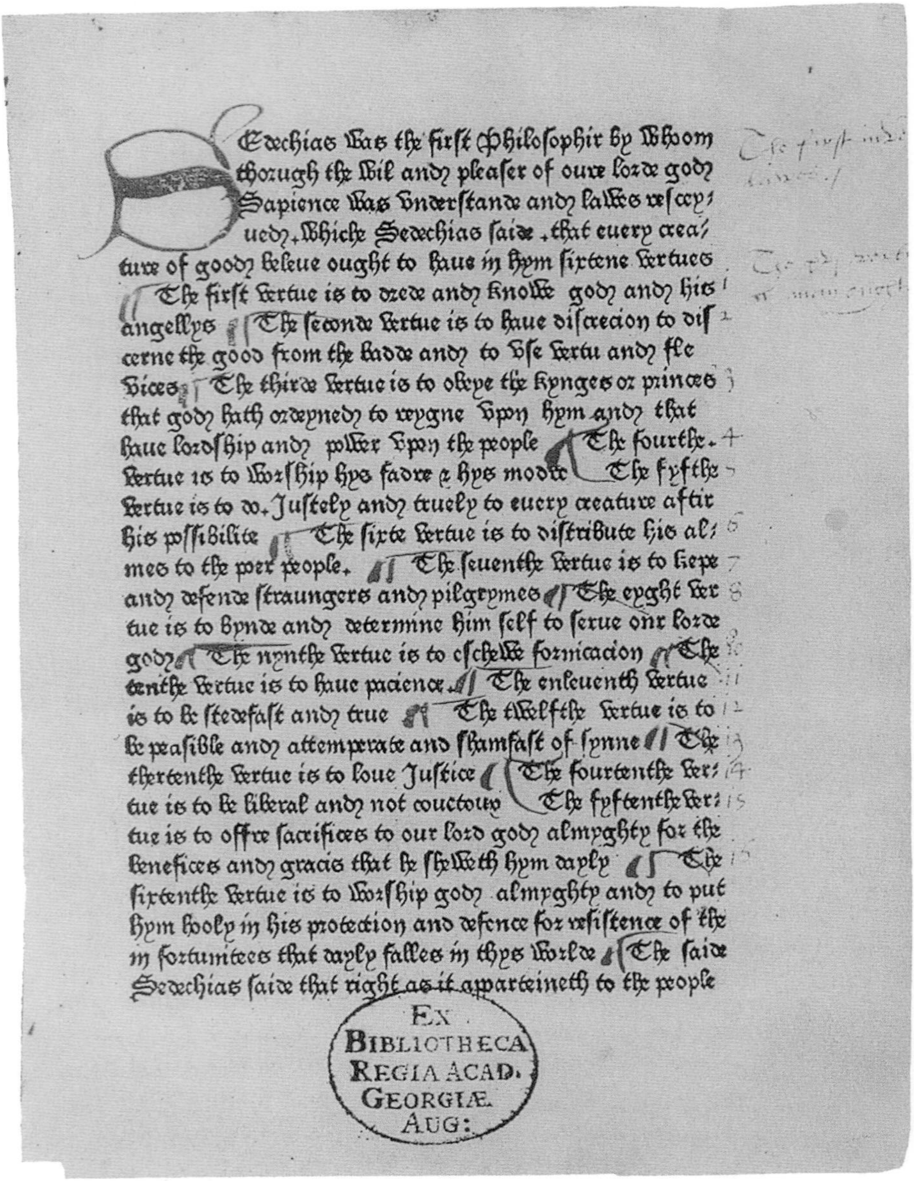

Sedechias was the first Philosophir by whom
thorough the will and pleaser of oure lorde god
Sapience was vnderstande and lawes resceyued. Which Sedechias saide, that euery creature of good beleue ought to haue in hym sixtene vertues
The first vertue is to drede and knowe god and his
angellys ¶ The seconde vertue is to haue discrecion to discerne the good from the badde and to vse vertu and fle
vices ¶ The thirde vertue is to obeye the kynges or princes
that god hath ordeyned to reygne vpon hym and that
haue lordship and power vpon the people ¶ The fourthe
vertue is to worship hys fadre & hys modre ¶ The fyfthe
vertue is to do, Iustely and truely to euery creature aftir
his possibilite ¶ The sixte vertue is to distribute his almes to the pover people. ¶ The seuenthe vertue is to kepe
and defende straungers and pilgrymes ¶ The eyght vertue is to bynde and determine him self to serue our lorde
god ¶ The nynthe vertue is to eschewe fornicacion ¶ The
tenthe vertue is to haue pacience ¶ The enleuenth vertue
is to be stedfast and true ¶ The twelfthe vertue is to
be peasible and attemperate and shamfast of synne ¶ The
thertenthe vertue is to loue Iustice ¶ The fourtenthe vertue is to be liberal and not couetous ¶ The fyftenthe vertue is to offre sacrifices to our lord god almyghty for the
benefices and gracis that he sheweth hym dayly ¶ The
sixtenthe vertue is to worship god almyghty and to put
hym hooly in his proteccion and defence for resistence of the
misfortunes that dayly falles in thys worlde ¶ The saide
Sedechias saide that right as it aparteineth to the people

Plate 26: The Dictes and Sayengs of the Philosophers, Westminster, William Caxton,
second edition 1479 (GW 8322). Göttingen State and University Library.

Vum multæ res i philosophia nequaq̃ satis adhuc explicatæ sint:
tū pdifficilis Brute quod tu minime ignoras:& perobscura quæ-
stio est de natura deorū:quæ ad agnitionē animi pulcherrima est:
& ad moderandā religionē necessaria.De qua tam uariæ sunt do-
ctissimorū hominum tamq; discrepātes sentētiæ:ut magno argu
mento esse debeat:causam idest principiū philosophiæ esse scien-
tiam:prudēterq; Academicos a rebus incertis assensionem cohi
buisse. Quid temeritate fortius?aut quid tā temerariū:tamq; idignū sapiētis gra
uitate atq; costantia:q̃ aut falsum sentire:aut quod nō satis explorate pceptum sit & co-
gnitū:sine ulla dubitatione defendere.Velut in hac quæstione pleriq; quod maxie ueri
simile est:& quo omnes duce natura uehimur:deos esse dixerūt.Dubitare se pithagoras
nullos esse omnino.Diagoras melius:& Theodorus Cyrenaicus putauerūt. Qui uero
deos esse dixerūt tanta sunt in uarietate:ac dissensione cōstituti:ut eorū molestum sit an
numerare sententias.Nā & de figuris deorū & de locis atq; sedibus & actiōe uita multa
dicitur:deq; his suma philosophorum dissensione certatur. Quod uero maxime causa
remq; cōtinet est:utrū nihil agant:nihil moliantur:an ab omni curatione & administra-
tione rerum uacent:ā contra ab his & a principio omnia facta & constituta sint:& ad in
sinitū tēpus regnantur:atq; moueātur.Imprimisq; magna dissensio est:eaq; nisi diiudi-
catur:in sumo errore necesse est homines atq; in maximarū rerū ignoratōe uersari.Sūt
enim philosophi & fuerūt:qui omnipo nullā habere cēserent rerū humanarū pcuratio-
nem deos:quorū si uera sententia est:quæ potest esse pietas:quæ sanctitas?quæ religio?
Hæc enim omnia pure ac caste tribuenda deorū numina ita sunt:si animaduertantur ab
his:& si est aliquid a diis immortalibus hominū generi tributū.Sin aūt dii neq; possunt
iuuare:nec uolūt:nec omnino curant:nec quid agamus aiaduertunt:nec est quod ab his
ad hominū uitā permanere possit:quid est quod ullos deis immortalibus cultus:hono-
res:preces adhibeamus?In specie autē sictæ simulationis sicut reliquæ uirtutes:ita pie-
tas inesse nō potest:cū qua simul & sanctitatem & religionē tolli necesse est:quibus sub
latis pturbatio uitæ sequitur & magna cōfusio.Atq; haud scio an pietate aduersus deos
sublata fides etiā & societas generis humani & una excellētissima uirtus iustitia tollat.
Sunt autē alii philosophi:& hi quidē magni atq; nobiles:qui deorum mēte atq; ratione
omnem mundū administrari & regi censeant:neq; uero id solū sed etiā ab eisdē uitæ hominum consuli & puideri.Nam & fruges & reliqua quæ terra pariat:& tempestates ac
temporū uarietates cæliq; mutationes:quibus omnia quæ terra gignat:maturata pube
scentia diis immortalibus tribui generi humano putāt:multaq; quæ dicēt in his libris
colligūt:quæ talia sunt:ut ea ipsa dii immortales ad usum hominū fabricare pene uideā
tur.Contra quos Carneades ita multa disseruit:ut excitaret homines nō socordes ad ue
ri inuestigandi cupiditatē.Res enim nulla est:de qua tantopere nō solum docti sed etiā
indocti dissentiant:quorū opiniones quū tam uariæ sint:ranq̃ inter se dissidentes:alterū
psecto fieri potest ut earū nulla alterū certæ non potest:ut plus una uera sit.Qua quidem in causa & beniuolos obiurgatores placare:& inuidos uituperatores confutare pos
sumus:ut alteros repræhēdisse pæniteat:alteri sed didicisse gaudeant.Nam qui admo-
nent amice docendi sunt:qui inimice insectantur repellēdi.Multum autem fluxisse ui-

a

Plate 27: Cicero: de Natura deorum, Venice, Philippus Pincius, 1494 (GW 6904), fol 1r.
Göttingen State and University Library.

Plate 28: Terence: Comoediae, Strasbourg, Johann Grüninger, 1496 (HC 15431), fol 1r.
Göttingen State and University Library.

| MENEDEMVS. | CHREMES. | **In hac scena. XXII.** |

MENEDEMVS. CHREMES.
SOSTRATA. CLITIPHO.

Nimuero Chremes nimis grauiter cruciat ado
lescentulū:nimis ҫ inhumane:exeo ergo vt pacem conci=
liem.optime ipsos video.CHRE.Ehem menedeme. cur
nō accersi iubes filiam:& ҫd dotis dixi firmas? Sostr.Mi
vir obsecro te ҏne facias.CLI.Pater obsecro vt mihi igno=
scas.MENE.Da veniam chreme.sin te exorem CHRE.
Egone mea bona vt dem Bachidi dono sciens:non faciā.
ME.At id nos nō sinemus.CLITI.Si me viuū vis pater
ignosce.Soft.Age chremes.MENE.Age queso ne tam
obfirma te chremes.CHRE.Quid istuc? video nō licere
mihi:vt cœperam:hoc pertendere.MENE.Facis ҏvt te de
cet.CHRE.ea lege hoc adeo faciam:si id faciat:quod ego
hunc æquum censeo.CLI.Pater omnia faciam.impera.
CHRE.Vxorem vt ducas.CLITI.Pater.CHRE.Nihil
audio.ME.Ad me recipio:faciet.CHRE.Nihil etiā au=
dio ipsum.CLI.Perij.SOSTRA.An dubitas Clitipho?
CHRE.Immo vtrū vult.MENE.Faciet omia. SOST.

Interuenit persona cuius gratia pax concilieꝰ ita
vt omnia tranquilla sint.& composita prout co
medie finis postulat.

a ¶ Enimuero.Hoc loquitur Menedemus solus
apud se.Enimuero:nonnunqꝫ principium est ali
quid per iram dicturi.   b ¶ Hem.Interiectio per
cipientis eum quem volebat.   c ¶ Accersi.Be/
ne accersi quia proprie accersitur vxor dū ad vis
ducitur.   d ¶ Mi vir.te.Putat sostrata id quod
erat fictum esse verum timebatꝗ ne pater peni/
tus exheredaret filium omnia tribuens filie.
e ¶ Obsecro.Nil significantius.Nam orare ҫ pla
cidos petere.Obsecrare vero iratos rogare.
f ¶ Ne facias.Hec timebat ne omnia bona illi tra
deret.   g ¶ Sciens.Quod peius esse ҫ si nesciret
h ¶ Age.Vt sit aduerbium hortantis q.d.age ig
nosce ꝗ   i ¶ Ne tam obfirma te.Id est noli te tam
obstinatum ostēdere.Ille enim dicitur se affirma
re in aliquo proposito qui obstinate ac pertinaci
ter in illo perseuerat tanꝗ immobilis truncus.&
est translatio sumpta a repagulo:obfirmando.
k ¶ Pater.Tantum dicit hoc verbum non statim
volens dare responsum tanꝗ prius deliberaturꝰ
l ¶ Ad me recipio.Hoc dicendi genere sæpius.Ci
cero vtitur in suis epistolis.& precipue comme=
daticiis vt cerne facile est nemo enim negat recipe
re interdum sumi pro promittere.

                 p   iij

Plate 29: Terence: Comoediae, Strasbourg, Johann Grüninger, fol 85r.

Arma : Multi uarie dixerunt cur ab armis Virgilius coeperit : omnes tamen in hanc sententiam af
sentire manifestum est : quum cum constet aliunde sumpsisse principium : sicut in premissa eius
uita monstratum est . Per arma autem bellum significat : et est tropus metonymia . Nam arma qui
bus in bello utimur pro bello posuit : sicut toga qua in pace utimur : pro pace ponitur : Vt Cicero:
Cedant arma togę : idest bellum paci .   Arma utrumque: figura usitata est : ut non eo ordine respó
deamus : quo proposuimus : nam prius de erroribus Aeneę dixit : post de bello, hac autem figura etiam

in prosa utimur . Sic Cicero in uer
nnis : Nam sine ullo sumptu no
stro coriis tunicis frumentoque sup
peditato maximos exercitus nostros
uestiuit: armauit .   Virum
quem non dicit : sed ex circunstan
tiis ostédit Aeneam .   Cano : po
lysemus sermo est Tria enim signi
ficat : aliquando laudo : ut Regem
que canebant . Aliquando diuino :
ur Ipsa canas oro . Aliquando can
to : ut hoc loco . Nam proprie can
to significat : quia cantanda sunt
carmina .   Troię : Troia regio é
asię : Illum ciuitas est Troię . Pleru
que tamen usurpant poetę . et pro ci
uitate uel regioné uel prouinciam po
nunt . Iuuenalis : Et flammis asia
ferroque cadentem .   Qui prius:

RMA: VIRVMQVE

CANO : TROIAE

QVI PRIMVS

AB ORIS

taliam fato profugus lauinaque uenit
L ittora: multū ille et terris iactatus et alto

Querunt multi cur Aeneam primum ad italiam ueniffe dixerit : cum paulo post dicat Antenorem an
te aduentum Aeneę fundaffe ciuitatem . Constat quidem : sed habita temporum ratione perite Virgi
lius dicit . Namque illo tempore quo Aeneas ad Italiam uenit finis erat italię ufque ad Rubiconem
fluuium : Cuius rei meminit Lucanus : ut Et gallica certus Limes ab aufoniis difterminat arua coloni
Vnde apparet Antenorem non ad Italiam ueniffe : sed ad Galliam cifalpinam : in qua Venetia est.
Postea uero promotis ufque ad alpes Italię finibus nouitas creauit errorem . Plerique tamen quęstioné
hanc uolunt ex sequentibus folui : ut uideatur ob hoc addidiffe Virgilius ad lauina littora : ut non
significaret Antenorem . Melior tamen est superior expofitio .   Italiam : At quidem hoc exigit :
ut nominibus prouinciarum prepositionem addamus : ciuitatum nunquam : Tamen plerunque paucæ
fo ordine rectum est . Nam ecce hoc loco detraxit prouincię prepofitionem dicens : Italiam fato uenit:
pro ad italiam uenit . Tullius in uerninis : Ea die Verres ad meffanam uenit . Sane sciendum est ufur
pari ab auctoribus : ut uel addant : uel detrahant prepofitiones . Nanque ait Virgilius : Siluis te tyr
rhene feras : pro in siluis . Vt ergo illic detraxit loco prepofitionem : sic hic prouincię : et est figura .
Italia autem pars Europę est . Italus enim rex siculorum profectus ab loca quę fę
iuxta tyberim : et ex nomine suo appellauit Italiam . Ibi autem habitaffe siculos : uti Luarolauini
um est: manifestum est : Sicut ipse alio loco dicit : Siculi ueteresque sicani . Item Et gentes uenere sica
nę .   Fato profugus : Fatum ad utrunque pertinet : et qɔ fugit : et qɔ ad Italiam uenit . et bene addi
dit fato : ne uideatur aut causa criminis patriam deferuiffe: aut noui imperii cupiditate .   Profuguf
autem proprie dicitur qui procul a fedibus suis uagatur : quasi porro fugatus . Multi tamen ita diftin
unt : ut profugos effe dicant eos : qui exclufi necessitate de suis fedibus adhuc uagantur et fimulac m
uenerint fedes non dicantur profugi : sed exules . Sed utrunque falfum est : Nam et profugus lectus est :
qui iam fedes locauit : Vt in Lucano : Profugique a gente uetusta Gallorum celtę mifcentes nomen
iberis : et exules qui adhuc uagantur : Vt in Saluftio : qui nullo certo exilio uagabantur : adeo exili
um est ipfa uagatio .   Lauinaque uenit littora : hęc ciuitas tria habuit nomina . Nam prius Laui
num dicta est a Lauino Latini fratre . Poftea Laurentum a lauro inuenta a Latino : dum adepto im
perio post fratris mortem ciuitatem augeret . Postea Lauinium a Lauinia uxore Aeneę . Ergo Lauina
legendum est : non Lauinia : quia post aduentum Aeneę Lauinium nomen accepit . Ergo aut Laui
num debuit dicere : sicut dixit : aut Laurentim: quamuis quidem superfluę effe prolę fim uelint :   Lit
tora : Laurolauinium constat . viii. miliarrius amari remotum . Nec nos debet fallere quia dixit lauia
littora . Littus enim dicitur terra quęq; mari uicina: sicut ipse Virgilius in quarto: C ui littus arandū : qui
per naturam littus arari non poffit. Ergo sciendum est littus uocari et terram .   Multum ille: collifio est .
et ille hoc loco abundat. Est enim interpofita particula propter metri necessitatem: ut stet uerfus. nam si de
trahas ille stat fensus. qui primus enim ad omnia pofsumus trahere: sic alio loco: Nunc dextra in geminas
ictus: nunc ille finistra. Est autem archaifmos.   Et terris iactatus: fatigatus est enim apud thraciam men
stro illo: quod e tumulo Polydori fanguis emanauit: apud cretam pestilentia: apud strophadas infulas har
pyiis . Tempestate uero et in primo: et in tertio :et proprie locutus: nam iactamur in mari fluctibus: fatiga
mur in terris . et bene duorum elementorum mala uno femone concludit .   Et alto: medo mari . Altum
tamen sciendum est qɔ et superiorem : et inferiorem altitudinem significat . Náq; mensure nomé altitudo .

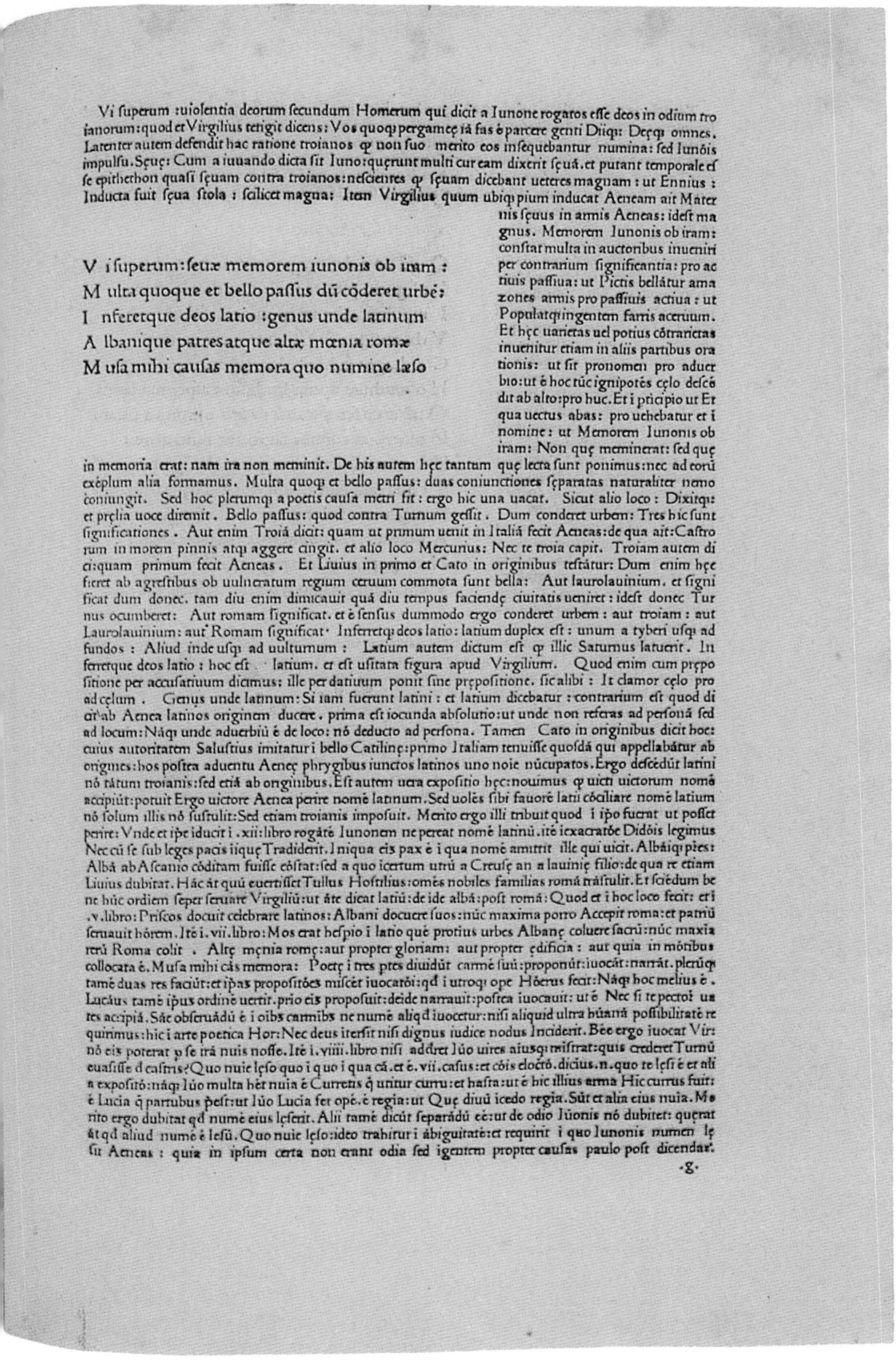

Vi ſuperum :uioſentia deorum ſecundum Homerum qui dicit a Iunone rogatos eſſe deos in odium tro ianorum:quod et Virgilius tetigit dicens: Vos quoq pergameę iā fas ē parcere genti Diiq: Deęq omnes. Latenter autem defendit hac ratione troianos ꝙ non ſuo merito eos inſequebantur numina: ſed Iunōis impulſu. Sęuę: Cum a iuuando dicta ſit Iuno:quęrunt multi cur eam dixerit ſęuā. et putant temporale eſ ſe epithethon quaſi ſęuam contra troianos:neſcientes ꝙ ſęuam dicebant ueteres magnam : ut Ennius : Inducta fuit ſęua ſtola : ſcilicet magna: Item Virgilius quum ubiq pium inducat Aeneam ait Mater nis ſęuus in armis Aeneas: ideſt ma gnus. Memorem Iunonis ob iram: conſtat multa in auctoribus inueniri per contrarium ſignificantia: pro ac tiuis paſſiua: ut Pictis bellātur ama zones armis pro paſſiuis actiua : ut Populatq ingentem farris aceruum. Et hęc uarietas uel potius cōtrarietas inuenitur etiam in aliis partibus ora tionis: ut ſit pronomen pro aduer bio:ut ē hoc tūc ignipotēs cęlo deſcē dit ab alto:pro huc. Et i pcipio ut Et qua uectus abas: pro uehebatur et i nomine: ut Memorem Iunonis ob iram: Non quę meminerat: ſed quę in memoria erat: nam ira non meminit. De his autem hęc tantum quę lecta ſunt ponimus:nec ad eorū exēplum alia formamus. Multa quoq et bello paſſus: duas coniunctiones ſęparatas naturaliter nemo coniungit. Sed hoc plerumq a poetis cauſa metri fit : ergo hic una uacat. Sicut alio loco : Dixitq: et pręlia uoce diremit. Bello paſſus: quod contra Turnum geſſit. Dum conderet urbem: Tres hic ſunt ſignificationes. Aut enim Troiā dicit: quam ut primum uenit in Italiā fecit Aeneas:de qua ait:Caſtro rum in morem pinnis atq aggere cingit. et alio loco Mercurius: Nec te troia capit. Troiam autem di cit:quam primum fecit Aeneas. Et Liuius in primo et Cato in originibus teſtātur: Dum enim hęc fieret ab agreſtibus ob uulneratum regium ceruum commota ſunt bella: Aut laurolauinium. et ſigni ficat dum donec. tam diu enim dimicauit quā diu tempus faciendę ciuitatis ueniret : ideſt donec Tur nus ocumberet: Aut romam ſignificat. et ē ſenſus dummodo ergo conderet urbem : aut troiam : aut Laurolauinium: aut Romam ſignificat· Inferretq deos latio: latium duplex eſt : unum a tyberi uſq ad fundos : Aliud inde uſq ad uulturnum : Latium autem dictum eſt ꝙ illic Saturnus latuerit. In ferretque deos latio : hoc eſt latium. et eſt uſitata figura apud Virgilium. Quod enim cum prępo ſitione per accuſatiuum dicimus: ille per datiuum ponit ſine prępoſitione. ſic alibi : It clamor cęlo pro ad cęlum. Genus unde latinum: Si iam fuerunt latini : et latium dicebatur : contrarium eſt quod di cit ab Aenea latinos originem ducere. prima eſt iocunda abſolutio:ut unde non referas ad perſonā ſed ad locum: Nāq unde aduerbiū ē de loco: nō deducto ad perſona. Tamen Cato in originibus dicit hoc: cuius autoritatem Saluſtius imitatur i bello Catilinę:primo Italiam tenuiſſe quoſdā qui appellabātur ab origines:hos poſtea aduentu Aenęę phrygibus iunctos latinos uno noie nūcupatos. Ergo deſcēdūt latini nō tātum troianis:ſed etiā ab originibus. Eſt autem uera expoſitio hęc:nouimus ꝙ uicti uictorum nomē accipiūt:potuit Ergo uictore Aenea perire nomē latinum. Sed uolēs ſibi fauorē latii cōciliare nomē latium nō ſolum illis nō ſuſtulit:Sed etiam troianis impoſuit. Merito ergo illi tribuit quod i ipō fuerat ut poſſet perire: Vnde et ipe iducit i .xii. libro rogātē Iunonem ne pereat nomē latinū. itē i exacratōe Didōis legimus Nec cū ſe ſub leges pacis iiquę Tradiderit. Iniqua eis pax ē i qua nomē amittit ille qui uicit. Albāiq pres: Albā ab Aſcanio cōditam fuiſſe cōſtat:ſed a quo icertum utrū a Creuſę an a lauinię filio:de qua re etiam Liuius dubitat. Hāc āt quū euertiſſet Tullus Hoſtilius:omēs nobiles familias romā trāſtulit. Et ſciēdum be ne hūc ordiem ſeper ſeruare Virgiliū:ut āte dicat latiū:de ide albā:poſt romā: Quod et i hoc loco fecit: et i .v. libro: Priſcos docuit celebrare latinos: Albani docuere ſuos:nūc maxima porro Accepit roma:et patriū ſeruauit hōrem. Itē i. vii. libro: Mos erat heſpio i latio quē protius urbes Albanę coluere ſacrū:nūc maxia rerū Roma colit. Altę męnia romę:aut propter gloriam: aut propter ędificia : aut quia in mōtibus collocata ē. Muſa mihi cāš memora: Poetę i tres ptes diuidūt carmē ſuū:proponūt:iuocāt:narrāt. plerūq tamē duas res faciūt:et ipas propoſitōes miſcēt iuocatōi:qđ i utroq ope Hōerus fecit:Nāq hoc melius ē. Lucāus tamē ipus ordinē uertit. prio eis propoſuit:deide narrauit:poſtea iuocauit: ut ē Nec ſi te pectoř ua tes accipiā. Sāc obſeruādū ē i oibs carmibs ne numē aliqđ iuocetur:niſi aliquid ultra hūanā poſſibilitatē re quirimus:hic i arte poetica Hor: Nec deus iterſit niſi dignus iudice nodus Inciderit. Bēe ergo iuocat Vir: nō eis poterat ꝑ ſe irā nuis noſſe. Itē i. viiii. libro niſi addret Iūo uires aiusq miſtrat:quis crederet Turnū euaſiſſe d caſtris? Quo nuie lęſo quo i quo i qua cā. et ē. vii. caſus:et cōis elocūō. dicius. n. quo te lęſi ē et ali a expoſitō:nāq Iūo multa hēt nuia ē Curretis ǭ utitur curru:et haſta:ut ē hic illius arma Hic currus fuit: ē Lucia ǭ partubus ꝑeſt:ut Iūo Lucia fer opē. ē regia:ut Quę diuū icedo regia. Sūt et alia eius nuia. Me rito ergo dubitat qđ numē eius lęſerit. Alii tamē dicūt ſeparādū eē:ut de odio Iūonis nō dubitet: quęrat āt qđ aliud numē ē leſū. Quo nuie lęſo:ideo trahitur i ābiguitatē:et requirit i quo Iunonis numen lę ſit Aeneas : quia in ipſum certa non erant odia ſed igentem propter cauſas paulo poſt dicendas.

V i ſuperum:ſeuæ memorem iunonis ob iram :
M ulta quoque et bello paſſus dū cōderet urbē:
I nferetque deos latio :genus unde latinum
A lbanique patres atque altæ mœnia romæ
M uſa mihi cauſas memora quo numine læſo

·g·

Fols 60v/61r (opening of the Aeneid). Göttingen State and University Library.

Plate 31: Virgil: *Opera*, edited by Sebastian Brant, Strasbourg, Johann Grüninger, 1502.
Wolfenbüttel, Herzog August Library.

German humanism came about through direct encounter with the Italian humanism of the mid-fifteenth century in various places, at courts and government offices, schools and universities. It appealed to rank-conscious nobility, patricians and persons of lower birth for whom education opened the path of advancement. At first it was taken up by the secular intelligentsia, but then found a response in so-called "monastic humanism" and in the renewal of Christian training (especially in the Upper Rhineland).

The frequently cited "early humanism" of around 1400 at the Prague court of Charles IV influenced art and architecture, but initially it had little literary resonance. The reception of its most important literary document, the *Ackermann aus Böhmen* (1400) by Johann von Tepl (*c.* 1350–1415), a disputation between the ploughman of the title and Death, only really began seventy years later with its appearance in print: it came out as one of the first books in the vernacular, with woodcuts illustrating key scenes printed together with Albrecht Pfister's text in Bamberg in about 1470, and was followed by 16 further reprintings in rapid succession in Bamberg, Strasbourg, Basle, Augsburg and Heidelberg. In 32 conversational exchanges, Johann von Tepl keeps before our eyes man's rebellion against the inevitable fate of death; the elements of medieval dialectics are retained throughout the debate, but humanistic overtones are present in a new evaluation of the relationship of man to his creator. This many-faceted text from a transitional period is of fundamental importance for the development of prose style in the German language. Its wide reception in printed form shows its popularly instructive character for a lay readership and its use as edifying monastic reading matter as well.

Just as Rudolf Agricola (1444–85), Conrad Celtis or Peter Luder (1415–72) were moulded through their personal experiences of Italy into protagonists of humanist ideas and neo-Latin literature – which they spread within the "sodalities" they founded in German lands – so the earliest representatives of humanistic literature in the vernacular became confirmed in their approach through personal contacts with Italian humanists. Two scholars who propagated humanistic ideas in German – each in his specific way – in the second half of the fifteenth century, were the Ulm doctor and writer Heinrich Steinhöwel (1411–79) and the Chancellor to Count Ulrich of Württemberg, Niclas von Wyle (1415–79). As contemporaries, they became the first major literary translators at work in the German-language area. Steinhöwel methodically brought out all his works in print from 1471 with Günther Zainer in Augsburg, and from 1475 onwards with that printer's brother Johann in Ulm. Steinhöwel's Latin and German *Aesop* (1476) from Zainer in Ulm (see Plate 44) has as an appendage the short story *Guiscardus und Sigismunda* translated at second hand by Niclas von Wyle from a translation into Latin by Leonardo Bruni (1369–1444) from the Italian of the *Decameron* by Giovanni Boccaccio (1313–75).

With the publication of his *Translationen oder Tütschungen* in Esslingen in 1478, Niclas von Wyle turned to the literary public with new humanistic role models: the prince qualified through learning and the noble lady who was also his equal in erudition took centre stage in his translations. Niclas von Wyle's close personal relationship and correspondence with Enea Silvio Piccolomini during the latter's occupation in the service of Frederick III in Vienna (before he was elected to the papacy as Pius II in 1458) was to prove formative for him. Piccolomini's letters and discourses were regarded by his contemporaries as examples of style just as much as for the intellectual stimulation and analysis of Italian Renaissance humanism they provided. Niclas von Wyle was bilingual like all the scholars of his age, although he used Latin only in his letters: one can best describe him as a propagator of the fund of humanist ideas in the German language. He laboured over his principal work, the *Translatzen*, between 1461 and 1478; it consists of a collection of eighteen different tales by the Italian humanist writers Poggio (Giovanni Bracciolini), Enea Silvio Piccolomini, Leonardo Bruni, Francesco Petrarch, Nicolosia Sanuda, Gasparino Barzizza and Buonaccorsa da Montemagno. These tales had circulated widely in manuscript, but thanks to their translation and issue as single printed texts they came into great demand as reading matter. The translator did his best to make German correspond to the stylistic ideals of Latin and to imitate his Latin copy as exactly as possible. The resultant German conformed so closely to Latin syntax and word order that it could only be understood by those educated in Latin. Some of the translations contain a special humanistic agenda, especially the tenth *Translatze*, a treatise on upbringing, which Eneo Silvio Piccolomini had composed in 1443 for the 16-year-old Duke Sigmund of the Tyrol. On his own part, Niclas von Wyle dedicated this exhortatory letter and mirror for princes to Margrave Karl of Baden, and recommended it for bringing up his three sons. They should address themselves to studying the classics, and make positive use of the theoretical and practical wisdom they conveyed.

The sixteenth *Translatze* is a panegyric on women, whose virtues and wisdom he praises, and in doing so adopts the examples of the wisest, most learned and cultivated women given by his author Nicolosia Sanuda, and nominates as his own example of a remarkable contemporary woman the Countess Palatine Mechthild.

In his documented collaboration with the printers Günther and Johann Zainer in Augsburg and Ulm respectively from 1471 onwards, the Ulm city physician Heinrich Steinhöwel planned the publication of his translations in a more organised way than Niclas von Wyle had done. Steinhöwel had urged Johann Zainer to set up a press in Ulm and supported him financially for life whilst at the same time retaining a say in his publishing programme. Among his most successful translations is the tale *Griseldis* from Boccaccio's *Decamerone*; Steinhöwel knew it from a Latin reworking by Francesco Petrarch under the blunt title *De oboedientia et fide uxoris* (1373). This widely circulated tale tells of a poor man's daughter who is married by a prince who subjects her to almost unendurable trials. Steinhöwel's very free translation was printed in 1471 by Günther Zainer in Augsburg (H 12817) and twice reprinted in that same year; an illustrated edition came from Johann Zainer in Ulm in 1473, followed by a further ten new editions by 1500.

Steinhöwel's most extensive publication was a Latin-German edition of the late-classical Aesop's *Fables* which he brought out as a richly illustrated folio with Johann Zainer in 1476 (GW 351; see Plate 44). This composite volume contained Aesop as handed down through the Middle Ages, enriched from a newer fable collection by Rinuccio da Castiglione issued from Milan in 1471 and some of Poggio's *Facetiae*. Steinhöwel alternates these Latin texts with his own free prose renderings in German. This bilingual edition is decorated with over two hundred woodcuts which make it a particularly fine example of the reception of late classical and humanistic fables in print (see Plates 42–4).

A third early humanist calls for mention, who, besides translating into the vernacular, engaged in the the gathering and restoration of classical Latin poetry and instructional writings: Albrecht von Eyb (1420–75). The intellectual cast of mind of this Eichstätt canon had been formed during a 14-year stay in Italy, where he had become acquainted with the *studia humanitatis*. By 1459 he had compiled a floreligium of rhetorical, poetical and historical writings which Johann Sensenschmidt of Nuremberg first printed in 1472 under the title *Margarita poetica*. He intended this anthology as a book of samples of classical rhetoric, letter-writing and poetry. The lengthy extracts from the works of Virgil, Juvenal, Ovid, Statius, Prudentius as well as Cicero, Valerius Maximus and Apuleius and the newer Italian humanists Petrarch and Poggio pursued the twin aims of making rhetoric native to Germany and so improving its use there, whilst encouraging the wisdom implicit in these texts to be applied in relevant areas of life, thereby contributing to an intellectual renewal. Albrecht von Eyb's compilation has its own specific character and a particular linguistic and philosophical cast that merits closer analysis: but no doubt his contemporaries for the most part regarded it as a straightforward anthology of extracts from classical and humanistic texts not yet available complete in individual editions. The *Margarita* went through at least fifteen editions between 1472 and 1503. In his epilogue, Albrecht von Eyb explained the need to be familar with classical poetry, for only he with such knowledge possessed "the education worthy of a free man".

The *Ehebüchlein*, or "Little Marriage Book" – to take a single example from von Eyb's tracts in German which display his erudition and familiarity with classical, medieval and humanist writers – was issued in 1472 by Anton Koberger in Nuremberg under the explicit title *Ob einem Manne sey zu nehmen ein eheliches Weib oder nicht* (whether a man should marry or not). Apart from the theological context, he stresses the importance of marriage for society and the well-being of the partners. In parallel to this re-evaluation of marriage, the status of women and their cultural significance is seen from a fresh angle with reference to important women in history.

Albrecht von Eyb's translations are distinguished from those of Niclas von Wyle by their livelier prose and a freer handling. He does not translate from Latin slavishly, but "according to the sense and meaning of the material". Albrecht von Eyb belongs accordingly not only to the mediators of classical literature and culture from the Latin, but also to the early creators of literary German.

PRINTING IN GREEK AND HEBREW

Greek texts were only rarely printed in their entirety during the incunabula period, and at first only Greek grammars and dictionaries were typeset in that language (GW 7812–18). The first edition of Homer in Greek appeared in Florence in 1488 (H 8772). This picture changes only after 1495, when Aldus Manutius began to print with Greek types in Venice: by 1498 we find him with Theocritus and Hesiod and nine comedies by Aristophanes in his programme. Prior to this, most Greek authors were known only in Renaissance Latin translation, and this applies to Herodotus and Thucydides or Plutarch (1470, H 13125). The Iliad, for example, had been twice printed in Lorenzo Valla's translation. In 1495 Aldus was ready – in his initial year as publisher – with the first in a five-volume edition of Aristotle (GW 2334; see Plate 36), and in the following ten years he brought out Thucydides, Herodotus, Sophocles, Euripedes, Demosthenes and Plutarch's *Moralia*. He had his own Greek types cut for this purpose in close imitation of fine calligraphic models. Aldus had to close down his printing office between 1509 and 1512 on account of the war against Venice by the League of Cambrai; but in the final three years of his life to 1515 he published Pindar, Plato, Hesychius, Athenaeus and the Attic orators.

Through establishing the "New Academy", a learned society for Greek studies in 1500 in Venice, attracting the best Greek scholars, and making a critical selection of the most suitable texts, Aldus contributed significantly to the textual history of the ancient Greeks. His "head readers" were the Cretans Markos Musurus (Professor of Greek at the

University of the Venetian State in Padua) and Johann Gregoropulos. A great many manuscripts which served Aldus as printer's copy are preserved in the Bibliothèque Nationale in Paris and in the Library of Beatus Rhenanus in Sélestat, and these, taken together with the printed books, are important testimony in the history of text transmission.

There were a number of universities in Italy where Greek studies had been possible since the mid-fifteenth century, including Florence, Rome, Bologna, Ferrara, Pavia and Padua. In addition to that, Greek was also taught at Latin schools in Italy. But the situation was altogether different in German-speaking lands, where reservations concerning the Greek language (and the intellectual outlook associated with it) were manifold. As late as 1521, a monk had cautioned from the pulpit that one should beware this newfangled tongue known as Greek as it was the mother of all heresies, that at that very time a book in that language, calling itself the New Testament, was to be found in many hands, and that this was full of thorns and snakes!

This warning concerned the *Novum Testamentum Graece* of Erasmus of Rotterdam, which had been published by Johann Froben in Basle in the spring of 1516 in two folio volumes, containing the original Greek text with its Latin translation and surrounding commentary. Four further printings of this important edition, which was to form the basis for Luther's *Bible* translation, appeared in 1519, 1522, 1527 and 1535, each time with textual changes and additional notes. In a preamble, Erasmus explained his hermeneutical principles and his future intention of making the *Bible* accessible to ordinary people in the vernacular. This Greek New Testament was the first integral Greek printing in German-speaking lands. In 1515 the first chair in classical Greek was established at Leipzig University. Up until then, interested humanists had had to choose either between an education in Italy or private studies with a scholar such as Conrad Celtis in Vienna.

The Nuremberg patrician and autodidact Willibald Pirckheimer (1470–1530) made himself proficient in Greek from grammars and dictionaries and acquired the Greek writers little by little. Pirckheimer constantly stepped up his efforts to master Greek, and with such success that he is still regarded today as one of the leading intermediaries between Greek literature and Germany. Lucian's treatise *How to write history* was among his first renderings into Latin, and this translation was printed in 1515 in Nuremberg by Friedrich Peypus (1485–1535) so that it could be held up as a model to German humanists to spur them on to greater historical labours. Not by chance did he dedicate this work to the emperor Maximilian I, who was eager to record the history of the empire and of the Habsburgs for posterity. He undertook several literary projects for Maximilian I, including the Ehrenpforte and Triumphzug, on which he worked between 1515 and 1517 together with his friend Albrecht Dürer, who produced the monumental woodcut plates.

A translation of Lucian's Piscator seu reviviscentes printed by Friedrich Peypus in Nuremberg in 1517 carried a dedicatory preface, the Epistola apologetica. In it, Pirckheimer drew an idealized picture of the modern theologian, who should have a comprehensive grasp of all the sciences; he should be well versed in grammar and Latin, Greek and Hebrew letters, know both Aristotelian and Platonic philosophy, and be at home with the quadrivium and the writing of history. The close connection between theology and humanistic studies is clearly apparent from this curriculum drawn up by Pirckheimer.

Among Pirckheimer's most significant translations for the history of learning are Plutarch's Moralia, issued in 1513 by Friedrich Peypus in Nuremberg, and Ptolemy's Geographia of 1525, with large-scale illustrations, from Johann Grüninger in Strasbourg in co-operation with Anton Koberger in Nuremberg.

The medieval rediscovery of the classical languages was accompanied by that of Hebrew, which had largely lain buried. At the end of the fifteenth century, Hebrew manuscripts were brought together and edited in Italy: Avicenna's Canon medicinae, for instance, printed in Naples in 1491 by Azriel ben Joseph Ashkenazi Gunzenhauser (GW 3113). The first Hebrew professorships in Germany date from 1518 in Wittenberg, Erfurt and Leipzig, 1520 in Rostock, 1521 in Greifswald, 1522 in Heidelberg, and 1525 in Tübingen and Freiburg. The Reformation initially encouraged Hebrew studies, but these were soon scaled down to become a mere adjunct to theology. Printing in Hebrew is to be found from the begining of the century in the works of assorted humanists, and the first attempt to expound the Hebrew language from the Christian standpoint came in 1506 with the Rudimenta hebraica of Johann Reuchlin, printed in Pforzheim by Thomas Anshelm (see Plate 38). An abridged Hebrew grammar had appeared in the anthology *Margarita philosophica* by Gregor Reich (1467–1525) from Johann Grüninger in Strasbourg in 1503. The *Margarita* covered a compendium of book learning, and this reference work went through numerous editions between 1503 and 1517.

VADIAN AND THE PROVISION OF TEACHING TEXTS

The demand for reliable texts to work from in academic teaching can be explored through the example of the humanist Vadian (Joachim von Watt, 1484–1551) from St Gall, who taught philosophy and poetics in Vienna in the footsteps of Conrad Celtis after 1508. He particularly emphasised the need for good school editions in the dedication to his pupil Christophorus Crassus (c.1490–1549) which appears in his edition of Sallust's *De coniuratione Catalinae et bello Iugurthino historiae* (Vienna, 1511). Vadian published these texts in connection with his lectures on the historical writings of Sallust. He had observed whilst preparing these, as he put it in his dedicatory letter, in what a sorry state the available editions of Sallust, Lucretius and Pliny were to be found. He took particular exception to an edition which Pomponius Laetus, a pupil of Lorenzo Valla and founder of the Accademia Romana in Rome, had provided in Rome in 1490. In language bristling with metaphor, Vadian describes how in his need he had sought refuge in the new text edited by Aldus Manutius, and compared this resource – in Homer's words in the *Odyssey* – with a "rescue from a great disaster at sea". Vadian had a thousand copies of Aldus's edition reprinted by the printer-publishers Hieronymus Vietor (1480–1546) and Johann Singrenius (c.1480–1545) in Vienna in 1510.

The Elder Pliny's *Praefatio* to his *Naturalis historia*, dedicated to the emperor Vespasian, should be mentioned as one of Vadian's most important editions (Vienna, 1513). In his own dedication to his colleague Georg Collimitius (1482–1535), Vadian gives a detailed account of the only available, and in his opinion inadequate, editions from the Italian humanists. He intends to make his a reliable version that will safeguard the text for the benefit of students.

One of Vadian's mathematical and astronomical editions was of the *Sphaera* attributed to Proklos Diadochus (410–485 AD), which had also appeared in Latin translation in a collection of *Scriptores astronomici veteres* published by Aldus Manutius in 1499. Vadian had this printed and published on its own in 1511 by his friends Vietor and Singrenius. Here, once again he gave prominence in his introduction to protecting the text as the basis for future commentary, and to making classical texts available for the "less well-to-do young". Students were also well served by further reference works, dictionaries and collections of historical documents which were entrusted to him. In this way Vadian edited in 1513 a small publication with glosses (ascribed to Luctatius Placidus) to Ovid's *Metamorphoses*, and dedicated it to his younger brother Melchior as he felt himself "responsible for his intellectual development". And as the writings of Ovid could shape mental aptitudes, he wanted to do all he could to contribute to their spread.

The special role of classical texts in learning and the instruction of pupils becomes apparent from Vadian's dedicatory epistle to the Vienna Boys' Choir. He had dedicated his edition of the seventh book of the Elder Pliny's *Naturalis historia* to them. Calling upon Plato – and in close accord with the ideas of Pico della Mirandola – Vadian wrote that a good knowledge of human nature should be the basis for all debates on philosophy and natural history.

Vadian translated not only classical writings, but also those of Italian and German humanists such as Lorenzo Valla or Conrad Celtis. He issued Celtis's poetical works (*Odes, Epodes, Carmen saeculare*) in 1513 through his Viennese publisher Lukas Alantsee (d. 1522) in an edition printed by Matthias Schürer of Strasbourg. Here, once again he underlined in his preface that these texts should serve not only for the cultivation of the young, but for the promotion of virtue in general. However, the theological faculty in Vienna did not see it that way, and summoned the publisher Alantsee in 1514 to defend himself on account of the immoral and unchristian content detected by some religious orders.

For the Viennese university professors, and their printers in turn, it became apparent how interdependent were scholars, with their concern for the best textual foundations, and publishers, who counted on the scholars for advice.

The procurement of Greek and Hebrew texts for teaching purposes remained difficult for a long time. Reuchlin complained in 1520 that he had found no single printed Greek or Hebrew book available during his lectureship in those subjects at Ingolstadt. Two years later, Reuchlin reported from his position at the University of Tübingen that he had obtained several hundred Hebrew Bibles from Venice, mainly for use as teaching material. He had furthermore only imported editions of Xenophon at his disposal. In 1524 Melanchthon had access to just a single copy for his lectures on Demosthenes, from which he had to dictate a few lines at the start of each lecture in order to be able to comment on them. It is true that printing was up and running to provide great numbers of cheap books, but it took a long time before all scholars and students could be furnished with texts in Greek and Hebrew typography.

Nevertheless, it is possible to confirm that Latin teaching texts had been available in appropriate numbers since about 1480. Outwardly, by this date book design had broken away from manuscript production, the title page and colophon had developed, and octavos and quartos were largely supplanting folio formats. The individual illumination of copies was being replaced by woodcut illustrations printed with the text. Book prices sank during the 1470s to between a half and a quarter of their starting level. Above all, a change came about in the titles on offer: after the Bible editions, liturgical and simple instructional texts, grammars and dictionaries which dominated the early years, it was now the writings of the humanists and editions of the classics which found favour with the printer-publishers.

Printing made possible the transmission of knowledge through affordable text editions which combined literary accuracy with suitable appearance. The advancement of philology through the possibilities opened up by printing and the necessity of teaching from reliable texts were emphatically proclaimed above all by Joachim Vadian, in an introductory poem to a Viennese impression by Vietor and Singrenius in 1511. Because Vadian here goes beyond contemporary topicality and places the invention of printing in a world historical context, and characterises it as a cultural quantum leap that is only to be compared with the discovery of writing by the ancients, it is worth giving the full text in the original Latin and in translation:

Aegiptii quos fertilis fovet Nilus.
Hermem suum subinde laudibus tollunt
Quod litterarum primus ipse repertor
Dederit Nepotibus scientiae lumen.
Agenoris natum vigil beat Graecus
Cadmum / figurae cultioris auctorem:
Phoenice dum suis refert Characteres:
Quos Atticus coluit lepor bona fruge
Dum posteris tam digna lectu compegit.
Latina lingua gloriatur Carmentem
Quae mater et nutrix veteris est Euandri
Cum patriam linguens novas sedes quaerit
Latio attulisse formulas: quarum est usus
In litteris politioribus. Verum
Germanus is qui litteras fudit Stanno
Docuitque tantum comprimi semel praelo
Quantum celerrimae manus die longo
Scribunt: beatus et perennitur foelix
Praecellit Hercle cuncta priscorum inventa
Quanto melius animum polire quam corpus.
Iam Chalcitypus humanus est: siquidem scribit:
Iam quod legas praestat benignitas aeris:
Et quo frequenter percolas diam mentem.
Si vivat Hermes gratias ageret Rheno:
Et Cadmus ipse si rederit ex umbris:
Carmentis ipsa / si veniret ex Orco
Cum Graeca cernerent rudi imprimi plumbo.
Hebraeque et quaecunque sunt prius scripta:
Tam insigniter quam nunc latina cuduntur.

An iambic by Joachim Vadian
on the well-deserved praise of printing

The Egyptians showered with favours from the fertile river Nile
never tired of extolling their god Hermes, for as the prime

inventor of letters he had bestowed the light of knowledge on posterity.

The Greeks praised Cadmus, son of Agenor, for his attention as creator of a more developed form of writing. The characters which he caused his brother Phoinix to bring home to his countrymen raised Attic sensibilities to a higher plane and combined them with literature worthy to be handed down to future generations. Latinists attribute to Carmenta, mother of the ancient Evander, the honour of bringing to Latium those characters employed in polite letters, when she left her native land in search of a new residence.

The Germans, however, cast single letters from metal and showed that through a single pull of the press the highest daily output of the nimblest scribe could be exceeded, thus out-shining all the inventions of the ancients put together; praise and glory to them!

And how much more highly are mental labours to be valued than physical ones? Even if a man still writes (by hand) today, he is in a sense already a printer. For what one reads and by what means one's god-given brains are fed will be attended to from now onwards by the quality of metal alloy.

If Hermes still lived, so would he thank the Rhine, as would Cadmus returned from the realm of shades or Carmenta back from the underworld, if all were able to see how Greek, Hebrew and everything that was earlier written by hand now gets printed metallically just as excellently as does Latin.

The national argument most frequently used in praise of the invention of printing – that Gutenberg's invention now enabled the Germans to share in the intellectual world of the classics – was placed by Vadian in a world historical context. In the form of a four-stage progression which culmi-nated in Gutenberg's invention of moveable letters, the Egyptian god Toth (re-cast as the mythological Hermes), who was looked upon as the inven-tor of written signs, is first recalled. Then Cadmus, descendant of the pro-genitor of the Phoenicians, Agenor, and considered since Herodotus to be the inventor of the Greek alphabet and thus father of Western cul-ture. The Arcadian naiad Carmenta, who migrated to Italy with her son

Evander, finally serves as the inventor of the earliest Latin alphabet, which had 15 letters. With his word-play on *litterae politiores*, Vadian alludes not only to the cultivated Latin of classical literature, but also to the neo-Latin humanistic poetry of his own day which was also described by those same words. Vadian intended to bridge the gap between the works of Roman antiquity and the present in using this term, but he further plays on *litterae politiores* to refer to the use of roman type (as opposed to black letter) for the works of his contemporaries.

Gutenberg cumulated all mankind's former advances through his invention, which now made it possible in a single printing operation to publish many times more than any diligent copying could yield. It was not these new quantities alone, but above all the quality and accuracy of publication, that vouched for the fact that education could now shed a universal light.

Vadian shows how in the year 1511 printing had not only spread right across Europe, but that it was already possible to set and print with Greek or Hebrew types. The extremely close bond between technical history and intellectual history is tersely expressed in Vadian's poem: only through the discovery of letter forms and the new scope to multiply them endlessly could knowledge and culture be globally disseminated.

A FEW DISSENTING VOICES

The arguments brought on the humanist side were almost exclusively in favour of printing, but there were isolated voices opposed to it. The verdict of Abbot Johannes Trithemius in a publication descriptively entitled *De laude scriptorum* (1515) is well known. He begins with the question of durability, since for him the manuscript still remains associated with vellum, but printing with that relatively new material, paper:

> Writing, if set down on vellum, will last for a millennium;
> however printing is on paper, and so how long will it last? It
> would be much if printing in a paper volume were to survive for
> two hundred years in the opinion of many by reason of the
> material on which it is printed. Let the future decide that. But
> even if many printed books shall become available, yet they

will never be printed to the extent that one can't easily find something to copy that has not already been printed [. . .] He who gives up the occupation of writing for the sake of printing, is no true friend of manuscript transmission: since at best he fixes his gaze on the present and takes no pains to provide for future generations [. . .] When compared to the handwritten book, the printed one can never be placed on the same level. The printer generally takes little care over the spelling and layout of his books. But he who transcribes, goes to much trouble in these matters.

The scholarly contention that insufficient care is exercised in the composing room is widely shared by the humanists. Their general concern is expressed in a complaint which Erasmus of Rotterdam makes in his introduction to Lorenzo Valla's *Annotationes* to the Latin translation of the New Testament, namely that: "in earlier times a single writing mistake would only affect one copy, but now it appears in an edition of thousands".

The printer-publishers acknowledged this danger, and that is why Peter Schoeffer reassures his customers in a list advertising books in stock of 1472: "No one should refrain from purchasing these books on the grounds that they may be disfigured through slipshod workmanship or downright errors [. . .]. All may see with what care and attention and how much mental and physical labour the texts of these books have been read and revised." But the very fact that the correctness of the text needed to be emphasised in this way shows clearly how prevalent this criticism had become.

Theological suspicions were directed not against printing as such, but rather against the translation of the "holy" Greek and Latin tongues into German and against possible misuse. In one of the first censorship pronouncements, on 22 March 1485, the Archbishop of Mainz, Berthold of Henneberg, gave his views on translations from Greek or Latin into German:

Although people may come to acquire erudition thanks to the so-called divine art of printing by turning to the books of the various sciences which are readily available in ample measure, we have nevertheless heard how certain men, tempted by greed after fame and fortune, have misused this art and steered that which had been given to mankind for the cultivation of life into the paths of corruption and falsification. Then we had to see books containing the order of the Mass, and sundry others, that were written on divine matters and the cardinal issues of our religion, translated from Latin into German and falling into the hands of common folk, not without bringing dishonour to religion.

The respectability of printing is not in question, but care has to be taken that:

the unsullied purity of godly writings shall be preserved. And so we command that no work, whatever its kind and to whichever science, art and knowledge it refers, that has been or shall be translated from Greek, Latin or any other language into German, publicly or secretly, directly or indirectly, shall be printed or such printing offered for sale, without the appointed doctors and masters of the university of our city of Mainz or such in our city of Erfurt respectively, being allowed to examine it and issue a permit for it to be printed or offered for sale.

The threatened penalty was excommunication, forfeiture of the books and a fine of 100 gold gulden. A proper concern for textual accuracy in translation has here become confused with the prevalent fear of theological texts in the vernacular.

In a papal bull – dated two years before Luther's first reformatory stirrings of 1515 – Leo X brought this concern to the point where he denounced anew the spread of texts in the vernacular. He had this to say about translations: "Errors of faith just as pernicious contain teachings contrary to Christian religion and matters aimed at the reputation of high-ranking dignitaries, so that to risk printing and selling writings, from the reading of which no edification is to be derived, will lead readers instead into the gravest errors in faith as well as in their lives and morals. Out of this, as teachers' experience proves, manifold troubles issue forth which it is to be feared will grow worse from day to day." Accordingly, censorship was enacted to the greater glory of God, and for the welfare of the faithful the supervision of the printing of books was instituted, "so that in future thorns may not grow together with the good seeds nor poison be mixed with medicines".

Despite the high-flown language, the fear of the Church establishment that it will lose power and influence with the spread of theological and religious knowledge in the vernacular is evident. By contrast, the only arguments raised by their humanisic contemporaries against printing were bibliophilic ones relating to the aesthetics of handwriting and a literary reminder that the mass production of texts in a printing office must be at least as well controlled as in a scriptorium. But beyond that, all the evidence from letters, introductions and the published books themselves speaks for the fact that printing clearly corresponded to the educational endeavours of the humanists.

Popular instruction in the vernacular

From the first books of Gutenberg up until 1500 – the year laid down on purely bibliographical grounds for the end of the incunabula (Lat. *incunabula*, cradle) period – some 30,000 different publications appeared that are still traceable today. Eighty per cent of these were written in Latin, the obligatory European language of the Church and the learned community. Naturally, this had one tremendous advantage for the many printing offices spread right across Europe, in that their marketing area was not confined to a single narrowly encircled territory. That is why the Frankfurt book fair, for example, developed at so early a date into an emporium for books from France, the Netherlands and Italy.

Only the remaining 20 per cent of printing was in the vernacular, although this share was to continue to rise. Early romances for light reading were published in German, alongside short dogmatic writings, herbals and guides to living. The domination of the book market by Latin was not broken until the end of the seventeenth century, with the Reformation in Central Europe during the sixteenth century playing no inconsiderable part in this.

But the circulation of narrative fiction in the German language may be dated back to the manuscripts of the late Middle Ages. The circumstances surrounding its reception began to alter, and this new readership was no longer exclusively made up from ecclesiastical and titled circles; it came from crafts and tradespersons in the towns and from lay intellectuals at the courts of the nobility. An outward sign of this steady rise in reading numbers is offered by the late-medieval manuscript workshop of Diebold Lauber of Hagenau in Alsace, in which up to five scribes and sixteen illustrators were active at times between 1427 and 1467. From "publisher's advertisements" and numerous surviving manuscripts we are very well informed about his publishing repertoire of 38 titles. Lauber manufactured his manuscripts on a production line, down to their pen-drawn decoration. We find him offering "typological" *Bibles*, courtly and heroic epics, religious and instructional texts, juristic and natural historical writings. Eighteen manuscript copies of the "typological *Bible*" alone have survived: a popular, vernacular pairing of texts, in which stories from the Old Testament are supported and enriched by tales from apocryphal and secular history, omitting the prophetical books. Konrad von Mengenberg's *Buch der Natur* belongs to the natural history category, and the *Schwabenspiegel* or *Belial* are legal texts. Knightly epics are represented by Wolfram von Eschenbach's *Parzival* and Gottfried von Strassburg's *Tristan*. Lauber was equally successful at marketing an "art of dying", prayer books, the *Zehn Gebote* or ten commandments with commentary, the *Legende der heiligen drei Könige* or the *Pfaffen Amis* by Der Stricker. Lauber produced stock in advance, and so needed to advertise his wares. His texts were always clearly set out, and came complete with table of contents, headings and, of course, pictures. The coloured pen-drawings were executed on a production line as well, making use of multi-functional picture types.

These titles satisfied the prevailing public taste very well, which explains why light reading in the vernacular found its way into print so early on. The works of Wolfram von Eschenbach came out in 1477 from Johann Mentelin in Strasbourg, as did Gottfried von Strassburg's *Tristan*. The early Augsburg printer Günther Zainer had learned his skills from Mentelin in Strasbourg, from whence he returned to Swabia with both the technology and a successful publishing plan. Augsburg became a publishing centre for the German prose romance in the 1470s and 1480s; besides Zainer, Johann Bämler, Anton Sorg and Johann Schönsperger the elder devoted themselves to this genre. Anton Sorg printed *Tristrant* in 1484 and *Wilhelm von Österreich* in 1481 and 1491. From 1483 onwards, Schönsperger printed the romance *Pontus und Sidonia* (the translation is attributed to Eleonore of the Tyrol) at least four times, the *Alexander* romance at least nine times from 1472, and the story *Griseldis* again on nine occasions. Texts frequently reappeared in pirated editions from Strasbourg; thus we find a printing dating from *c.*1489 of the *Troja* (Troy) romance that had already appeared from Bämler, Sorg and Schönsperger from 1474 onwards. In addition to the literature of the late Middle Ages in German, translations of popular works from the Italian fifteenth century were undertaken, such as the above-mentioned Petrarch romance *Griseldis*, or *Florio und Biancefora* after Boccaccio. Favourites among romances modelled on French tales included *Melusine* by Thüring von Ringoltingen alongside *Pontus und Sidonia* or the *Ritter von Turn* in Marquart von Stein's translation.

Since the early nineteenth century these texts have come under the general heading of "chapbooks", but modern literary criticism prefers to call them "prose romances". In his study *Der Mythos vom Volksbuch* (1977), Joachim Kreuzer concludes that the term "Volksbuch" (popular or chapbook), which dates back to the romantic era, evokes the wrong connotations with reference to the conditions in which these texts came into being as well as those under which they were distributed and read. The more neutral description "prose romance" makes it clear that these texts are no longer in verse form (and thus for recitation), but rather in prose, which indicates that they were meant for the private reader. Quite a number of the Middle High German epics were rendered from verse into prose after the invention of printing. The contemporary term for these texts was "Historia", which denoted romance-like tales that hopefully would be taken for true. The connecting element was the notion of truth in popular historiography and the edifying character of these credited stories. In support of this feigned writing of history, sources of evidence were cited, eyewitness reports in the case of *Alexander des Großen Historie* by Johann Hartlieb, or biographical references and alleged surviving documents for *Eulenspiegel* or for *Doktor Faustus*. Taken as a group, "Historia" represents an attempt to combine truths and what might pass for truth into a credible didactic message, for instance in *Melusine* the warning of the fragility of human happiness, or with *Fortunatus* the moral: "wisdom instead of riches". Actual places, dates and distance measurements contribute to the air of authenticity.

These Augsburg editions were provided as a rule with powerfully stated woodcuts that illustrated the narratives in a lively manner. The representation of emotions through stereotypes, frequent enough in the storytelling, was repeated in the woodcuts: as a sign of love, a box containing a heart would be presented, and farewells and welcomes would take place at a town wall or by the sea shore. The woodblocks themselves were often sold on, crudely sawn down to fit new formats, and used again in different contexts. A moral exhortation accompanied the earliest of these histories ("Here ends the book and history of how the rich, delightful and mighty city of Troy was destroyed through the destiny of God. As an example to the whole world"), but this was soon replaced by an emphasis on entertainment value ("Hereinafter follows the history of Lord Tristan and the fair Isolde of Ireland, which history well merits an opening speech, though it be unused, since readers and listeners are vexed by long preambles . . .").

The vernacular prose romance of the fifteenth century in German is inconceivable without the translated output, or rather the stimulus to translate, provided by two ladies of the German-Austrian higher nobility: Elisabeth of Nassau-Saarbrücken (1393–1456) and Eleonore of the Tyrol (1430–80). Both were politically active and were deeply involved with French and Latin literature. One of the translations of *Pontus und Sidonia*, a prose romance originating in France around 1400, can be traced back to Eleonore. It describes the flight of the king's son Pontus, driven from his native Spain by the Moors, who foils many plots and in the end wins the favour of the princess Sidonia of Britain through heroic deeds. Johann Schönsperger printed this "fair history" in 1483, 1485, 1491 and 1498. Plate 39 is taken from the 1498 edition and depicts the wedding of Pontus and Sidonia. This woodcut is still crude in style, with no attempt to achieve spatial recession or represent the landscape, and with only the simplest shadings, but it is enlivened by the contemporary colouring, which was probably added in the printer's workshop.

Whilst the framing story runs along the classical lines of a journey in search of a bride, with the overcoming of various dangers and the testing of the hero through adversities, Sidonia represents an emergent type of self-confident heroine who behaves autonomously within the personal and political scope available to her.

Similarly, Elisabeth of Nassau-Saarbrücken succeeded in carrying the knightly romantic style over into a realistic treatment of contemporary themes with her translation of a French *chanson de geste* into a German prose romance. She translated *Huge Scheppel* into German in 1437. The titular hero is Hugo Capet, son of a prince and a butcher's daughter. Great heroic exploits win him the hand of the daughter of Ludwig, last of the Carolingians (here put forward as the son of Charlemagne). In a second part, which only survives in the German version, the hero has to fend off many envious persons. Because of his lowly origins and unfeigned honesty, the hero of the title became well known and achieved widespread popularity. *Hug Schapler*, the first of Elisabeth's translations, appeared as a "truthful historie" in a re-working by

Konrad Heindörffer from the Strasbourg printing office of Johann Grüninger in 1500. Grüninger printed and published liturgical and theological texts as his main line of business, alongside numerous editions of the classics. His German-language publications are distinguished by their magnificent woodcut illustrations (see Plate 40). Lively depiction and an effect of recession are due to the fine hatchings, reminiscent of copper engraving, which make any kind of colouring superfluous. The publicity value of the narrative illustration underlines a new function for the title page, which gives a short and sharp summary of the contents in five lines, and advertises in a single size of type that this "true history" will prove a "good read" (*"lieplich lesen"*).

Alongside these translations from French and Italian, and the renderings of Middle High German epics into early New High German prose form, there are "original romances" in the vernacular to be met with increasingly after 1500, such as *Fortunatus* (1507), the *Eulenspiegel* (c. 1510), or the *Historia von D. Johann Fausten* (1587). Besides their issue as individual titles, collections of these tales and novelettes began to appear in the sixteenth century, like, for instance, the enormous compendium *Das Buch der Liebe* which Sigmund Feyerabend brought out in Frankfurt in 1587.

However, the favourite prose for German readers was not drawn from this fictional literature alone, but from instructional matter in the form of fables and early textbooks. Herbals, medical guides and encyclopaedias reached out to a new public in the towns.

ENCYCLOPAEDIAS

Take your way, oh book, and soar swiftly through the air;
Never was anything printed to compare with you.
A thousand hands grasp out for you with eager love,
You are constantly read with busy purpose.
In you, human affairs follow the deeds of the gods,
Each page is adorned with splendid decoration.
You report the primal dawn and creation of matter,
All that has ever happened, you make completely known.

In this bookseller's advertisement (the original is in Latin) from the year 1493, a masterpiece of book art is being launched with a poem: a chronicle of the world from the pen of the Nuremberg town physician Hartmann Schedel. With humanistic erudition, a compendium of received and contemporary knowledge is provided in word and picture, and made further accessible through extensive and detailed indexes. Relating to actual events in time, whether warlike threats or natural disasters, this work is recommended as a comprehensive manual for any educated person prepared to read not just the orthodox theological interpretation, but also empirically based knowledge when this is reliably presented. The totality of scientific culture, for which the antique world had already coined the term "encyclopaedia", is contained in this monumental work, which above all possesses great clarity and vitality through its illustrations.

Some 1400 copies of the Latin version and about 800 copies of the German edition of the *Weltchronik* were produced in 1493 in Nuremberg by Anton Koberger's large enterprise there. The *Nuremberg Chronicle* has remained famous to this day for its numerous woodcut views of towns, sometimes the earliest ones extant. It is true that only a small proportion of these are authentic: for instance, one and the same woodblock does duty for Mainz, Naples, Aquila, Bologna and Lyons, for – according to the medieval tradition of praising towns – they all had to be protected by high walls, situated on a river to facilitate trade and close to a mountain range to ensure a good climate. But other views, such as those of Regensberg or Nuremberg, are still highly regarded for their faithful recording of detail. A consortium was formed in Nuremberg for this production. Michael Wolgemut and his stepson Wilhelm Pleydenwurff created the woodcuts in their workshop, and since Albrecht Dürer was a pupil with them from 1486 to 1489, this has led to much speculation as to whether the young Dürer may have been involved in the preliminary drawings for these woodblocks.

The impetus for the project came from two Nuremberg citizens known to be patrons, Sebald Schreyer and Sebastian Kammermeister. The wealthy dealer Schreyer was a councillor and master of St Sebald's church between 1482 and 1503. Together with his brother-in-law, the mining entrepreneur Kammermeister, he carried the financial risk of this book.

Hartmann Schedel, who had been commissioned by them, divided his chronicle into seven "ages of the world" in accordance with the story of the Creation. And when he presents different creation myths at the outset, he nevertheless leaves us in no doubt about the scriptural dimension: "But all these things were not made by Jupiter, but by the architect of the world, the source of redemption, whom we call God." The first age interprets the Creation story (see Plate 41), and the second age begins with the building of Noah's ark and ends with the departure of Lot and the destruction of Sodom. The third age contains the stories of Abraham, Moses, Joseph and King Saul. Here, wide-ranging accounts of the history of Greece and the ancient gods are introduced, as well as descriptions of the cities of Paris, Mainz, Venice and Padua, since Schedel traces their respective foundations back, directly or indirectly, to the Trojans.

The fourth age starts with King David and Solomon, and ends with the destruction of Jerusalem. Rome's history is slipped in here, with further digressions on ancient poets and philosophers. The fifth age extends from the Babylonian captivity as far as the beheading of John the Baptist, although Persian history, Alexander's campaigns and a further stretch of Roman history engage the author's special interest as well.

The sixth age takes us from the birth of Christ to the present, thus comprising some 1500 years; it also makes the longest chapter, with over 300 pages. The next few pages are left blank to give each reader the chance to write up entries which will carry the chronicle forward with events taking place during his or her lifetime. In this chapter, most of the authentic townscapes are to to be found in the order of their foundation dates: Regensburg, Vienna, Nuremberg, Metz, Geneva, Constantinople, Budapest, Strasbourg and so forth.

The seventh age once again contains scriptural meditations on the end of the world, corresponding to the opening chapter. The map of Germany included at the end of the book is the first map of Central Europe to appear in print, and is a reworking of the so-called Cusanus Map of 1439 by the Nuremberg cosmographer Hieronymous Münster (1437–1508).

This encyclopaedia is of the greatest interest to us on book historical grounds, since the handwritten layouts for both the Latin and German versions have been preserved in their entirety in Nuremberg City Library. These let us follow the preparatory writing out of the text and the preliminary sketches for the illustrations as well. Anton Koberger had to raid the riches of his previous book production, and especially his German Bibles, in order to make up the huge number of 645 woodblocks that were called upon for the 1809 illustrations.

Hartmann Schedel put together his text from various sources; in another of his books he states his working principle: *Colligite fragmenta, ne pereant* ("Gather up the fragments that remain, that nothing be lost"), in the words of the miracle of loaves and fishes. By these means, the encyclopaedia offered a comprehensive synthesis of the state of knowledge of its time, still framed in theological modes of thinking, but alert to contemporary experience. Consequently, we find all sorts of matter being extracted from this printed chronicle throughout the sixteenth century, as often in other historical-geographical descriptions of the world such as Sebastian Münster's *Cosmographey* (Basle, 1550) as in current collections of tales for which it provides the basis for fictional travel descriptions. For instance, Dr Johann Faust (when his legend first assumed a fixed literary form in 1587) took an unusual route for his journey through the air on a winged horse; he went from Trier to Paris and thence by way of Mainz to reach Naples. This lets us glimpse how the still unknown author of the *Historia von D. Johann Fausten* made up this early flight plan at his writing desk whilst leafing through the pages of the *Schedelsche Weltchronik* (fols 23–42). In other words, the itinerary follows the sequence of the woodcuts exactly. The author of this story, written a full century later and published in 1587, took over not just the order of the woodcuts, but relied on the chronicle for factual data on various large European towns, their trading structure and the local etymology for place names. This prominent example makes clear the importance of this vast Nuremberg book enterprise for the cultural, intellectual and book history of the early modern period.

It is also possible to trace Anton Koberger's far-flung trading connections, with copies sold to Florence, Venice, Bologna, Milan and Lyons and, perhaps less predictably, to Graz, Vienna and Buda or to Breslau, Krakow and Danzig. The final account of sales which has survived shows that besides his own business partners, there were booksellers, booktraders and bookbinders, and merchants and traders involved in this distribution, among them factors of the Fugger trading and banking houses in Augsburg and Nuremberg, and individual clerics and academics who acted as agents.

It was natural enough for Gutenberg's invention to be honoured in such an encyclopaedia. Schedel praises it for its capacity to mediate, and counts it among mankind's greatest advances:

> The art of printing first took place in the city of Mainz on the
> Rhine in AD 1440, from whence it spread to all parts of the world.
> By its means the riches of literature and wisdom contained in the
> books of the ancients – long unknown to the world and buried in
> the grave of ignorance – have again been brought to light [. . .].
> If this art had been discovered and employed sooner, undoubtedly
> many books of Livy, Cicero or Pliny and other highly learned
> men would not have been lost through the ravages of time. And
> as the inventor of that art and craft of printing now merits no
> small amount of praise, who can say with what measure of praise,
> honour or renown are to be esteemed those Germans who,
> through their enlightened, ingenious and apt knowledge of
> printing have discovered how the long closed fountains of untold
> wisdom, whether human or divine in origin, can be made to flow
> forth to all mankind.

FABLES

The fable is particularly suited to conveying the basic constants of human
behaviour, ethical standards and the practical conduct of life. Already in
his Rhetoric, Aristotle thinks highly of the fable as a means of convinc-
ing through a contrived example. The fable belongs on the one hand to
animal literature, on the other hand to instructive literature which gives
advice through disguising truth as fiction. This fictionality is asserted by
protagonists drawn predominantly from the animal kingdom, which
from time to time behave like humans; by constructing particularly
compelling examples which relate to the human condition, the didactic
aspect of this modest literary form is predetermined. It follows that
these pointed exemplary tales may be prefaced or concluded by spiritual, moral or political advice at some length: "And the moral of this
story . . .".

So it is not surprising that among the few early German-language
texts of the incunabula period, editions of fables should be repeatedly
encountered. A mere six years after the invention of printing, the first
vernacular text – and the earliest illustrated book – was printed by

Pfister in Bamberg: Ulrich Boner's collection of fables, Der Edelstein. Another collection appeared fifteen years later, the Latin-German edition known as the Ulm Aesop compiled by Heinrich Steinhöwel.

The fable collection Der Edelstein by Ulrich Boner, a Dominican from Berne, was completed in 1349 and strove to be a "mirror of life's wisdom". The hundred examples from Aesop are drawn from the world of animals and plants, and only to a limited extent from human life. The rhymed Middle High German fables are so grouped that a natural progression through the morals can be followed. Often morals are juxtaposed in pairs, so that each enhances the other's effectiveness: kernel and shell, faithful and unfaithful spouses, deserved and undeserved ridicule, treachery and uprightness, success and failure, greed and contentment. Moral teaching is opposed to "deceit, trickery, underhandedness, hypocrisy, envy, avarice, miserliness, bickering, violence, vanity", and argues instead for "freedom, honour, and skill". The title comes from a fable which tells of a cock who finds a precious stone in the dirt but does not recognise its worth and asks a grain of seed in exchange for it, for that at least he can eat. Just like this precious stone, the poem is meant only for prudent and sensible folk, and not for fools who lack proper insight. The same moral is pointed out in a second fable, with which this printed book starts out. It tells of apes who only long for the sweetness of the nut kernel, as the shell is too hard and bitter for them. This can be seen in Plate 42, and the book opens on to this page without any preamble, since most early editions were printed without any title page in the modern sense.

Boner states in his epilogue that his work has been "zu tütsche bracht von latein", that is, taken from Latin into German. This should not be taken as meaning a literal translation, but rather that the originals have served him as a general source. He names his authorities for some of the examples in the text, and in Fable 55 he mentions Aesop as the begetter of the genre in antiquity.

Boner takes over pre-existing content, and paraphrases it for his readership. He clothes familiar material in the costume of the age for the instruction and entertainment of his public, and to make it accessible to them. He treats his sources very freely for the most part, and writes at length, occasionally using pentameters in verse in contrast to his patterns. A constant in fable writing is that animals embody human attributes and characteristics: the lion is proud, the fox is cunning, the ass is stupid, etc. People and animals are representatives of a type, bearers of a projected character. Boner generally uses rhyming couplets of four metrical feet. This is not apparent from the look of the page, as the text is not set as verse, but run-on in a justified measure to save space. Reading is not easy, not just because of this typesetting convention, but on account of the author's clumsy versifying. Beauty of language and elegance of expression generally elude him. Add to this the fact that a printed version of the second half of the fifteenth century has been based on a manuscript exemplar that was already more than a century old and thus out of fashion.

Nevertheless, one can speak of a vogue for manuscripts of the *Edelstein* in the fourteenth and early fifteenth centuries, as a good two dozen copies and additional fragments are extant. So it is not surprising that early printing seized upon *Der Edelstein*, since it generally took its cue from the "bestsellers" of the manuscript era. Early printing in Bamberg is linked to the name of Albrecht Pfister. He brought out some nine titles between 1460 and 1464, among which are the *Vier Historien* (free adaptations of the Old Testament stories of Joseph, Daniel, Judith and Esther), a German and a Latin *Biblia Pauperum*, and the *Belial* of Jacobus de Theramo; and then in about 1470 there came Johann von Tepl's *Der Ackermann aus Böhmen*. All Pfister's publications are set in large missal-type, and he printed almost exclusively in German. Furthermore, all his works contain woodcut illustrations, and this was something quite new in the early days of printing. The Boner edition is preserved in a unique and complete copy in the Duke August Library at Wolfenbüttel. It was completed – so the colophon tells us – on St Valentine's Day 1461: "At Bamberg is this little book finished after the birth of our Lord Jesu Christ in the years that are numbered 1400 and in the 61st, it is true, on St Valentine's Day. God protect us from his plague. Amen."

Der Edelstein is printed in the B36 types (those of the 36-line *Bible*), which in their monumentality suit neither the text nor the illustrations. The font available for typesetting comprised 192 letters, punctuation marks, contractions and ligatures. Following a manuscript tradition that was still very much alive, a rubricator has marked the opening capital of each verse line and added large initials in red to enhance readability. Otherwise, capitals are only used at the beginning of lines of verse, and then only in so far as typographic sorts were provided: "W" and "Z" are missing altogether, which can be taken as an indication that this fount was originally cast for setting Latin texts. In the same way, the lower-case "w" is missing, and Pfister gets round this by setting an unpointed "i" against a "v" as a makeshift "w", but since there is no linking stroke between these characters the deception is easily spotted. Each sheet was passed through the press three times: first for the text, then for the woodcut showing the main scene, and finally for the woodcut with the figure of the narrator. This can be seen from Plate 43, where the pictorial woodcut has fallen below its allotted space and overprinted the text, so that the narrator block has had to be repositioned to overprint both. It would require further technical experimentation before the leaden type material and the wooden illustrations could be transferred to paper in the same impression.

The woodcuts in the single surviving copy were hand-coloured at the time. They are simple in style, and do not show any interiors or detailed representations of architecture or landscape. The animal drawing is crude: it is hardly possible to tell a wolf from a dog, or a horse from a donkey. The lion is closer to a heraldic beast, and unlikely to scare anyone.

The figures of the narrators are recurrent leitmotifs, and we find this tradition in the earlier Boner manuscripts. A few of the pictorial subjects are derived from these medieval manuscripts, although we are not able to point to one particular manuscript which may have served as the model for this edition.

THE ULM AESOP

Printing came to Ulm on the direct initiative of the humanist and city physician Dr Heinrich Steinhöwel, who lived there from 1450 until his death in 1478. His extensive literary activity centred on making humanist texts available in translation for a German public. His first opus was a translation of a Latin prose romance dating from late antiquity which he completed in 1461, and which he published as König Apollonius von Thyrus with the Augsburg printer Günther Zainer in 1471.

His next work was to become one of the key publications of early humanism in South Germany, his famous translation of Petrarch's Latin reworking of the *Griseldis* story from Boccaccio's *Decameron*. The first edition appeared, also in 1471, from Zainer in Augsburg, and went through two new impressions within a year. Steinhöwel got to know Günther Zainer's younger brother Johann through this involvement, and persuaded him to move to Ulm, promising to support him financially in setting up a printing office. On 11 January 1473 the first dated edition left the new press at Ulm. It was a work of Steinhöwel's from his main professional field of activity: *Das büchlein der ordnung der pestilenz*, the first printed book about the plague by a contemporary writer, and one of the earliest of all medical texts in German.

Although the *Aesop* edition contains a printer's mark, there is no date given, but a comparison of the typefaces used allows it to be reliably assigned to the winter of 1476/7. The *Aesop* became his most successful book. This Latin-German volume comprises 171 chapters in eight parts, starting with a novelistic *Vita Aesopi* and followed by the body of the text, which divides 80 fables of similar extent but different provenance into four books. As in the remainder of his translated output, Steinhöwel makes very free use of the source material. By inserting proverbs, rhymes, popular sayings and allusions to real events, he often makes his versions half as long again as the originals and adapts the book for a broader reading public. It is clear how much interest this compilation generated from the fact that it ran through about twenty editions before 1500, for which the woodcuts were taken, directly or indirectly, from the Ulm edition. The book's European reputation, however, was based on a Latin version produced by Anton Sorg of Augsburg in 1480. In Zainer's edition, after an initial woodcut portrait of the author, we find 190 woodcuts which in their diversity of subject matter provide a panorama of late medieval life. People are shown in modern costume, and detailed information is given for the furniture and interiors. Animal scenes are enacted in front of landscape backdrops, although these are still formally simplified. Differentiated colouring of the various picture planes manages to convey an effect of spatial recession (see Plate 44). For most of the fables, no pictorial references would have been needed, nor anything that would have been difficult for the artist who drew on the blocks or the woodcutter to have found in Ulm. An exception has to be made for the Bamberg edition of Ulrich Boner's *Der Edelstein*, from which we can detect a few borrowings, as for example in the fable of the wolf and the crane, with its lateral reversal of the wood-cut from Boner's fable of the wolf and the stork. The two surviving copies of this book – equally popular and valuable on account of its decoration - are hand-coloured throughout: even the hundred initials (outline Lombardics) have been coloured in. It is highly probable that this work was carried out in Ulm, perhaps even to the printer's commission and in the workshop responsible for the illustrations.

PRACTICAL BOOKS

It is of great interest for the history of science that, thanks to printing, technical literature was not only disseminated in Latin for theoretical teaching purposes within the universities, but that the literature of the seven free arts – grammar, rhetoric, dialectics, astronomy, geometry, arithmetic and music – appeared in large print runs in the German vernacular for an educated urban public. Peter Schoeffer published a *Herbarius* in Mainz in 1484 (probably in imitation of the first herbal produced in Rome in 1483), and stated in a preface that it was expressly intended for the general public. The sole concession to those ignorant of Latin was that the German names appeared in the captions to 150 woodcuts of plants, otherwise the text was kept in Latin throughout. In the following year, though, he did bring out in German a more elaborately designed *Gart der Gesundheit* with 381 woodcut illustrations. Next to woodcuts in simple outline are to be found blocks with lively hatching and three-dimensional effects. The hand-colouring, typical for the period and probably organised by the publisher, gives the pictures clarity and vitality. The relation of this extensive text to numerous illustrations makes this herbal a masterpiece of layout (see Plate 45). This 'garden of health' describes 382 plants, 25 animals and 28 minerals under their Latin names in its total of 435 chapters. The author, the Frankfurt city physician Johann Wonnecke of Kaub, falls back on German sources from the twelfth to the fourteenth centuries. Starting with an Augsburg reprint in its year of first publication, 1485, the *Gart der Gesundheit* met with a tremendous reception that continued with 15 further incunabula editions and 55 others through to the eighteenth century. The Mainz printer-publisher Jacob Meydenbach translated it in 1491 and published it in that same year as his *Hortus Sanitatis*, a volume of more than 900 pages containing 1073 woodcuts. Copiously illustrated herbals were also printed in Italy and France during the incunabula period.

Plants were the the focus of attention, not for themselves, but for their healing properties, and similar success was to attend books of popular medical advice. The Augsburg physician Bartolomäus Metlinger published his *Kinderbüchlein* in 1473 with Günther Zainer, and it went into more than thirty printings by 1571. Metlinger had studied in Padua – as was the general custom – and had learned the anatomical presentation of clinical pictures from his teacher there, Paulo Bagellardi. Beyond that, the text offered instruction on baby care and tips for bringing up children. His introduction is expressly addressed to "fathers and mothers".

Hieronymus Brunschwig (c.1450–1512) turned to the practical side of medicine with *Dis ist das Buch der chirurgia. Hantwirkung der wund artzeney* (1497). This first medical text book in German and with clear illustrations was intended for doctors, medical students and nurses. An experienced publisher was found in Johann Grüninger of Strasbourg, who had already introduced a variety of large-format woodcuts of the best quality in his publications. The 61 woodcuts are printed from only 18 different blocks. Two equally large blocks predominate, which yield several pictorial variants when combined with others. We have already noted the successful hatchings in his woodcuts for Terence (Plate 28) and the *Hug Schapler* romance (compare Plate 40). They gain their effect from black and white contrast and from the grey values achieved by hatchings, so that additional colouring may be dispensed with. This medical textbook was also reprinted many times. Grüninger himself reissued it in 1513 with 60 new woodcuts.

Even more strongly practical in orientation was a guide to midwifery by the city physician of Frankfurt and Worms, Eucharius Rösslin, published by Martin Flach in Strasbourg in 1513. As a scholar concerned with the theoretical aspects of medicine, this doctor wrote a compendium on childbirth for lay persons. Doctors or surgeons seldom took the trouble to attend births, which were left almost exclusively to "wise women". This manual in German enjoyed enormous success, and over a hundred editions are known over the following decades. Because Rösslin put this guide together from many sources, and had little or no practical experience of his own, it contains a mass of false information. Thus he writes that it is normal for the baby to emerge head first, "its face bent backwards so that it is looking towards the heavens or towards the navel of its mother". In reality, the normal presentation of the back of the head is such that the face is aligned straight downwards. In this matter Rösslin follows the Church father Albertus Magnus, who is equally unlikely to have had any personal experience. His book advises on the conduct of the mother during pregnancy, on nutrition and childcare. A birthstool is recommended, and clearly shown as a diagram and in use, normal and abnormal foetal positions are discussed in detail, and the necessary actions of the midwife explained. Our Plate 46 shows two contingencies, in one of which the misplacement of a single baby in the uterus (drawn as a bottle-shape) calls for the midwife's intervention: "You should straighten up the child and set all to rights." In the case of the correctly aligned twins, the midwife should: "draw them out one after the other". All possible complications of the birth are fully debated, including miscarriages and Caesarean sections.

The final chapter concerns the nursing of healthy and sick-born children, and recommends breast-feeding. A Latin-German glossary rounds things off, so that the many Latin technical terms in use can be easily followed by the German reader.

Other texts were devoted to the specialised subjects of pure and applied mathematics, such as Adam Riese's *Rechenung auff der Linihen* (1518), or a *Geometria deutsch* (Nuremberg, 1498) by the master of the cathedral works at Regensburg, Matthäus Roritzer. Albrecht Dürer's writings on art theory hold a prominent position for their application of mathematics to the pictorial arts, above all his *Underweyssung der messung* (Nuremberg, 1525) and his *Vier Bücher von menschlicher Proportion*, published in 1528 by Hieronymus Andreae in Nuremberg. These last became a milestone in the literature of art, for they put the teaching of human anatomy on a systematic basis, clearly exemplified in words and pictures. We owe the coinage of many new words to his striving after a precise technical vocabulary. These treatises on proportion were distributed throughout Europe in the Latin translation of Joachim Camerarius

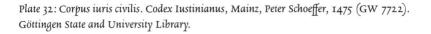

Plate 32: Corpus iuris civilis. Codex Iustinianus, Mainz, Peter Schoeffer, 1475 (GW 7722). Göttingen State and University Library.

BEATISSIMO PATRI PAVLO SE
CVNDO PONTIFICI MAXIMO,
DONIS NICOLAVS GERMANVS

On me fugit beatiſſime pater, Cūcg ſummo

Plate 33: Ptolemy: Geographia, Ulm, Lienhart Holl, 1482.
The enlarged initial shows Nicholas Germanus, an unknown Benedictine monk
from the circle of Nicholas of Cues presenting the volume to Pope Paul II.
Leipzig University Library.

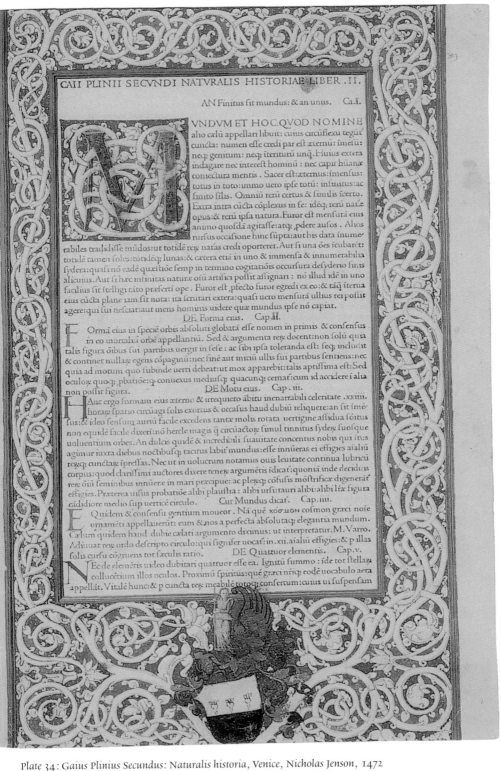

CAII PLINII SECVNDI NATVRALIS HISTORIAE LIBER .II.

AN Finitus sit mundus: & an unus.　Ca.i.

VNDVM ET HOC.QVOD NOMINE
alio cælū appellari libuit: cuius circūflexu tegūt
cuncta: numen esse credi par est æternū: imetu:
neq; genitum: neq; iteriturū unq̃.Huius extera
indagare nec interest hominū : nec capit hũanæ
coniectura mentis . Sacer est:æternus:imensus:
totus in toto:immo uero ipse totī: infinitus:ac
finito silis. Omniū rerū certus & similis icerto.
Extra intra cūcta cōplexus in se: ideq; rerū natũ
opus:& rerū ipsa natura.Furor est mensurā eius
animo quosdã agitasse:atq; ,pdere ausos . Alios
rursus occasione hinc sūpta:aut his data inume-
rabiles tradidisse mūdos:ut totidē reg; natas credi oporteret.Aut si una ões icubaret:
totidē tamen soles:totidēq; lunas:& cætera etiã in uno & immensa & innumerabilia
sydera:quasi nõ eadē quæstiõe semp in termino cogitatiõis occursura desyderio finis
alicuius.Aut si hæc infinitas naturæ oĩū artifici possit assignari : nõ illud idē in uno
facilius sit itelligi:cito præferti ope . Furor est ,psecto furor egredi ex eo:& tãq̃ iterna
eius cũcta plane iam sit nota: ita scrutari extera:quasi uero mensurā ullius rei possit
agere:qui sui nesciat:aut mens hominis uidere quæ mundus ipse nõ capiat.

DE Forma eius.　Cap.ii.

Ormã eius in speciē orbis absoluti globatã esse nomen in primis & consensus
in eo mortaliū orbē appellantiū. Sed & argumenta reg; docent:non solū quia
talis figura ōibus sui partibus uergit in sese : ac sibi ipsa toleranda est: seq; includit
& continet nullaq; egens cōpagniū:nec finē aut initiũ ullis sui partibus sentiens:nec
quia ad motum quo subinde uerti debeat:ut mox apparebit:talis aptissima est:Sed
oculoq; quoq; ,pbatiõe:q̃ conuexus mediusq; quacunq; cernat:cum id accidere i alia
non possit figura.

DE Motu eius.　Cap. iii.

Anc ergo formam eius æterno & irrequieto ãbitu inenarrabili celeritate .xxiiii.
horæ spatio circūagi solis exortus & occasus haud dubiũ reliquere:an sit imē-
sus:& ideo sensum auriū facile excedens tantæ molis rotata uertigine assidua soitus
non equidē facile dixeri:nõ hercle magis q̃ circiactoq; simul tinnitus sydeq; suoq;ue
uoluentium orbes.An dulcis quidē & incredibili suauitate concentus nobis qui iris
agimur iuxta diebus noctibusq; tacitus labit mundus:esse innũeras ei effigies aialiũ
reg;q; cunctaq; ipressas.Nec ut in uolucrum notamus ouis leuitate continua lubricū
corpus:quod clarissimi auctores dixere tenes; argumētis idicat:quonia inde decidius
reg; oĩū seminibus innũeræ in mari præcipue: ac pleq;q; cōfusis mõstrificæ digenerāt
effigies.Præterea usus probatiõe alibi plaustra : alibi ursi:tauri alibi:alibi lræ figura
cãdidiore medio sup uerticē circulo.　Cur Mundus dicat.　Cap.iiii.

Quidem & consensu gentium moueor . Nã quē κοσμον cosmon græci noie
ornãeti appellauerūt: eum &nos a perfecta absolutaq; elegantia mundum.
Cælum quidem haud dubie cælati argumento diximus: ut interpretatur.M.Varro.
Adiuuat reg; ordo descripto circulo:qui signifer uocat:in.xii.aialiũ effigies:& p illas
solis cursu cöyruens tot sæculis ratio.　DE Quattuor elementis.　Cap.v.

Ec de elemétis uideo dubitari quattuor esse ea. Ignitũ summo : sde tot stellaru
collucétium illos oculos. Proximū spiritus:quē græci nĩq; eodē uocabulo aera
appellãt.Vitalē hunc:& p cuncta reg; meabilē totoq; consertum:cuius ui suspensam

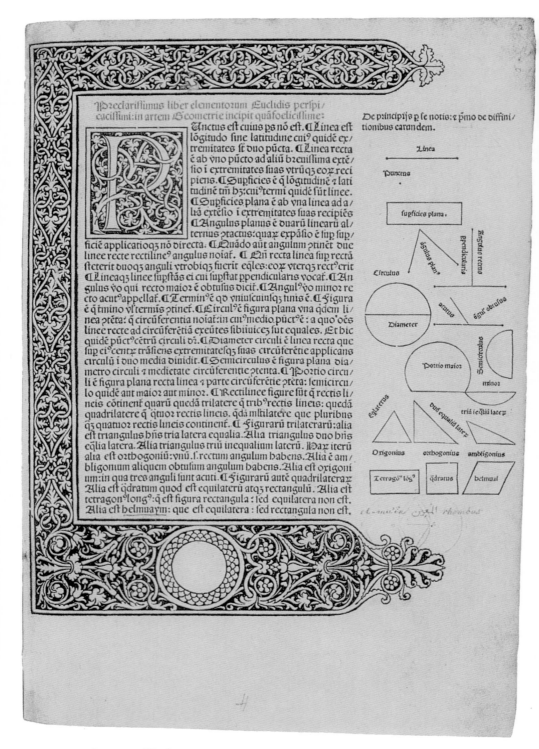

Plate 35: Euclid: *Elementa geometriae*, Venice, Erhart Ratdolt, 1482 (GW 9428), fol 2r.
Göttingen State and University Library.

ΑΡΙΣΤΟΤΕΛΟΥΣ ΠΟΛΙΤΙΚΩΝ,
ΤΟ Η.

Περὶ πολιτείας ἀρίστης τὸν μέλλοντα
ποιήσασθαι τὴν προσήκουσαν ζήτη-
σιν, ἀνάγκη διελέσθαι πρῶτον, τίς
αἱρετώτατος βίος· ἀδήλου γὰρ ὄν-
τος τούτου, καὶ τὴν ἀρίστην ἀναγ-
καῖον ἄδηλον εἶναι πολιτείαν· ἄ-
ριστα γὰρ πράττειν προσήκει τοὺς ἄ-
ριστα πολιτευομένους ἐκ τῶν ὑπαρχόντων αὐτοῖς· ἐὰν μή τι
γίγνηται παράλογον. διὸ δεῖ πρῶτον ὁμολογεῖσθαι τίς ὁ πᾶσιν
ὡς εἰπεῖν αἱρετώτατος βίος· μετὰ δὲ τοῦτο, πότερον κοινῇ
καὶ χωρὶς ὁ αὐτὸς ἢ ἕτερος· νομίσαντας οὖν ἱκανῶς πολλὰ
λέγεσθαι ἐν τοῖς ἐξωτερικοῖς λόγοις περὶ τῆς ἀρίστης ζωῆς,
καὶ νῦν χρηστέον αὐτοῖς· ὡς ἀληθῶς γὰρ πρός γε μίαν διαίρεσιν
οὐδεὶς ἀμφισβητήσειεν ἂν, ὡς οὐ τριῶν οὐσῶν μερίδων, τῆς
ἐκτὸς καὶ τῆς ἐν σώματι, καὶ τῆς ἐν τῇ ψυχῇ πάντα ταῦτα ὑπάρχειν
τοῖς μακαρίοις· οὐδεὶς γὰρ ἂν φαίη μακάριον τὸν μηδὲν μόριον ἔ-
χοντα ἀνδρίας μηδὲ σωφροσύνης, μηδὲ δικαιοσύνης, μηδὲ φρο-
νήσεως. ἀλλὰ δεδιότα μὲν τὰς παραπετομένας μυίας, ἀπε-
χόμενον δὲ μηθενὸς ἂν ἐπιθυμήσῃ τοῦ φαγεῖν ἢ πιεῖν τῶν ἐσχάτων· ἕ-
νεκα δὲ τεταρτημορίου διαφθείροντα τοὺς φιλτάτους φίλους·
ὁμοίως δὲ καὶ τὰ περὶ τὴν διάνοιαν οὕτως ἄφρονα καὶ διεψευ-
σμένον, ὥσπερ τι παιδίον ἢ μαινόμενον· ἀλλὰ ταῦτα μὲν λεγόμενα

υυυυ

Plate 37: Ptolemy: Geographia, Ulm, Lienhart Holl, 1482 (HC 15539), double-page map of Italy. Leipzig University Library.

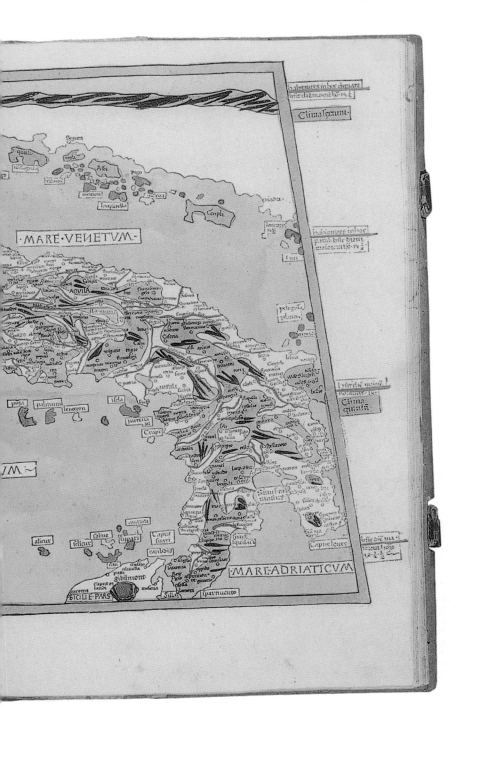

viri   nomen   et dixit

Genitiuo   הָאִישׁ   viri.Ruth.ij.   וַתֹּאמֶר שֵׁם הָאִישׁ

viro   fiet   fic·

Datiuo   לְאִישׁ   viro.Efter.vi.   כָּכָה יֵעָשֶׂה לָאִישׁ

dei   virum

Accufatō אֶת אִישׁ virū.iiij.Regū.vij.   אֶת אִישׁ הָאֱלֹהִים

iniquo   a uiro

Ablatiuo   מֵאִישׁ   a uiro.p̄s.xviij.   מֵאִישׁ חָמָס

IN NVMERO PLVRALI

uiros   viris   uirorum   uiri   uiri

אִישִׁים vel אֲנָשִׁים הָאִישִׁים לָאִישִׁים אֶת אִישִׁים

viris a

ALIVD

מֵאִישִׁים

verbo a   uerbum   uerbo   uerbi   uerbum

דְּבַר הַדָּבָר לִדְבַר אֶת הַדָּבָר מֵהַדָּבָר

a uerbis   uerba   uerbis   uerborum   uerba

דְּבָרִים הַדְּבָרִים לַדְּבָרִים אֶת דְּבָרִים מִדְּבָרִים

Vbi in quibuſdam duplicem articulum reperies.

Huius itacꝫ declinationis primę cōmunis eſt regula.ut cuiuſcūꝗ ter/
minationis nomē maſculinū numeri ſingularis tibi propoſitū fuerit,
ſimpliciter ei cata paragogē addas iod et mem q̄d p̄ hirek ſonabit im
q̄d ſi regat poſt ſe caſum,aut ei cohęreat ,pnomē ſubiūctiuū.q̄d dicīus

affixum.deponit mem finale.exemplū Deute.i. אֵלֶּה הַדְּבָרִים

Ideſt hęc ſunt uerba.iam hoc uocabulū nihil regit. ſed pſalmo.xxxiij.

בְּדִבְרֵי יְהֹוָה ideſt uerbo dn̄i.hęc uox uerbū,regit poſt ſe gt̄m

ſcilicet dn̄i ut infra de regimine ac cōſtructiōe dicemus.nūc q̄d ad hāc

Plate 38: Johann Reuchlin: De rudimentis Hebraicis, Pforzheim, Thomas Anshelm, 1506.
From the reprint, Hildesheim.

bent. vnd als Pontus sölichs vernam vnd er auch nit anderst begerē
was. antwurt daraff vnd sprach. Er dancket dem künig vnnd seiner
landschafft fast vnd wie der künig sein erster herr wär gewesen. vnd
het jm vil eer vnd güts erbotten. vnnd vil mer dann er nymmer kund
vnd mocht verdienen. vnd weñ er darzü würdig vnd geschickt wäre
das er die aller mächtigesten frawen in aller dyser welt möchte geha-
ben. so wolt er Sydoniam dar für nemen. vnd dancket aber fast vnd
vil dem künig. vnnd den herren vnnd freyen die do waren von seinem
land vnd sprach er wär gehorsam vnnd willig gefallen zü thün. dann
er hett sy lieb für alle ander. dye wurden fro von seiner antwurt. vnnd
giengen vnd sageten die mär dem künig der ein groß wolgefallen dar
ab het. vnd schicket von stundan nach dem bischoff. vnnd liessen sy gegen einander versprechen.

Und darnach am montag vermäheln. es ist nit zü fragen ob
Sydonia vnd Pontus groß freüd hetten. wann sy hetten zü
tausent malen grössere freüd in jrem hertzen dañ sy beyde außwendig erzeygten. vnd yederman klein vnd groß reych vnd auch arm
er freüten sich an jrer hochzeyt. Pontus der was weyß vnd wolt auch
nyemandts vnwill haben. vnd gieng zü dem burgunde vmnd zü des
hertzogen brüder ymbert cholans. vnd zü dem grafen montbeliart die
do kōmen waren. vnd beredt sich gegen jn vnd sprach. Die abenteüer
die vngeuerlich geschehen wär die wär jm fast leyd von des herrē tod
wegen. vnnd fürwar als er mit jm stach das er nit west wer er wär.

i iij

Plate 39: *Pontus und Sidonia*, Augsburg, Johann Schönsperger, 1498 (H 13289).
Göttingen State and University Library.

Ein lieplichs lesen vnd ein zwarhafftige Hystorij wie

einer (ð da hieß Hug schäpler vñ wz metzgers gschlecht) ein gewaltiger küng zü Franckrich ward durch sein grose ritterliche mänheit. vnd als die geschrifft sagt so ist er ð nest gewessen nach Carolus magnus sun künig Ludwigē

Plate 40: Hug Schapler, Strasbourg, Johann Grüninger, 1500 (H 8970), title page. Göttingen State and University Library.

Els nun die werlt durch das gepew göttlicher weißheit der sechs tag: volendet vn himel vn erde beschafft
geordnet gezieret vn zu letst volbracht wordē sind. do hat der gloz wirdig got sein werck erfüllet vn am
sybendē tag von den wercken seiner hendt geruet. nach dē er die gantze werlt vnd alle ding die dar in sind beschaf
fen het do hat er auffgehört. nit als zewürcken muede. funder zemachen ein newe creatur d materi oder gleichnus
nit vergangē wer dañ er hört nit auff zewürcken das werck der geperungen. vnd der herr hat den selbē tag gebe
nedeyet vn geheiligt vnd ime geheyssē sabathū. das nach hebreyscher zügē ein rue bedeüttet darumb das an dē
selben tag ruet võ allem werck das er gemacht het. do võ auch die iuden an dem tag võ aigner arbait zeferen er
kant werde. Dē selbē tag habē auch etlich haidenische völker voz dem gesetz farlich gehaltē. vnd also fein wir
zu end der göttlichen werck kome. darumb so söllen wir die in dem alle sichtliche vnd vnsichtliche ding sind fore
chten liebhaben vnd eren. vnd von dem herren des himels. von dem herren aller güter. dem gewalt gegebē ist
in himel vnd erden. die gegenwürtigen güter. souer die gut sind. vnd auch die waren seligkait des ewigen lebēs
suchen.

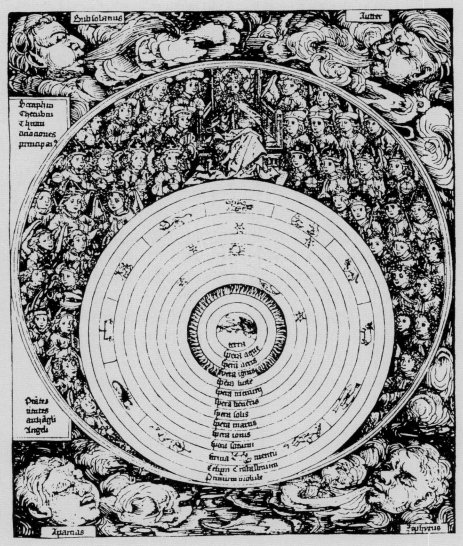

Plate 41: Hartmann Schedel: Weltchronik (The Nuremberg Chronicle), Nuremberg,
Anton Koberger, 1493, fol 5v (the seventh day of Creation), woodcut by two different hands –
the wind gods in the corners are attributed to the young Albrecht Dürer.

Ins mals ein affe kam gerāt·Do er vil guter
nuſſe vant·Der hette er geſſē gerne·Im waſ
geſagt von dem kerne·Der wer gar luſtiglich vn
de gut·Geſwert was ſein thūmer mut·Do er der
pitterkeit entpfāt·Der ſchalē darnach zu hant·Be
greiff er der ſchalē hertikeit·Von den nuſſen iſt mir
geſeit·Sprach er das iſt mir worden kunt·Si ha
ben mir verhonet meinen munt·Hyn warff er ſie
zu der ſelben fart·Der kerne der nuſſe ſm nye wart·
Dem ſelben affen ſein gleich·Beide jung arm vnde
reich·Die durch kurze pitterkeit·Verſchmehē lan
ge ſuſikeit·wenne mā das feuer enzunte wil·So
wirt des rauches dick zu vil·Der thut einem in den
augen we·wen man darzu bleſet mee·Biß es en=

Plate 42: Ulrich Boner: Der Edelstein (The precious stone). Bamberg,
Albrecht Pfister, 1461 (GW 4829), fable 1. Wolfenbüttel, Herzog August Library.

Vil leute das gros wúder nam · waū er mit eisen
bedecket wart · So verlos er auff der selben vart ·
Sein schwere vnd alle sein krafft · Do sprach des
keisers meisterschafft · Der stein ist here euch gleich
waū uber alle küigreich · Ist here ewr gewalt · Als
des steis manigfalt · Die weil ir mugt das lebē ge-
hā · So mag euch nyemāt widerstā · So seit ir schwe
re als der stein · Alle dise werlt was euch cleis · Aber
waū ir gewallet nyder · So kumpt ewr krafft nit
wider · Als schnelle ewr haubt wirt bedacht · So
habt ir verlorn ewr macht · Darumb so rat ich ·
Das ir seit bedechtiglich · waū ir seit totlich · Das
sage ich euch sicherlich · Vnd sullet euch richtē auff

Plate 43: Ulrich Boner: Der Edelstein, Bamberg, Albrecht Pfister 1461, fable 72.

aper legē foltēt · to fprach die katz · wie wol du vil
vnd gnůgfam antwůrt haft · fo bin ich toch nit in
mainung / daz ich faften welle · ¶ Dife fabel wyfet
dz die böfen von natur wā fie ettwaz böfes in iere
gemůt feczent / ob fie wol nit vrfach findent das
glimpfflich ze volbringen · toch ftand fie nit von ir
angenomen boßhait ·

¶ Fabula · v · de Vulpe et rubo ·

STultū eft auxilium implozaē ab illis
quibus a natura datum eft obeffe / po
tius q̄ alys prodeffe · de hoc audi fabu
lam · ¶ Vulpes cum fepem quandam
afcenderet / vt periculum vitaret / quod
fibi imminere videbat · rubu manibus oprehendit
atq̃ tolam fentibus profudit · et cū grauiter faucia
foret / gemens inquit ad rubuz · vt me iuuares ad
te confugi · et tu deterius me periclitafti · Cui rubz
Errafti vulpes ait · que pari tolo me capere putafti
qua cetera capi confueuifti · ¶ Fabula fignificat / ꝙ
ftulte implozar auxiliū ab illis qbz natuale ē obeē

Plate 44: Heinrich Steinhöwel: Aesop, Ulm, Johann Zainer, 1476.

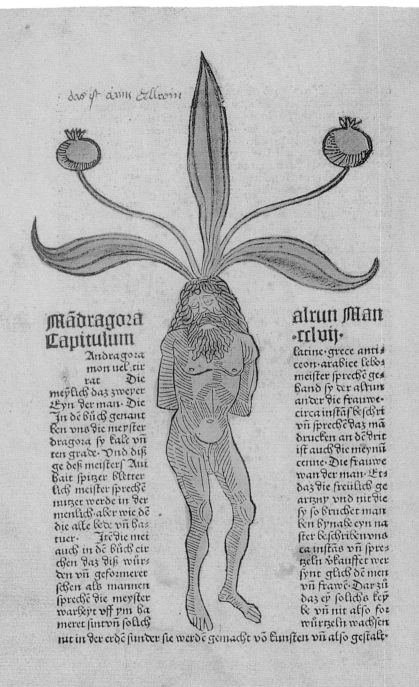

das ist ewm Alroin

Mādragora Capitulum

Andragora mon vel.tir rat Die meyslich daz zweyer Eyn der man. Die In de buch genant ten vns die meyster dragora sy kalt vn ten grade. Vnd diß ge deß meisters Aut kait spitzer bletter lich meister spreche nutzer werde in der menlich.aber wie de die alte kede vn ka tuer. Jre die mei auch in de buch ein chen daz diß wur den vn gefozmeret schen als mannen spreche die meyster warheyt vff ym ka meret sint vn solich

alrun Man .cclvij.

latine grece anti ceon arabice lebos meister spreche ge kand sy der alrun ander die frauwe circa in stas beschri vn spreche daz ma drucken an de drit ist auch die meynu cenne. Die frauwe wan der man. Et daz die freilich ge artzny vnd nit die sy so bruchet man ken bynak eyn na ster beschriben vns ca in stas vn spretzeln verkauffet wer synt glich de men vn frawe. Darzu daz ey solichs ker k vn nit also fo wurtzeln wachsen

nut in der erde sunder sie werde gemacht vo kunsten vn also gestalt.

Plate 45: *Gart der Gesundheit* (Garden of health), Mainz, Peter Schoeffer, 1485 (H 8948). Leipzig University Library.

Rosegarten

Item ob das kind geteilt lege
oder vff seinem angesicht/ So
soll die hebam leichtlich ynlasse
ir finger/vñ das kind in der sei
ten der müter vmbkere Oder ob
sie ein handt mag ynlassen /soll
sie das kind ordnen vnd richten
also/Welche theil des leibs dem
vßgäg aller nechst seind/die sel
ben soll sie halte vnd vßfüren.
doch sol sie aller meist dz haupt
süchen/halten vnd vßfüren.

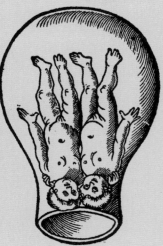

Item ob der kinde mer
dañ eins wer/als zwyling
vnd sich gleich erzeugten
mit den höuptern/So sol
die hebam eins nach dem
andern vßfüren/besonder
das erst empfahen /als ob
stadt/vnd das ander nitt
verlassen.

E.iij

Plate 46: Eucharius Rösslin: Der Schwangern Frauwen vnd Hebammen Rosegarten,
(The pregnant woman's and midwife's rosarium), Strasbourg, Martin Flach, 1513.
From the facsimile, Dietikon-Zürich, Stocker 1976.

(1532–34), and Michelangelo, among others, encountered them in this form in Italy; a French translation appeared in 1557, an Italian in 1591, and a Dutch one in 1622.

The humanistic recourse to the classical texts of antiquity and a new opening-up of the empirical method brought about a creative climate for fruitful research and development at university level. Lay admission to the universities and the new political power of the civic elite formed the background for vernacular texts to flourish. Printing brought the means to satisfy these educational needs with (relatively) large editions at reasonable prices. This gradual increase in the share of literature in the vernacular was a prelude to its furious growth-rate during the century of reformation.

Broadsides and the "latest news"

Communication changed radically in the fifteenth century. After centuries of restriction to oral discourse, the sermon and the manuscript, new possibilities for the multiplication of religious and secular knowledge were now opening up because of the woodcut and the manufacture of paper in Central Europe. Religious instruction had an age-old tradition, that ran in parallel with preaching, based on the pictorial exposition of spiritual and theological content through its iconographical transfer to church windows or bronze church doors and instructional columns. We think of such magnificent pictorial cycles as those contained in the stained glass of Canterbury and Bourges cathedrals. The chancellor of the University of Paris, Johann Gerson (1363–1420), who worked tirelessly for the reform of religious life in France, recommended at the beginning of the fifteenth century that: "instructional panels should be hung in churches in order to remedy the religious ignorance of the people". Nicholas of Cues renewed this suggestion three decades later in Germany. He must have discovered on his visitations to the German dioceses in 1451 and 1452 that even the basic prayers of the faith were all too frequently unfamiliar, thus he had so-called "Lord's prayer tablets" set up in several churches. One such wooden notice board has been preserved in Hildesheim. It opens with these words: "When the German cardinal Nicholas of Cues was sent to Germany during the pontificate of Nicholas V and in the year following upon the golden year (1451), he reproached the common lay people above all because they could not speak the 'our father' and the creed properly. Therefore he instructed that these should be written out and prominently displayed in the churches. This has been done, and so here follows the Lord's prayer . . .".

Nicholas of Cues might equally well have made use of another method of spreading religious imagery or prayer texts – and one which had been known about for at least fifty years – the single-sided woodblock print transferred to paper by burnishing. A celebrated early example, known as the Buxheim St Christopher, has survived from 1423 (see Plate 47). This popular image with its accompanying Latin couplet followed by that specific date was cut in wood and an impression taken by rubbing.

The picture contains further details from the legendary life and miracles of this saint which would have called for explanation by an instructor. Even the text would have needed to be translated, for it contains the crucial words which reveal the reason for the special position occupied by Christopher in popular devotion: "on the day that you look upon the image of the holy Christopher, you will not die a sudden death". Fear of the *mors repentina* or *mala* – that sudden or evil death which leaves no time for repentence, atonement or conversion – was a horror of which hell-fire preachers made much. This explains the wide distribution of images of St Christopher on church windows, frescoes or stelae, especially in southern Germany.

This saint's image reproduced on paper attests to new and exciting possibilities: in theory, every household could now hang its own St Christopher in a devotional nook, thereby transferring its uplifting powers out of the public arena of the church and into a private and domestic setting. That is why devotional pictures became favourite subjects for the new woodcutting technique. First the illustration and its text would be drawn in reverse on the woodblock by an artist, and then a craftsman would cut away the non-printing areas of the image, the printing surface would be inked, and a dampened sheet of paper placed over it and rubbed down with a burnisher. This relief printing process would yield 200–400 impressions, and possibly more, according to the type of wood used. The cracks which developed in some of the lines show what heavy demands were made of these woodblocks.

As well as St Christopher, we find prints of other patron saints and devotionalia, such as St George, St Barbara, St Catherine, St Michael and St Francis, and of course Madonnas and Crucifixion scenes. By the middle of the century, metal as well as wood had come into use as a surface for cutting.

When several of these woodcut-printed sheets are bound together, then we speak of a "blockbook". Where this happens, the close relationship between visual and textual information called for careful planning, since all the text had to be laboriously cut into the woodblocks. Surviving examples all happen to postdate Gutenberg's invention, but the two techniques developed in parallel to each other. Shorter texts were chosen for blockbooks, such as the *Ten Commandments*, the *Song of Songs*, popular guides to dying of the *Ars moriendi* kind in Latin or

German, and of course the Biblia pauperum or "poor man's Bible". Here, the message of a sermon was delivered in a clear educational framework, in which connections between Old and New Testaments were highlighted and presented with verbal and visual economy. The example from a Biblia pauperum in German (Nuremberg, 1471, see Plate 48) shows the annunciation by an angel to the Virgin Mary flanked by two Old Testament prefigurations: on the left, Eve, who as Mary's anti-type was led astray by the serpent in paradise; and on the right, as a sign of God's power to intervene in the course of nature, the story of Gideon's conversion. Gideon asked God for a sign, and on the second morning found that the fleece layed out before the tent was dry whilst the ground all around it was wet with dew (Judges 6:36–40). The text below tells us to regard this as a sign of godly omnipotence, likewise that Mary: "ohnzerstörung irs leibs unnd der jungfrawschafft durch den heili-gen geist geschwengert ward" (without ravage to her body and virginity is made pregnant through the holy spirit). Further quotations from four prophets reinforce the links between the two testaments.

But worldly subject-matter also found its way into blockbooks as well: calendars and primers, for example, or Johann Hartlieb's Chiromantia, individual fables, and that most widely circulated of short Latin gram-mars – the Donatus – which we have already encountered.

Typographic broadsides can be traced back to Gutenberg, who printed an Aderlass- und Laxierkalendar (bloodletting and laxatives calendar) and a Cisianus or guide to the months of the year. Calendars became a reli-able mass-production line from the earliest days of printing. As single-sided prints, they could be hung up in the parlour and inspected daily, and for that reason alone very few copies have survived. Some calendars show no more than the dates, and symbols – perhaps to highlight Sun-days or the most propitious dates for bloodletting – for those less able to read. Additional text might be printed alongside in German or Latin to provide a calendar of events. A broadside belonging to the University of Göttingen, and unknown until quite recently, was printed for the year 1478 (see Plate 49). In the upper margin there is a "speech balloon" with the New Year's greeting "Ain gut sälig iar" which is decoratively supported by the newly born Christ-child, symbol of a new beginning. This same image is repeated within the coloured initial "D". In the six long lines which follow, the most important reference dates for 1478 are given: the initial for Sundays, followed by the golden number, and then the moveable feasts. The left-hand column gives a summary of the seasons, concentrating on the familiar festivals: "March begins the next day after Candlemas", "The month of August starts on the Wednesday after St James." The information in the right-hand column concerns the best days for bloodletting with regard to different generations and parts of the body: "On Monday after Mary's nativity good (for the) elderly (but) excepting the skin." Calendars of this kind ran into large editions of several thousand copies and were printed with undiminished success until well into the eighteenth century.

NEWS-SHEETS

Broadsides with sensational news, such as the latest information concerning theatres of war, freak births or glittering occasions of state, commanded a wide circulation. These were generally called "Newe Zeytung" after their main heading, and gradually the Middle High German term "Zeitung" (at first signifying just "news" or "tidings") gave its name to a new genre or medium. From the outset, this word was often qualified by an adjective such as "alarming", "happy" or "new". In contrast to the periodical press which first surfaced in the seventeenth century, these news-sheets were confined to a single topic and were aimed in each case towards a specific public. Most "current news-sheets" consisted of one news item – usually containing a woodcut, and not always one intended for the purpose – and a rhyming text in two or three columns purporting to be an eye-witness narrative. Without this widespread and popular medium, we would be at best ill-informed about many fifteenth- and sixteenth-century events, including certain natural catastrophies, legal proceedings, the campaigns against the Turks or the early history of the Thirty Years War. Many of the ruling houses exploited this new medium and commissioned writers to feature popular entertainments such as royal weddings and also to report on plans for the call to arms and the conduct of war. Emperor Maximilian I, whilst still regent, began to deploy this means of influencing public opinion. Quite a few publicists loyally disposed towards the empire supported his measures through the journalistic manipulation of natural occurrences.

As an instance of this, a meteorite impact in the neighbourhood of Ensisheim in Alsace was used by Sebastian Brant in order to support Maximilian's policies. On 7 November 1492 a meteorite fell to earth near Ensisheim. It weighed approximately 260 pounds. To this day a fragment of some 100 pounds is kept in Ensisheim town hall. It is the oldest existing meteorite fall for which there are sources and eye-witness reports, and many fragments are housed in the world's leading natural history museums. Sebastian Brant's broadside appeared in that same year from the Basle printer and publisher Johann Bergmann von Olpe, who identifies himself on the page through the initials J. B. and his motto: "Nüt on vrsach" (nothing without a cause; see Plate 50). An expressly prepared woodcut reproduces the exact trajectory of the meteorite, approaching from the west and striking the ground before the city gates of Ensisheim. The text is bilingual, Latin and German, and directed through its language and classical allusions towards a reasonably well-informed public. In building to a climax, Sebastian Brant talks of numerous strange phenomena in recent years which have culminated in this "thunder stone". The Latin text ends with the rather general wish that the misfortune to be expected as a result of this "fall of thunder" may strike evil enemies, whereas the German text speaks unequivocally of an evil omen for the French and Burgundians. The author then addresses a 22-line poem in German directly to Maximilian. He rouses him in theatrical language to advance against the French with the support of Austria and Germany, since fate is on his side. When this pamphlet came out, Maximilian was already on his way to Burgundy in order to exact revenge for a double personal insult: namely that Charles VIII of France had reputiated his marriage contract with Maximilian's daughter Margaret, and married Anne of Brittany, to whom Maximilian had been betrothed. In 1493 Maximilian regained a large part of Burgundy and part of his daughter Margaret's dowry.

This interesting broadsheet reports the meteorite impact in detail, and in its Latin text makes observations about meteorites from antiquity onwards. Sebastian Brant's vernacular text is less concerned to supply information, but comments on the significance of this portent and the support it gives to Maximilian's politics. This combination of an illustrative woodcut with text in two languages must have reached people from broad walks of life. We know of 25 surviving broadsheets in all in which Sebastian Brant comments on natural disasters and gives them a political slant.

The new medium of the broadside was not only available to report sensations, but also to warn against fraud, and counterfeit money in particular. Plate 52 shows a broadside "warning against false gulden" that was probably printed in 1482 by Johann Zainer in Augsburg. A counterfeiter was executed in Göttingen in 1481, after some four tons of forged coin had been confiscated. In order to warn against the circulation of such coinage, 11 identical pamphlets appeared in Augsburg, Basle, Magdeburg, Munich, Nuremberg, Reutlingen and Ulm, closely describing the forged coins and illustrating the obverse and reverse of each. This broadside offered factual information whilst gratifying morbid curiosity about criminal activities, thereby contributing to the prehistory of the popular press.

A BROADSIDE VIEW OF THE NEW WORLD

The news of Columbus's discovery of America, so momentous to us today, did not at the time generate quite the interest that we would have imagined. With hindsight, we know that it represented a decisive breakthrough into a "new world", whereas contemporaries had long grown used to hearing of the discovery of "new islands" in the western oceans by the Portuguese and Spaniards: the Canary Islands were found in the fourteenth century, and several times over in the course of the fifteenth century they learned of new, hitherto unknown peoples along the coasts of Africa, in the Cape Verde Islands and in Guinea. "New peoples" and "new islands" were constantly making news in those days, so when Christopher Columbus's letter appeared in print in 1497 under his title *Von jüngst gefundenen Inseln* . . . (Concerning the islands recently discovered in the Indian Sea) then – however spectacular this publication may seem to us today – it simply joined a long sequence of reported discoveries. His text had appeared in Spanish back in 1493, the same year as the Latin version was published in Rome, Basle, Paris and Antwerp, but it took until 1497 for a German version to reach Strasbourg. Sebastian Brant picked upon this intelligence in his *Narrenschiff* of 1494, and reported on the cultural differences and strangeness of a new people whom he likened to images from the "golden lands" woven into myth:

> Indeed we've since worked out a far way
> To lands beyond both Thule and Norway
> Such as Iceland and Lapland too
> Which in earlier times we never knew
> And lands by Portugal discovered
> And golden isles which Spain uncovered
> Inhabited by naked folk
> Of which the ancients rarely spoke.

The earliest illustrated news-sheets reported these discoveries too, and jumbled up imaginary figures of globetrotters from antiquity such as Herodotus with the narratives of the Portuguese mariners.

The letters of the Florentine scholar Amerigo Vespucci were accorded a very different reception after 1503. Vespucci made it clear that he was dealing with fundamentally new phenomena that were quite unknown to the ancients. He reported in a vivid and down-to-earth manner, giving precise geographical information and a wealth of cultural detail. His Paris publication of 1503 was followed by printings at Venice, Augsburg and Rome in 1504 and no fewer than 25 further editions over the next couple of years, 18 of them from German-speaking regions. The scholarly cosmographers Martin Waldseemüller and Mathias Ringmann based their *Cosmographiae introductio* (1507) on this weighty report, and in it they named the new continent "America" after its author. The single-sided news-sheet *Das sind die new gefunden menschen*. . . (These are the new-found people or race, in form and appearance as they stand here, through the Christian king of Portugal most wondrously discovered) has survived in this unique copy from 1505 (see Plate 51). It shows the landing of three ships of conquest in the New World, with aborigines who are gigantic in relation to the landscape. The woodcut, which takes up about half the page, is faithfully cut according to Vespucci's text: even the colouring follows the information given there. People are depicted from the viewpoint of a European whose attention has been caught primarily by their nakedness and the variety and unaccustomed form of their bodily decoration. Nudity is not interpreted as a positive way of being different, but as a sign of moral degeneracy, just as their (apparent) lack of any economical or political system earns the reproach that: "they live according to nature". The exaggeration of this immorality gave rise to accusations of cannibalism, which are increasingly vented in later pamphlets. A report that syphilis had been introduced to Europe by sailors returning from America also gained ground, together with dark rumours concerning aphrodisiacs. The plunder and "Christianisation" of this continent was justified by the blanket judgement that: "they uphold no regime, have no temples, and obey no laws".

EMPEROR MAXIMILIAN I

Maximilian I (1459–1519) was the first monarch to introduce all the benefits of printing for the furtherance of his rule in a systematic way. He had been chosen king of the Romans at the diet in Frankfurt in 1485, and crowned in Aachen. The death of his father Frederick III in 1493 left him sole ruler of Germany, and he strove at once for a crusade against the infidels and a campaign to be crowned as emperor in Rome – both lifelong aims which he pursued in vain. After many setbacks in campaigns in Northern Italy, he assumed the title of Roman Emperor Elect in the cathedral of Trentino. Decisions of great consequence for the centuries that lay ahead had to be taken under his rule, which affected, among other matters, the reform of the empire, the new regulation of armies and authorities (at the diet of Worms, 1495), and the extension of Habsburg marriage politics to Burgundy, Hungary and Poland (laying the foundations for the Austro-Hungarian monarchy in 1515). His reign was marked by constant menace from the Turks, and Luther's first appearance before the diet of Augsburg in 1518, at which the succession of Maximilian's grandson Karl V was settled with help from the Fugger family of bankers.

The arts and sciences experienced a marked upturn during Maximilian's reign, which the humanists celebrated as the beginning of a "golden age". He opened the University of Vienna to humanistic studies, and encouraged Latin poetry through specific commissions and the crowning of poets, giving attention to national literature in the vernacular (the *Ambraser Heldenbuch*) whilst at the same time endeavouring to imitate the Renaissance culture of the Italian princely courts (with the sequences of woodcuts for the *Triumphzug* and *Ehrenpforte*). Printing offered him a means of emulating the cultivation of these Italian princes with his "paper triumphs". He was open-minded towards any kind of technical, scientific or artistic innovation, and took the same interest in printing as he did in gun-making.

His interest in printing developed at two levels: on the one hand through the publication of pamphlets to influence public opinion in the direction of active political engagement, and on the other hand to manipulate his posthumous fame by compiling voluminous epics.

The pamphlets of Maximilian I

Whilst as a rule it was still customary during the reign of Frederick III for all official publications to be sent out under seal to a chosen circle of recipients (*litterae clausae*), Maximilian issued the majority of his announcements to the diet, proscriptions, mandates and patents as open letters (*litterae patentes*). Public dissemination through notice boards in town halls or announcements from the pulpit must have accounted for a significant part of a large edition of some three to four hundred copies at a time. In this way, the pulpit became an indispensible organ for communication and helped with the enforcement of the legal system: war and peace were announced from there, as were the imperial tax regulations. This fusion of spiritual and political interests is apparent to an exceptional degree in the appeal to engage in a crusade against the Turks, as can be seen from an advertisement recruiting entrants to the order of St George in 1494. The far-reaching audience this was intended to reach is listed comprehensively: "We send each and every of our and the holy empire's electors, spiritual and worldly, prelates, counts, freemen, gentlemen, knights, servants, captains, magistrates, guardians, administrators, officials, village mayors, lord mayors, judges, councillors, citizens and parishioners, and otherwise all others of our and the empire's subjects and followers of whatever dignity, rank and occupation, who come forward or are shown this our royal letter or copy thereof to see or to read, our every grace and every good."

A theoretically unlimited public throughout the empire, who read these writings or heard them read out, would be provided with full commentary on current political happenings: convocations of the diet contained detailed war reports, tidings of victory were broadcast in the form of royal mandates. Apart from the Turkish question, recurrent themes included wars against changing alliances in northern Italy, the campaign for Rome and imperial coronation plans, as well as such signal diplomatic successes as the Austro-Hungarian double betrothal of 1515. "Feldmären", or tales from the front, also reached wider circles as printed folk-ballads, the most popular news medium of the age; a few ballads mostly by unknown authors betray their direct dependence on, or are themselves versifications of, official bulletins.

However, Maximilian did not confine the use of printed pamphlets as a means of influencing the formation of political opinion to within the empire, he was the creator of a special form of psychological warfare as well. During his long drawn-out struggle against Venice he made three attempts (in 1509, 1510 and 1511) to incite the Venetians against the Signoria by means of propaganda leaflets printed in Italian. He let favourable winds waft balloons carrying this early agit-prop behind enemy lines before his archers shot them down. In well-formulated language, these leaflets spoke of freedom and equality, and incited the populace to arise and overthrow the "tyrants".

Maximilian's concern for a memorial

Maximilian certainly used new means of communication to influence his contemporaries politically, but in addition he saw in them a way to plan his own immortality. He put it thus in his autobiography, Weißkunig: "He who makes no memorial in his lifetime has no remembrance after his death, and that same man will be forgotten with the tolling of the bell, and therefore the money that I expend on this memorial will not be lost."

The recording of historical events for posterity – caring for what he calls the memorial ("Gedechtnus") – became the real foundation for his literary and artistic endeavours. He wanted to preserve traditions and at the same time to offer a model for his successors. Not actions alone but their *archiving* became in his eyes a vital task for every ruler. In his autobiography in Latin and its German translation as the Weißkunig, he attempted to assemble the materials for future historians. It is true that the Weißkunig remains skeletal, for at every turn he lacked sufficient space for narrative, and events were often inaccurately recounted. Complex historical situations were reduced to tournaments and battles between parties identified only by their heraldic colours, and the political background and diplomatic exchanges went unmentioned. We are left with 236 historically faithful woodcuts which were produced between 1514 and 1516 by Hans Burgkmair, Leonhard Beck, Hans Schäufelein and Hans Springinklee, among others. The *Weißkunig* encountered no contemporary reaction for it was not printed until 1775.

Maximilian did, however, have the Augsburg court printer Johann Schönsperger the elder print about forty copies on vellum and three hundred on paper of his verse epic *Theuerdank* in 1517. This epic poem, consciously modelled on medieval heroic literature, relates 80 of Maximilian's adventures on his journey to marry Mary of Burgundy (their identities are concealed behind the allegorical presentation). The individual adventures are loosely related to the courtship, and their outcome – carrying off the noble bride – is revealed, contrary to standard practice, in the opening chapter. A storyteller called Ehrenhold leads the hero through the 80 adventures that three malicious opponents with the expressive names "Fürwittig", "Unfallo" and "Niedelhart" have in store for him. Sir Theuerdank overcomes all perils, even natural catastrophes and diseases, through presence of mind, wisdom and courage. The marriage is postponed until after the capture of the Holy Land and the blessing of God which will follow from that achievement.

The fraktur typeface was specially designed by Vincenz Rockner, likewise the calligraphic flourishes which recall the manuals of the writing masters (see Plate 53). In order to keep up this imitation of handwriting, a few of the lower-case characters and most of the capitals have alternative versions: "D", "E", "J" and "M" had no fewer than eight variants cut and typecast for each. The large initials and flourishes to the ascenders and descenders were set and printed from a separate forme, and not from metal type but from woodcuts, so that a richer black resulted from the wood taking up and transferring the ink more effectively. Tell-tale cracks to some of the flourishes demonstrate that wood was used. The woodcutter Jost de Negker, who had come to Augsburg from Antwerp shortly beforehand, may have cut these, and he was also responsible for most of the 118 woodcut illustrations. Maximilian chose to have the *Theuerdank* printed, not because this was a quick and simple means of reproduction, but because he wanted to imitate a manuscript in print, and so increase its exclusiveness.

Printing and the Reformation

"Dr Martin Luther said: Printing is *summum et postremum donum*, that through which God drives the objectives of the evangelists forward. It is the last flame before the extinction of the world." With this enthusiastic encomium on printing, Johann Aurifaber closes his *Table-talk* (*Tischreden oder Colloquia Doctor Martin Luthers*) of 1566, in which he passes on the ideas of the Reformation in popular form through lively quotations. Aurifaber (1519–75) discerns in Luther's graphic dictum the central role of printing in the spread of Reformational doctrines, and above all of the Bible itself. The quotation also reminds us indirectly of the bilinguality of literature in the fifteenth and sixteenth centuries; works in Latin predominated, although nearly three times as much vernacular literature appeared between 1518 and 1526 as did between 1501 and 1517.

GERMAN BIBLES BEFORE LUTHER

The history of printing is inextricably bound up with the spread of the Bible: in the early 1450s it was the *Vulgate* – St Jerome's translation, which had been the standard one since late antiquity – that Gutenberg chose to be the first printed book of any substance and which he produced magnicently in a stately textura typeface. During the remainder of the fifteenth century, 94 editions of the complete Vulgate appeared in all, of which 22 were closely modelled on the *Gutenberg Bible*. The first book to be printed in Strasbourg was also a 49-line *Vulgata* (GW 4203) of about 1460, a copy of which in the university library at Freiburg is known to have been rubricated in 1460 and 1461. It was produced by Johann Mentelin, Strasbourg's first printer. Mentelin came from present-day Sélestat, where he is on record as a "Goldschreiber" (lit. "writer in gold") and notary. He was awarded Strasbourg citizenship in 1447, probably began to print there from about 1458, and went on to produce in 1466 the earliest complete Bible in German, based on a lost translation of more than a century earlier. This followed the Latin model so doggedly that its German text can only be grasped by someone who knows

Latin grammar as well. Furthermore, an example (Genesis 1:3–4) shows that its choice of words was already old-fashioned:

dixitque Deus	fiat lux	et facta lux
Vnd got der sprach.	liecht werde gemacht	Vnd das liecht ward gemacht.
And God said.	Let there be light	and there was light.

et vidit Deus lucem	quod esset bona.
vnd got der sache daz liecht	das es ward gut.
And God saw the light	that it was good.

Mentelin set the text to a column depth of 61 lines in a very small point size of a still clumsy-looking Gothic-roman typeface, so that the overall extent could be brought down to 812 pages. The order of the books is broadly conventional for the Vulgate, except that he places the Acts of the Apostles after Hebrews rather than after the Gospel according to St John.

The text area is generously laid out with wide column separation and de luxe margins, and the interlinear spacing is correctly judged for the typesize, so that excellent reading conditions are created despite the small typeface. Here, as in his other books, Mentelin makes no use of initials or woodcuts, but leaves spaces for a rubricator to insert the initials. Our specimen page (see Plate 54) shows the opening of the first book of Maccabees: the rubricator added the running headline and the opening of the Prologos by hand, as well as the seven-line initial for the prologue and the eight-line initial to the first book.

Despite its antiquated language, this version of the Bible went through 13 further printings, 9 of them in Augsburg alone. Individual words which had totally fallen out of use were replaced in the second printing by Heinrich Eggestein in Strasbourg (1470) and the third by Jodokus Pflanzmann in Augsburg (1475), but a thorough text revision with the help of the Vulgate was not undertaken until it came to the fourth edition, printed by Günther Zainer in Augsburg in 1476. In his publisher's announcement of 1476 – and one of the first printed book trade advertisements of all – Zainer described it as follows:

The book of the German Bible with pictures, corrected with great industry and made faithful. Thus all words incomprehensible or

foreign to German, such as there were in the first little *bibles*
to be printed, have all been taken out, and it has been set and
made after the Latin.

Besides improving and modernising the text, Zainer added illustrations
to a German *Bible* for the first time. There were 73 pictorial initials for
the openings of each biblical book, and these illustrated 45 biblical scenes,
or showed portraits of the authors or the presentation of apostolic letters. (See Plate 55 which shows the presentation of the apostle Paul's letter to the Ephesians.) It so happened that these initials occupied a dispro-
portionate two-thirds of the column width. The prologues themselves
open with square initials decorated with lilies of the valley (the initial
"P" appearing twice on this page) which are printed alongside the running headlines in black and the chapter headings in red. Zainer's accom-
plished Gothic-roman creates a restful and well-balanced page, to which
the generous whites between columns and between sections contribute.
The evenly spaced lines and the quality of the typeface are more apparent from our second example, with its expressive initial for the opening of Isaiah, showing the tree of Jesus coming forth out of the stem of
Jesse (Isaiah 11:1–9, see Plate 56). Günther Zainer used this woodblock
again in a second edition of 1477, and after his death it is to be found
once more in an edition printed by Anton Sorg in Augsburg in 1480.

We are led from this style of illustrative book decoration towards the
narrative woodcut – which does not merely edify Christians, but active-
ly encourages reading and facilitates understanding of the *Bible* –
through two *Bibles*, in Low German and the Lower Rhenish dialect
respectively, which made their appearance in Cologne in 1478 and were
probably printed by Bartholomäus von Unkel to the order of a publishing consortium formed by Messrs Johann Helmann and Arnold
Salmonster from Cologne and Anton Koberger of Nuremberg. The Low
German edition (GW 4307, see Plate 57) has 113 illustrations, whereas the
other version (GW 4308) has 123. The woodcuts were evidently influenced
by the "author portraits" (evangelists, prophets and apostles) of Zainer's
edition, but they are also related to miniatures in manuscript *Bibles* and
story *Bibles* from the Cologne-Netherlandish region. The plainly narrative character of these illustrations and a detailed introduction that

exhorted every Christian to read the Bible are evidence of a drive on the part of the *devotio moderna* to bring the word of God within the reach of the laity as well. The publishers were probably Brethren of the Common Life and Carthusians from Cologne, who referred in their introduction to those pictorial representations handed down in churches and monasteries which served in the same way for the instruction of the faithful. The translation from Latin into these two dialects, which were spoken in the diocese of Cologne, shows these current initiatives being put into effect. Dominant, two-column woodcuts stamp their image on these Bibles, which are decorated with further ingenious marginal borders. Plate 58 shows the creation story from Genesis, with the creation of Eve from Adam's rib. This pictorial subject, taken over from manuscript illumination, became highly popular as a woodcut and was widely circulated in countless Bibles, and appeared in encyclopaedias as well. The creation picture shows God the Father in a circle of archangels contemplating the created firmament, with waters, winds, and animals and plants in a hilly landscape. The four blocks which make up the border were re-used a number of times, at the start of the volume, for example, and for the opening page of Revelation.

These woodcuts enjoyed further circulation through the great Nuremberg publisher Anton Koberger, who had been a partner in the Cologne Bible enterprise. He had acquired the woodblocks in Cologne, and had 109 of them printed and at least partly coloured in his own workshops for his Bible of 1483. The text relied on Zainer's edition, improved once again with reference to the Vulgate. In the colophon (fol. 586v) Koberger hints at rather more: "prepared against the Latin text . . . and with splendid pictures". Koberger had at his disposal a far-reaching network of European business contacts, and had obviously printed a very large edition. He used a distinctive bastarda typeface for the text, which still has resemblances to an Upper Rhenish book hand, but already constitutes a clear early form of the fraktur which was taking shape in Nuremberg at the time. Such a typeface gives a page of German setting an entirely different look and texture from a contemporary page of Latin set in roman. Whilst the running headlines and chapter headings are printed with the text, spaces are left free for the large initials, which, in the Göttingen University Library copy, have been richly painted in a variety of techniques (see Plate 59). The woodcut of the creation story taken over from the Cologne Bibles has a ground of gold leaf and has been painted over in transparent colours in which blue, green and yellow tones prevail. The second pictorial example (Plate 60) shows the opening of Luke's gospel: the evangelist is depicted with his symbolic calf, and there are allusions to the special significance of the childhood of Jesus for Luke in the scenes of the birth at Bethlehem, the three kings and the presentation in the temple.

These editions were as handsomely decorated by hand as if they had been manuscripts, and accordingly sold for a high price which made their aquisition by the "common man" out of the question. Simpler "utility Bibles" were printed by Johann and Silvan Otmar in Augsburg between 1507 and 1518, in which woodblocks from Johann Schönsperger's edition of 1487 were recycled.

The total of 18 German-language Bibles before Luther is a remarkable one, and if their impact was restricted, then this was largely due to high prices, outmoded language, and a word-for-word approach to translation that adhered too closely to the Latin model, blurring comprehension and garbling sense. These German versions were only really accessible to those who could have read the Latin text in any case. Added to this – as the Church pressed its claim to be the sole interpreter of the scriptures – the necessary incentive to purchase these editions was lacking.

The fundamentally new significance that Luther conferred on the Bible for theological thinking and religious practice – the principle of the primacy of the Holy Scriptures in questions of faith (sola scriptura) and the empowerment of the laity to read the Bible for themselves and to decide between revealed truth and the fraudulent practices of the "old Church" – in addition to the creative power of the language in which his new German version had been hewn from the Latin original, secured for Luther's Bible translation an unprecedented resonance: from 1522 until Luther's death (1546), more than three hundred High German Bible editions appeared in an estimated total of more than half a million copies. One third of all German book production in the first half of the sixteenth century is accounted for by Luther's writings.

"I am a peasant's son, my greatgrandfather, grandfather and father were true-born peasants. I had as a matter of fact, as Philipp Melanchthon says, a supervisor, a local mayor and the sort you would expect to find in a village where someone has to be chief labourer over the rest. That was after my father moved to Mansfeld and became a smelter. I am from there." Luther's autobiographical sketch in his *Table-talk* (no. 6250) describes conditions in a struggling Thuringian copper-mining district and the social transformation of his family. A year after his birth on 10 November 1483 in Eisleben, his parents Hans and Margarethe Luder settled in Mansfeld, where his father had found work in the mining industry. With this occupational change came a rise in the economical and social fortunes of the family; his father became a master smelter in 1491, and as owner of a copper smelting furnace, became one of the four members of the Mansfeld village council elected to defend the rights of citizens against the local authorities.

Their son Martin at first attended the Latin school in Mansfeld, then went on to the cathedral school in Magdeburg in 1496, and after 1498 to St George's school at Eisenach. In the summer semester of 1501 he signed the matriculation book of the arts faculty at the university of Erfurt, by 29 September 1502 he had graduated as *Baccalaureus artium*, and he obtained his master's degree in January 1505. In the first semester of his ensuing legal studies at Erfurt he changed direction radically and entered the Erfurt convent of the Augustinian Eremites. He commenced theological studies at the university of Erfurt on their instruction after he had taken orders on 3 April 1507, and thus renewed his confidence in Aristotelian philosophy and the nominalist scholastic philosophy and theology of William of Ockham (c.1285–1349) and the Tübingen philosopher Gabriel Biel (c.1410–95), and his opposition to those doctrines based on revelation – with their sharp separation of reason and faith – against which he was later to take a hard line.

In October 1508 the vicar-general of the order of Augustinian Eremites, Johann von Staupitz (c.1469–1524), moved Luther to their Wittenberg convent and immediately entrusted him with a lectureship in philosophy at the university in that town. He travelled to Rome in 1510/11 with a brother of the order on a mission on behalf of dissenting convents, in order to settle differences concerning the organisation of the order. His observations of the condition of the Catholic Church there under Julius II, which he was later to style his "Roman experience" (where, amongst other matters, a plenary indulgence had been issued in 1506 for the building of St Peter's, against which many countries, led by the German rulers, had spoken out), laid the foundation-stone for his critique of the venal power of the papacy.

In October 1512, under the presidency of Andreas Bodenstein of Karlstadt a doctorate in theology was conferred upon Luther and he took over the chair of biblical exegesis (lectura in biblia) from his religious mentor Johann Staupitz. Staupitz had moulded Luther in the spirit of Augustine and the devotio moderna of the late Middle Ages. As professor of biblical exposition, Luther concentrated in the years which followed on the interpretation of the Psalms (1513–15) and the epistles to the Romans (1515–16). The Pauline doctrine of sin and forgiveness stood at the heart of his strict inquiry, which was strongly aligned to the actual text of the Bible. He had both texts freshly printed for his lectures, with extra space between lines and generous margins so that his listeners could note down the elucidations; Luther's own copy of the Psalter with his handwritten notes is today kept at the Herzog August Library in Wolfenbüttel.

THE MAIN TEXTS OF THE REFORMERS

Luther's new theological approach is particularly apparent in his appraisal of the justice of God and his theory of the justification of man. He taught that God's justice is not a judgmental but rather a forgiving justice which can be received by the faithful alone, and in this he set himself not only against scholastic theology but also against the practice of piety at the time. His first writing in the vernacular dealt logically with the seven penitential psalms (Sieben Bußpsalmen, 1517), in which he drew the seriousness of penitence and judgment into the foreground and preformulated the attack on the "justification through works" of scholastic theology. These arguments culminated in his Disputatio contra scholasticam theologiam of September 1517, in which he turned against the easy remission of sins typical of his age and the thesis that every "common" man could find God through his own resources. He spoke instead of man's fundamental sinfulness, and the necessity of grace for salvation. From this position it was but a small step to condemning the Church's system of indulgences out of hand. In the well-known 95 *theses* – which Luther addressed on 31 October 1517 to Archbishop Albrecht of Mainz (who was responsible for farming the sale of indulgences from the pulpit), and which mark the beginning of the Reformation – he laments the false and deadly security which indulgences produce through deception (*Theses* 31, 49, 52); works of love and prayer are to be more highly valued than indulgences (*Theses* 41 and 74). In the letter to Archbishop Albrecht, he uses the surname "Luther" that is familar today, whereas up until then he had used the family name Luder. The fact that between 1517 and 1519 he made use of the Latinized Greek name "Eleutherius" (the free one) in parallel to this shows that it was a conscious and programmatic decision to be known as "Luther". He made an etymological connection with "Eleutherius", and incorporated the idea of Christian freedom into his own persona. This may be verified through a further letter which he wrote on 11 November 1517 to his Erfurt friend Johann Lang, which he signed "Fr[ater] Martinus Eleutherius, imo dulos et captivus nimis, Augustinianus Wittenbergensis", which translates as "Brother Martin, the [through God] free one, or much more servant and prisoner [of God], Augustinian in Wittenberg", thus anticipating the fundamental idea of his tract on freedom of 1520, Von der Freiheit eines Christenmenschen: "A Christian man is a free ruler over all things and subject to nobody. A Christian man is a willing servant to all things and subject to everyman." This apparent contradiction, based on St Paul (I Corinthians, 9:19), resolves itself through reflection on the dual nature of each person. The "inner man" has no need of worldly, external things: "The gospel alone, the word of God", "Only the faith makes devout, free and holy." The concept of freedom which Luther acknowledged through his change of name as early as 1517 signals that he was conscious of new beginnings in his own theological argumentation.

Counter to Luther's original intentions, the 95 *theses* (couched in Latin) had spread rapidly; in order to formulate these more understandably for wider circles, he brought out his sermon on indulgences and grace (*Sermon von Ablaß und Gnade*) in March 1518, which created such interest that it had to be reprinted 25 times in the space of two years. True Christians, who felt repentant for their sins, would perform the "works of satisfaction" as a matter of course; in contrast to which, indulgences only created "lazy and imperfect Christians", Luther explained in plain language. Those who would rebuke him as a heretic because of these theses were: "dark minds, who had never even smelt the *Bible*, had never read Christian teaching and had never understood their own teachers, but were well nigh rotting with their gaping and threadbare scholastic opinions . . .".

Only two months after that, proceedings against Luther commenced in Rome; on the instructions of Pope Leo X (*reigned* 1513–21) he was examined by Cardinal Cajetan (1469–1534) on the fringes of the diet at Augsburg, but he refused to recant; in December Luther's sovereign, the elector Frederick of Saxony, rejected Cajetan's application either to hand him over to Rome or to banish him from his territories. The furious exchange of discussions, lectures and sermons reached its climax in the 1519 "Leipzig disputation" which took place between the Ingolstadt professor of theology Johann Eck, Andreas Karlstadt and Luther. Luther treated the justification doctrine so broadly that he threw out every authority of the Church other than the *Bible*, reduced the office of the Church to a purely functional significance, and concluded that even Councils could err. Pope Leo X demanded of him that he retract all his *theses* within sixty days in a bull which threatened excommunication, *Exurge Domine* of 15 June 1520, whilst Luther published his most important Reformational works: *An Address to the Christian Nobility of the German Nation, On the Babylonian Captivity of the Church of God*, and *On the Liberty of a Christian Man*. Of these tracts alone, 36 editions appeared in barely two years in the German, Dutch, English, Spanish, Czech and Latin languages. The papal nuncio Giralamo Aleandro (1480–1542) caused these and others of his writings to be burnt in Cologne and Mainz; Luther, on the other hand, burnt the excommunication bull and a copy of canon law in Wittenberg on 10 December. On 3 January 1521 Pope Leo X pronounced the anathema against Luther in the bull *Decet Romanum pontificem.* In April 1521 Luther was summoned to appear before Emperor Charles V (1500–58) and the diet of Worms. His journey through many places on the way became a triumphal procession; but for all that, imperial outlawry was pronounced against Luther in the edict of Worms, and the printing and distribution of his writings was forbidden. Luther was able to hide away as "Junker Jörg" at the castle on the Wartburg under the protection of elector Frederick from May 1521 until March 1522; numerous sermons and writings emerged from there, among them the *Magnificat verdeutscht und ausgelegt*, and, in the space of only eleven weeks from December 1521 to February 1522, his translation of the *New Testament* from the Greek.

PAMPHLETS

It was not only Luther's own writings that were printed as leaflets of four, eight or sixteen pages, but also those of his fellow combatants and supporters. The pamphlets of Ulrich von Hutten (1488–1523) or Hans Sachs (1494–1576) call for special mention. The dialogue form adopted from Latin literature proved to be particularly suited to broadcasting the new ideas of the Reformation because of its instructional nature. Fundamental questions of theology could be grasped by the man in the street when presented as a game of question and answer. Hans Sachs has a canon and a shoemaker in earnest disputation (Nuremberg, 1524); through their dialogue, the canon is exposed as a shallow and unreflective pedant, whilst the cobbler "Hans" is shown as a believer who holds to his Bible. They explore three problematical fields which Luther had already identified in his appeal *An den Christlichen Adel teutscher Nation* (Address to the Christian Nobility of the German Nation): the exclusive right of the Pope to interpret the Bible and to call a Council, and the supremacy of spiritual over temporal power.

Representatives of both confessional sides make their respective appearances in these prose dialogues and leave a record of their words and actions. Abstract theological questions do not always take centre-stage, and the effects of religious attitudes on daily life also feature in dialogues about usury, false fasts, or the oppression and exploitation of the peasantry. It follows that these leaflets have a fundamental importance for the study of the intellectual background to the Peasant's War of 1524–25. The leaflet containing the *Zwölf Artikeln aller Bauernschaft* was distributed through a massive first printing and numerous reprints. It originally set out to be a discussion document between the peasants and the towns and noble landowners in particular. In it, the peasants rebel against tithes, against serfdom and against labouring for their landlords, and argue for the natural produce of field, wood and river to be freely available to them.

In the first thirty years of the sixteenth century more than 9000 pamphlets appeared, and with the Reformation, this rose to represent a 17 per cent share of total production by title after 1517. Within a year the peasant's "twelve articles" had appeared in over 24 editions from 18 printers in 15 different towns. This had the effect of a seven-fold increase in its share of the market for vernacular texts between 1519 and 1522, from which the mounting circulation of its contents may be inferred. Even assuming that editions of only 500 copies were the norm, the public they reached would have been disproportionately greater, for leaflets were read out and discussed in many places within each community. We know that Luther's Reformational hymns were first circulated in editions of 400 copies, which were then announced before public services so that the faithful could have access to them. There is a Reformational flyer of 1524 demonstrating just how flexible this practice was, which opens with the paradoxical sentence: "Dear reader, if you can't read, then find a young man who can read this text to you." The spread of Reformational ideas was achieved through printing, but their impact was relayed to wider audiences with the spread of these texts from the pulpit and through song.

Broadsides, moreover – mostly large-format sheets printed on one side only, and furnished with a lively woodcut and a text (usually in verse) – took on a new quality. Our example (see Plate 61) shows the persuasive impact of a woodcut with a text which clarifies it and at the same time takes the instructive form of a dialogue: *Ein neuer Spruch, wie die Geistlichkeit und etlich Handwerker über den Luther klagen* (a new poem: how the clergy and certain craftsmen complain about Luther). At first, its author Hans Sachs lends rhetorical support to the complaining workers who had brought home good money during the previous century as contractors to the Church: the bell-founder, the cutter of vestments, etc. Whilst these classes now complain that the Reformation is leading to cut-backs in this outward show, Sachs succeeds in drawing attention to the true inner value of the faith, and in putting Luther forward in both text and woodcut as the go-between for the "common man", who is seen to be praised by God the Father for discharging that role. The verse form suggests once again that this text would have been recited and discussed by the congregation. Schooled by such broadsheets and pamphlets and introduced to Lutheran theology with its wealth of ideas, believers were motivated to become more familiar with the Bible. As the translation of the New Testament was issued in serial parts from the outset, the text could be acquired at affordable prices and in manageable sections, and could thus be disseminated more rapidly than would have been possible with the sale of a complete Bible. The secret of its bestselling status, however, rests surely with Luther's matchless achievement as a translator.

LUTHER'S TRANSLATION PRINCIPLES

Even if the immediate occasions for the translation were the enforced exile on the Wartburg and – according to Luther's own account – an urgent request from Philipp Melanchthon, the motivations nevertheless lay deeper. Luther's public and clear avowal of the Bible as the highest authority in questions of faith and his steadfast reasoning from the Bible had awakened a great need for an accessible translation. At the heart of his Bible translation stands a humanistic turning back to original sources, the Greek and Hebrew texts, in contrast to the translations which had gone before which relied on the Vulgata alone. He freed himself from the slavish imitation of Latinistic style, in that he conveyed "not word for word, but sense for sense", as Heinrich Steinhöwel (1412–c.1478) had already postulated for his own prose translations in the fifteenth century. In a circular letter on translation (Sendbrief von Dolmetzschen, 1530), Luther took on the "literalists":

> For one must not ask the letters of the Latin tongue / how
> German should be spoken / as these asses do / but instead / ask
> the mother in the home, the children in the alleys / the common
> man in the market about it and watch what comes out of their
> mouths / how they utter things / and interpret that, then will

they understand / and take note / that one is speaking with them in German.

For example, he does not translate Ex *abundantia cordis os loquitur* in a literal way as "Aus dem Überfluß der hertzen redet der mund" (out of the abundance of the heart the mouth speaketh, Matt. 12:34 KJV), but almost proverbially as "Wes das hertz voll ist, des gehet der munt über" (what the heart is full of, trips off the tongue). Ut *quid perditio ista ungenti facta est* comes out not as "Warum ist dise verlierung der salben geschehen?" (why was this waste of the ointment made? Mark 14:4 KJV), but as "Es ist schade um die Salbe" (it is a pity about the ointment). Freedom of wording finds its limits where the danger of falsifying the sense arises, as Luther explains:

> Again we have to linger / immediately after the words have been translated / over whether we could possibly have given other and clearer ones / for the reason / that something more is lying in the same words. (Summarien über die Psalmen und Ursachen des Dolmetschens, 1533)

If the literal sense of a sample can not be reproduced by a free translation (that is, if "something more is lying", or a richer, more subtle shade of meaning is encapsulated in the wording of the sample) then he brings this out through word-for-word translation. The supreme guiding principle for him was to convey the uncorrupted "meaning" of the text conscientiously: "auff mein bestes vermügen vnd auff mein gewissen" (to the best of my means and of my belief), as he puts it in the Sendbrief. It follows from this that writing is its own best interpreter (scriptura sui ipsius interpres), and therefore where translation problems occur, comparable places in the text have to be looked at together. He weighed up the individual line against the evidence of the Bible as a whole – the understanding of which he owed to his study of hermeneutics – and approached the analysis of questions of detail each time from the individual to the whole, from the letter to the spirit. The central example for the interdependence of linguistic and theological reasoning is his translation of Romans 3:28: "So we now hold / that a man is justified / without the deeds of the law / through faith alone." Luther defended himself vigorously against the objection that the word "alone" is not to be found in either the Greek or Latin texts, on the grounds that only by introducing "only" or "alone" could an "article of faith of Christian teaching" be clearly worded, namely the central message of St Paul that God is not to be influenced by good works in the distribution of his mercy.

The introduction of modal particles such as "alone", "though", "even", "only", "now", "yet" etc., is typical of Luther's style where it closely follows the spoken language. Along with sentence-rhythm, repetition, assonance and other means, they give his translations their sermon-like character. He was at pains "das Evangelium sprechen zu lassen" (to let the gospel speak). He specially favoured alliterations ("Der Herr ist mein Hirte", "Dein Stecken und Stab", Ps. 23; "Lasset euer Licht leuchten vor den Leuten", Matt. 5:16) and words linked through rhyme ("Rat und Tat", Prov. 8:14; "singen und klingen", Ecclus. 39,20). The quest for the right choice of words was lifelong, and he revised his translations several times: at first he had the phrase "und er fing zu erzittern und zu engsten" in St Mark's passion story, which changes in 1530 to "zu zittern und zu zagen" (to shiver and to shake, Mark 14:33). Similarly, he avoided the wooden nominative style of 1520, "und sie werden euer etliche zum Tod helfen" (and some of you shall they cause to be put to death, Luke. 21, 16 KJV) by changing in 1530 to "und sie werden euer etliche töten" (and they will kill some of you). Luther's wrestlings for the right word still bear fruit in everyday speech: words he invented, such as "Denkzettel" (memo or reminder note), "Feuereifer" (burning enthusiasm), "Herzenslust" (heart's content), "Morgenland" (the East) are still current, as are his turns of phrase "ein Buch mit sieben Siegeln" (a book with seven seals, Rev. 5:1), "seine Hände in Unschuld waschen" (to wash one's hands in innocence, Ps. 26:6), "der Dorn im Auge" (a thorn in the eye, Num. 33:55), or "im Dunkeln tappen" (grope in the dark, Deut. 28:29).

BIBLE TRANSLATIONS FROM 1522 TO 1546

Luther's Bible translations began with the New Testament, which he produced from the Wartburg. His source was a copy of the second edition of the original Greek text with Latin translation and *annotationes* by

Erasmus of Rotterdam which came out at Basle in 1519, and alongside which he used the familiar text of the *Vulgata*. There is no evidence that he referred systematically to any of the earlier German translations, although in rare cases he does incorporate a useful phrase which had passed into general currency. The accomplishment of the new version lay not merely in its language, but in Luther's interpretative additions by way of prefaces and marginal notes. In these prefaces he emphasises the separation of the New Testament from the Old Testament, the latter being "teaching and law", whereas the former on the contrary consisted of "gute Botschaft / gute Mehre / gute newe Zeytung" (gospel / good parables / glad tidings) which are revealed to the faithful through narrative sermons. The marginal notes contain definitions of terms, factual explanations and allegorical interpretations that concentrate on conveying the full meaning of the biblical words. With the parable of the kingdom of heaven, which is likened to a treasure hidden in a field or a merchant seeking goodly pearls (Matt. 13:44–46), Luther comments on the significance of the Bible: "The hidden treasure is the Gospel / that gives us mercy and justice on our merits / therefore it makes us joyful if we find it / that is / a good cheerful conscience / which we can not obtain through works alone." But direct confrontations with his opponents can also spill over into these notes, as when, for instance, he reprimands those who teach the commandments but do not follow them (Matt. 5:19) as a "herd of papists".

The book of Revelation has hardly any commentary, instead its metaphorical language was matched to 21 illustrations from Lucas Cranach's workshop. These were closely modelled on Albrecht Dürer's 14 woodcuts for the "Apocalypse" (1498 and 1511), but altered in a number of iconographical details and in order to correspond more strongly to the letter of the text. They exhibit a marked anti-Roman bias, which finds its climax in the identification of the whore of Babylon (i.e. the antichrist) with the pope.

In March 1522 Luther left the Wartburg and revised the translation as soon as he got back to Wittenberg with the help of the professor of Hebrew and Greek there, Philipp Melanchthon (1497–1560). After five months' printing time in the workshops of Melchior Lotter the younger, *Das Neue Testament Deutzsch* was published in folio format and in an edition of about 3000 copies by Lucas Cranach and Christian Döring in good time for the Leipzig autumn fair (29 September to 6 October 1522). The price of the so-called *September Testament* was about a gulden (although this would have varied according to condition, whether bound or otherwise), which would have represented about two months' wages for a schoolmaster, or the price of a calf. Nevertheless, the publishers were able to start printing a second edition immediately after the first had appeared, and this was ready on 19 December 1522 (the so-called *December Testament*); it contained several hundred improvements to word-selection and syntax, and the marginal notes were supplemented by more material of the kinds already noted. The work enjoyed no privileged protection, and in the following year 12 complete reprintings took place in Augsburg, Basle, Grimma and Leipzig: in 1523/4 no fewer than 14 authorised editions and 66 "piracies" appeared.

Whilst the printing of the *September Testament* was taking place, Luther began his translation of the Old Testament which was based once again on the original text and that of the *Vulgata*. This work was to extend over twelve years, which is partly explained by its considerably greater length and by the difficulty of making a new translation, this time from the Hebrew. But economic considerations also played a part, as editions of individual books from the Old Testament – which began to come onto the market from 1523 onwards – could be thought better value for money than the first complete *Bible*, which came out in 1534 from Hans Lufft in Wittenberg. The Hebrew language with its richness of imagery struck Luther as particularly suitable for translation into German. Nevertheless, problems of every kind arose in the process of "interpreting purely and clearly"; he often struggled for weeks to find the right expression in consultation with his colleagues, Melanchthon in particular, and some months he was only able to finish a few lines. However the reader confronts a problem-free and fluently readable text, unaware of those "Wackersteine und Klötze" (broken stones and stumps) that would have lain in his or her path: "Es is gut pflügen, wenn der Acker bereinigt ist" (ploughing is easy when the field is cleaned up). Just as he took pains over his translator's premise "sense for sense", so Luther was equally concerned to have the stylistic individuality of the examples in hand come across clearly, as when he re-phrased the Psalms, without any knowledge of Hebrew metrics, but in correspondingly free rhythms and with ingenious tone colours.

The notion of the biblical texts as a unified whole was increasingly emphasised in the prefaces: prophesies which are made in the Old Testament regarding Christ and salvation find their fulfilment in the New Testament; people and events were designated as prefigurations of the New Testament, following the example given by St Paul in which Adam is made a figure of the Christ that is to come (Rom. 5:14). Luther points this out movingly in his preface to the Pentateuch: "Here will you find the swaddling-clothes and the crib / in which Christ lay / there also the angel who guided the shepherds / scanty and poor are these swaddling-clothes / but dear is the beloved Christ / who lay therein."

The first part of the Old Testament, the five books of Moses, which appeared in 1523 from Melchior and Michael Lotter in Wittenberg, was once again furnished with woodcut illustrations from the workshop of Lucas Cranach which serve the text down to the letter and show such things as Noah's ark, the Ark of the Covenant or a seven-branched menorah. The historical books (Joshua to Esther), the poetic books (Job, Proverbs, Ecclesiastes, Song of Solomon) and the Psalter followed in 1524.

All these translated parts were brought together, revised, and finally published in 1534 as the first complete Bible, the Biblia / das ist / die gantze Heilige Schrifft / Deudsch, which included the translation of the apocryphal books (Judith, Tobit, Baruch, Maccabees, Esther) which had been newly undertaken for the most part by Melanchthon and Justus Jonas (1493–1555). There are altogether 118 woodblocks by the monogrammist MS from the Wittenberg workshop of Lucas Cranach, in this typographically ambitious volume from the printing house of Hans Lufft which enjoyed the protection of an electoral privilege against unauthorised reprinting. New editions with only minor improvements appeared in 1535, 1536, 1539 and 1540; a fundamental revision carried out from 1539 to 1541 resulted in the Wittenberg edition of autumn 1541 (known as the "Medium Bible" because of its large paper size); the illustrations were mostly undertaken by the MS monogrammist. This re-working was advertised on the title page: "Auffs new zugericht" (made as new), and much store was set on careful and faultless printing. Luther also introduced a "warning" in which he makes a powerful complaint against unlicensed and therefore unreliable reprinters: "As you solely seek [to gratify] your greed / ask yourself a little afterwards / how right or wrong it is to reprint something / as it has often happened to me / that I have read pirated reprints

/ and found them to be falsified / so that I have in many places failed / to recognise my own work."

The definitive text is the Biblia / das ist / Die gantze Heilige Schrifft: / Deudsch Auff Newzugericht. D. Mart. Luth., which Hans Lufft published in Wittenberg in 1545. As it was the final version to appear during Luther's lifetime, it assumed almost canonical status and – contrary to Luther's own intentions – it has barely changed over the centuries. A few of Luther's own corrections were, however, incorporated into the edition of 1546, which appeared posthumously and was seen through the press by his close colleague and proof-reader Georg Rörer (1492–1557, see Plate 62).

Between 1522 and 1546 it is possible to identify 430 part or complete editions, so that there must have been some half a million Luther Bibles in circulation by the middle of the century. Besides that, there were attempts by the "old" Church to stem the flow of Lutheran doctrines by issuing its own translations. On the instigation of Duke George of Saxony (1471–1539), who had already prohibited the Luther Bible for his own subjects in 1552, Hieronymus Emser (1477–1527) published with Wolfgang Stöckel in Dresden a New Testament that he had compiled from Luther's September Testament, earlier German Bibles, and by reference to the original sources. This was illustrated by re-using the woodblocks from the December Testament which Cranach had sold to him. In an afterword, Emser did his best to dissuade people from reading the Bible, which was not intended for the laity and belonged in the safe hands of the clergy, and to this end he fell back on the old arguments of the previous century: "That is why those lay persons (who will follow my advice) should now concern themselves more with a pious and godly life / than with the Bible / which is recommended only to the learned."

The Biblia / beider Allt vnnd Newen Testamenten of the Dominican Johann Dietenberger (c. 1475–1537) met with greater success. It appeared in Mainz and Cologne – with the backing of an imperial privilege – in 1534, and in fact before Luther's complete edition. This Mainz professor of theology also made use of Luther's translation, directly and indirectly (through Emser's extensive borrowings). As well as earlier German versions, but he provided additional summaries of content for the books, and marginal notes – for variant translations and other explanations – where he also noted "falsifications" in Luther's interpretation. Dietenberger's Bible survived until 1776 in a total of 46 editions.

Ｃ riſtofori faciem die quacunq́ tueris ·:·
Ｉlla nempe die morte mala nõ moꝛieris ·:·   Milleſimo ccccᵒ
                                              ｚ xᵘ anno ·:ẛ·

Plate 47: The Buxheim St Christopher, woodcut broadsheet dated 1423.
From a facsimile after the unique copy in the John Rylands Library, Manchester.

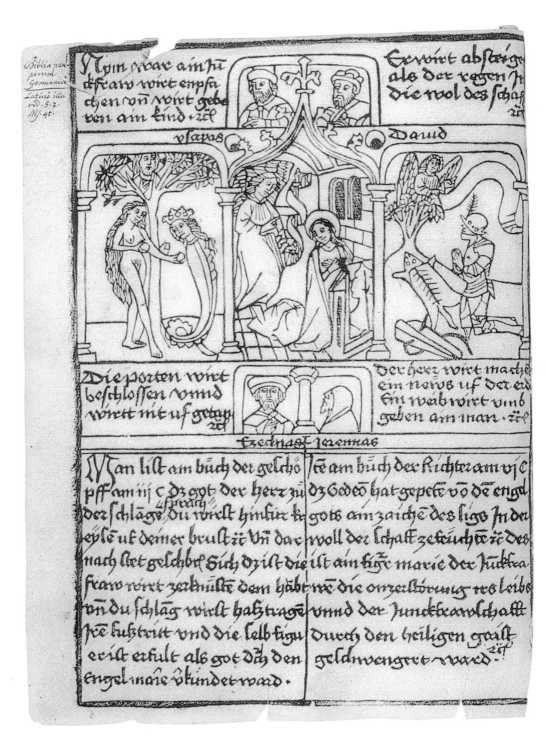

Plate 48: *Biblia Pauperum*, block-book, Nuremberg, Hans Sporer, 1471.
Wolfenbüttel, Herzog August Library.

Es jars als man zalt nach Christi geburdt·M·cccc·lxxviij·jar··So ist d·z·U· der suntäglich
büchstab·☙ Vnd xvj·die guldinezal ☙ Vñ von dē Christag biß auff der herren vaßnacht·v·
wochen vnd drey tag·☙ Die lxx·tāg vahent an am sant Anthony tag· Der herren vaßnacht
ist am nāchsten tag vor liechtmeß·Der ostertag ist ō nāchst sontag vor Marie verkündūng
Die kreüezwoch an sontag nach sant Marx tag·Der pfingstag ist der achtent tag nach des
heyligen kreüez tag·Das aduent vahet an An sant Andreas abent·

☙ Hornūg wirt new am achtende ō vnschuldige kindlin
morgē wenn es·ix·schlecht·liij·minut ☙ Der pruch am nā
chstē tag nach Anthony nach mittag·v·stund·lviij·mi·
☙ Merez wirt new am nāchstē tag nach Liechtmeß mor
gens frū so es·iij·schlecht·xxxix·mi·☙ Der pruch am erich
tag nach Valentini morgē so es·v·schlecht·xxviij·minut·
☙ Apptill wirt new an mitwoche vor Perpetue Felicita
tis nach mittag·vj·stund·xlviij·mi·☙ Der pruch am mit
woche nach Gedeudis v·stund nach mittag·liiij·minut
☙ May wirt new an sant Ambrosius abēt vor mittag so
es·vj·schlecht·lv·minut·☙ Der pruch am freitag vor Thi
burey morgen so es·vj·schlecht·xv·minut·
☙ Prachmon wirt new an des heyligen kreütz abent· iiij·
stund nach mittag·xxiij·minut·☙ Der pruch am sambstag
nach Seruacy·ix·stund nach mittag·xiij·minut·
☙ Der andprachmō Embolismalis wirt new am sontag
nach Urbani·vj·stūd nach mittag·liiij·minut·☙ Der pruch
an sant Veits tag wenn es·xj·schlecht·xlij·minut·
☙ Hāmō wirt new am nāchstē tag nach Petri vñ pauli
morgen wen es·vj·schlecht·xxxiiij·minut·☙ Der pruch am
mitwochen nach Margarethe am morgens frū wenn es
ij·schlecht·xxxviij·minut·
☙ Augstmon wirt new am mitwoche nach Jacobi nach
mittag wenn es·ij·schlecht·xxxvij·mi·☙ Hie wirt Eclipsis
solis das ist ein finstrein Also der mon wirt drew tepl der
sunne verdeckt ☙ Der pruch am donerstag nach Laurēti
nach mittag·v·stund·xlij·minut·
☙ Sāemō wirt new am donerstag nach Bartholomei·x·
stund nach mittag·v·mi·☙ Der pruch am sāpstag nach
vnserfrawē gepurd vor mittag so es·vij·schlecht·xxvj·mi·
☙ Der erst Herbst wirt new am sambstag nach sat Ma
theus tag morgens so es·viij·schlecht·lij·mi·☙ Der pruch
am sontag vor sat gallen tag x·stund nach mittag·xlv·mi·
☙ Der and Herbst wirt new an sontag vor Simonis vñ
Jude nach mittag·x·stund·vij·mi·☙ Der pruch an sant
Martins abent so es·xj·schlecht·xliij·minut·
☙ Der wintermō wirt new an dē nāchstē tag vor Kate
rine nach mittag so es·ij·schlecht·lv·mi·☙ Der pruch am
mitwoche nach Nicolai·v·stund nach mittag·xxj·minut·
☙ Jenner wirt new an dem heyligen Christ abent morgē
vor mittag wenn es·ix·schlecht·xxiiij·minut·

☙ Nun volgent die Aderlāssin·

☙ Hornung·☙ Am pfingstag nach ō obrost sittellāssig
ō jungen on die füß Am freitag vnd sampstag nach dem
obrost gūt den jūgen on das haubt·An der mitwochē vñ
donerstag vor sent Pauls ker mittel dē altē an sant pauls
ker mittel dē alten·An dem mōntag nach sant pauls ker tag
mittel dē alten·An der mitwochen nach sant Pauls tag
gūt lassen den alten·nicht die diech· ☙ Merez·
☙ Am freytag nach sant Agathe tag gūt ō junge on das

haubt·An sant Valentins abēt mittel dē junge oi dz hertz
An freytag vor sant Matheis tag gūt dē alten·An ō mit
woche nach Mathie gūt dē altē on die diech ☙ Aprill·
☙ An sant Gregori tag vñ den nāchstē darnach mittel dē
jūgen on das hertz·Am montag vnd erichtag vor vnsre
frawen kündig gūt dē altē nit die diech·Am sampstag
nach vnser frawen tag gūt lassen den alten· ☙ May·
☙ Am donerstag nach Ambrosy mittel dē jūgen on die
prust·Am montag vor Thiburey mittel den jungen·Am
montag vor sandt Jörgen tag gūt dē alten on die diech
An sampstag nach sant Jörgen tag gūt dē altē·An mō
tag nach sant Jörgen tag mittel den alten on die füß Gūt
erceney nemen· ☙ Prachmon
☙ An der mitwochen nach des heyligen kreüez tag mittel
den jungen on das hertz·Am freytag vnd sampstag vor
Urbani gūt den alten·An sant Urbans tag mittel dē altē
Am erichtag vñ mitwochen nach Urbani gūt den junge
nit das haubt· ☙ Embolismalis ander Prachmon
☙ Am aftermontag nach Bonifacy gūt den junge· Am
donerstag vor Viti mittel den jungen Am donerstag vnd
freytag nach Vit gūt den alten·An sant Johans abent
gūt dē alten on das haubt· ☙ Hāemō
☙ Am montag vnd erichtag nach sant Ulrichs tag gūt
den jungen·An sampstag nach Felicitatis gūt den junge
on die diech An sampstag vor marie Magdalene mittel
den altē on die füß·An montag vñ erichtag vor Magda
lene gūt den alten on das haubt· ☙ Augstmon
☙ An montag vor sant Sixt tag gūt den jūgen·Am sāpß
tag nach Sixti gūt den jungen on die diech·Am montag
Marie schidūg gūt dē altē on dz haubt· ☙ Sāemō
☙ An donerstag vnd freytag nach Egidy gūt den jūgen
on die diech An vnser frawen gepurd vnd den nāchstē
darnach gūt den jungen·Am mōtag nach Marie gepurd
gūt den alten on das haubt· ☙ Herbstmon
☙ An dem mitwoch vnd donerstag nach Michaelis gūt
den jungen on die diech·An montag vnnd erichtag vor
Dionisy gūt den jungen·Am donerstag vor dionisy mit
tel dē junge on die füß Am sampstag nach Galli mittel
den alten·on die hertz obe prust· ☙ Ander Herbst
☙ An sant Narcissen tag gūt den junge on die diech·Am
nāchsten tag nach aller heyligen tag gūt den junge· Am
freytag sampstag nach aller heyligen tag gūt den jungen
on das haubt·Am freytag sampstag nach Martini mit
tel den altē on die prust·Am freitag nach Elzabeth gūt
den alten· ☙ Wintermon
☙ An sant Andreas abent gūt dē junge Am freytag vnd
sampstag vor Nicolai gūt den junge on das haubt· Am
donerstag nach Lucie gūt den alten· Am sampstag vor
Thomae mittel den alten·An sant Thomas tag Gūt den
alten·An sant Siluesters tag gūt den jungē on dz haubt

Der tag vor vñ nach dē neüen vñ pruch ist nit gūt aderlassen·Darumb seind die selben zeichen hie nit beschriben

---

Plate 49: Calendar for the year 1478, with new year's greeting scroll "Ain gut sälig iar"
in head margin, broadside, Augsburg, Anton Sorg, 1477.
Göttingen State and University Library.

De fulgetra anni xcij, Sebastianus Brant.

Von Maximiliano.

Müt on v fach
.J. .B.

Komischem kuning:

Plate 50: Sebastian Brant: Der Donnerstein von Ensisheim
(The Ensisheim meteorite), broadsheet, 1492.

Das sind die new gefundñ menschñ oð volcker Jn form vñ gestalt Als sie hie stend durch dñ Cristenlichen

Künig von Portugall gar wunderbarlich erfunden.

Plate 51: Amerigo Vespucci: *Das sind die new gefunden menschen . . .*
(These are the new-found people or race . . .), Leipzig, 1505.
Wolfenbüttel, Herzog August Library.

Hie seind ʒe mercken die ʒeichen der falschen guldin ym
nyderland gemacht vñ seind Ettliche mincʒer ʒu Göttin
gen yn sachssen/vnd yn andern stetten verbant vnd auf
vier thunnen von yn gemincʒet·

Item die guldin auff der vier
herren schleg mit einem ʒwifal
tigen·w·Was stat oben an dem
mencʒer rad·Ist falsch·

Item die guldin mit einē apfel
vnd sant Johanns auff der an=
dern seiten Ein schilt mit einem
leo·Etlich seind falsch·

Item die guldin mit einē apfel
vnd die ander seiten sant Peter
mit einē steren an der brust·solt
stan sant Johañs auf den heim
burger schlag·seind falsch·

Item die guldin mit dē bischoff
mit einē grossen schilt auff den
kölnischen schlag/vñ die ander
seitten bey dem haubt ein b·mit
einem tittel·Etlich wöllent es
sey ein v·mit einem tittel seind
falsch·

Item die guldin mit einē apfel
vnd die ander seitten ʒwischen
den füssen ein kreucʒ mit einē
stern auff den franckfurter sch=
lag·Etlich wöllendt es sey ein
kron mit einē stern·oder ein gekrönter künig·sein falsch·

Item der vorgenanten guldin·Ist einer nitt besser/dann
fünff weißpfenning·vnd ist der raiff vmher guldin eins
halben halms dick Vnd das corpus ist gancʒ kupfferin/
vnd über gült·Vñ das kupffer ist so hart gemincʒet vñ
gesotten dʒ es wol klingt·Hierumb mag sy nyemant er
kennen an dem klang·noch an dem striche·   Vlm

Plate 52: "The signs of false gulden", broadsheet, Ulm, Johann Zainer, c. 1482.
Reproduced from Carl Wehmer: Deutsche Buchdrucker des 15. Jahrhunderts,
Wiesbaden, 1971, plate 54.

116

Tewrdannck hin zů der Künigin gieng
Gar freündlichen Sy Jn empfieng
Fůert Jn in Jr köstlich gemach
Darinn Sy stetz zů wonen pflag
Nam darzů etlich Jrgeheim Rede
Deßgleichen auch Tewrdannck der Held thet
Auf daffelb Sy anfieng vnnd sprach
Herz habe Jr Euch auf dise sach

P

Plate 53: Maximilian I: Theuerdank, Augsburg, Johann Schönsperger, 1517.
Woodcut by Leonhard Beck (showing contraction of marriage to Mary of Burgundy).
From the facsimile by Simon Laschitzer in the Jahrbuch der Kunsthistorischen Sammlungen der
Allerhöchsten Kaiserhauses, vol 8, Vienna, 1888.

prologus in machabeorū. i capitulū

Je zwei bücher machabeorū das
ist der streiter die do beruren vns
die streite die do seint geschehen
vnder den leitern oder fürern der
hebrepschen vnd vnder den beiden
der von persia: iedoch ist zu wisse
das dz ander bůch der streiter ist
ein send brief den gesendet hat judas machabeus vnd
die elttesten der iuden mit im zu jerlm. dē andern iudē
die do vmb vnd vm zu streit waren in den lande ge
gen der sunne aufgang. vnd die selben bücher sprech
en aus den streit der iuden der geschehen ist am sa
both. vnd auch der edeln hertzogen oder leitern vnd
furern die do brasen machabeus: vnd besunder iude
machabep wie der vber winden hat aus dem mann
en dise bücher iren namen haben. Vnd disse hpsto
ria beschleußet in ir die erlichen wercke der brüder
machabeop: vnder dem kunig antiocha die die hei
ligen gesetze haben geliret. Bittre marter vnd die
selbe hat nit beweint die milde ir můter do man sp
noigt mit der marter: sunder sp hat sp vil mer ver
mant frölichen zu der eren vnd wirdikeit der marē

S ist geschehen darnach als
alexander philipi el kunig in
macedo der des ersten reiche
in kriechen das er auf ging
von der erden eierim das der
schlug darium den kunig per
sarum vnd medop. er hůb vil
streite: vnd behielt die feste
nung ir aller: vnd ober die kunige der erd. Vnd
nam die raube der menig der beiden: vnd die erde
schweig in seiner angesichte. Vnd er samelte die
krafte vnd ein her als starck: vnd sein hertz ware er
höhet vnd erhaben: vnd er behielte die kunigreiche
der beiden vnd der würtriche vnd sp wurden im zins
haftig. Vnd darnach nider viel er in das bett: er be
kant das er wurd sterben. Er berieff die edelen sein
kinder die vn iungen eagen ernieret wur
den: vnd er deilt in sein reich do er denoch lebt. Alex
ander repschset xij iar: vnd starbe. Vnd sein ge
sellen behilten das reich ein iertlicher in seiner seat:
vnd sp ale satztē in auf kunigliche krone nach sein
em tod vnd ir süne nach in vil iare vnd die vbel
wurden gemanigualteigt in der erde. Vnd aus in
aus ging die wurzel der sunden der edel antioch
us ein sun des kunigs antiochi der zu rome was
gruessen ein pfant oder ein geisel: vnd er herschte
in dem C vnd xxxvij des kriechisch reichs. In den
tagen aus gingen aus ifrl die vngerechten süne
vnd sie gabē rat vil sprechen. See wir vnd besellē
wir einen punt des frides mit den beiden die neben
vns sein: wan darnach als wir von in sein gegäg
en haben vns funden vil vbel. Vnd dise rede was
gesehen gůt in iren augen. Vnd ir ettlich vō dem
volck ordentē das vestiglich vnd ab gingen zu dem
kunig: vnd er gab in den gewalt: dz sp deten die ge

reichtikeit der beiden. Vnd sp pauwtē ein gemeine
schüle in ierlm nach dem gesetze der beiden: vnd sp
liessen sich nit beschneiden: vnd gingent von dem
heiligen testament. vnd sp haben sich zu gefugt den
beiden: vnd gaben sich gantz dar zu das sp detn daz
vbel: vnd das reich ware bereit in dem angesichte
anthiochi: vnd er hub an zu reichsen in der erden
egipt: also das er reichtset vber zwei reich. Vnd er
ein ging in egipten in schwerd menig in den wege
vnd elephanten vnd die reitenden: vnd in grosser
menig der schiffe. Vnd er besellet den streit wider
den prolomeum kunig egipti: vnd prolome vorcht
sich vnd floh vor seinem antlitz: vnd es vielen vil
verwunter. Vnd er begreif die gemurten stete der
erden egipt: vnd er nam die raub der erden egipti.
Darnach als anthiochus hette geschlagen egiptum
er wider kere in dem hunderstein vnd xliij iare vnd
auf steige in irlt: vnd auf ging in ierlm in seiner
menige: vn in hoffart ein ging er in die heiligkeit:
vnd nam den guldin altar vnd den leucht des liech-
tes vnd alle sein gefesse vnd den tisch der brot furle
gung vnd die vaß der fuchten opffer vnd die schal
en der salben vnd die guldin morser vnd den fur
banck vnd die kronen vnd die guldin sprunge die
do was in dem angesichte des tempels: vn der zer-
mischet dise alle. Er nam silber vnd gold vnd die
begirliche vaß: vnd nam die verborgen schertze die
er vant: dise alle furt er hindan vnd ging in seine
erden. Vnd machet ein grose schlagung der mensch
en: vnd er redt in grosser hoffart. Vnd es ware ein
grosses clagen in irlt: vnd in einer ieztlichen seat.
Vnd die fursten erseuftzten vnd die elteschen: die
iungen vnd die iungfrawen wurden kranck: vnd
schön gestalt der weiber wurden verwandelt. Ein
ietzlich man nam ein dagen: vnd die do sassen an
dem ehlichen bett die wainten. Vnd die do fassen an
wegt vber die dar in wonten: vnd nach disem ein
ietzlich haus iacobs aus ioch das beruptenis. Vnd
nach eagen zwei iar sendet der kunig einen fursten
der zinß in die stete iuda: vn der kam in ierlm mit
grosser schar. Vnd er redt zu in fridsame worte in
falschkeit: vnd sp glaubten im. Vnd also bald viel
er auf die seat: vnd schlug sp mit grosser pflag: vn
verloß vil volckes aus irfl. Vnd nam die raub der
seat vnd er anzundet die mit fewer. Vnd zestört
ir heuser vnd ir mauren in dem vmb kreiß: vnd sp
fürten gefangen die frauwen vnd die kinder: vnd
sp besassen das vich. Vnd sp pauten die seat dauit
des mit einer grossen starcken muren vnd mit starck
en türne: vnd die ware in zu einer vestikeit. Vnd
do hin setzten sp das sündliche vnd heidnische volck
die vngerechten man: vnd sp wurden al zu searcke.
Dorumb sp legten dar in harnasch vnd speise: vnd
samenten den raub ierlm vnd legten die do selbst:
vnd wurden in zu einem grossen stricke. Vnd das
geschach zu einer lagunge der heiligen seat vnd in
einem bösen schmertzen oder dollong teuffel in irfl
Vnd sp verguffen das vnschuldig blůt durch den
vmkreis der heiligen seat: vnd vermeiligten die hei
ligkeit. Vnd die woner in ierlm flúhe durch it wil
len: vnd sp ware zu einer wonung der auslendisch

Plate 54: The first German Bible, Johann Mentelin, Strasbourg, 1466 (GW 4295), fol 301r.
Göttingen State and University Library.

creücz vnsers herre Jhesu christi durch ten
mit die welt ist gekreücziget vnd ich der
welt. Wañ in christo ihesu ist nit etwas
nütz die beschneydung noch auch die übre
wachsung aber die new creatur vnd alle
die da nachuolgent diser regel. Frid vnd
erbermd sey über sy vnd über israhel gots
Füro hin brüder keyner sey mir leydig
Wann ich trag das zeychen tes herren ihe
su in meim leyb. Brüder die genad vnsers
herren ihesu christi sey mit euwerem geyst
Amen.

¶Die epistel ad galathas hatt ein
ente. Vnnd hebt an die Epistel zü
ten Laodicern.
Das erst capitel.

Aulus tet nicht von ten
menschen noch durch ten
menschen aber durch ihe
sum christum. Den brü
dern die da seind zü Lao
dicy. Die genad sey mit
euch vnd ter frid võ got
vnsern vatter vnnd von tem herren ihesu
christo. Ich wirck gnad mein got durch
alles mein gebett. Darumb das ir seyt be
leybent in im vnnd zü volenten in gütten
wercken. Beytent ter verkeypssung an tem
tag tes vrteyls verwüstende euch nit mit
etlicher üppiger red das die croffen ot das
euch abkeret von ter warheit tes ewange
liums das da wirt geprediget von mir.
Vnd nun got ter macht die dinge die da
seind von mir dienent zü tem nutz ter war
heit tes ewangely vnd thünd die güttig
keyt ter wercke die da seind ter behaltsam
tes ewigen lebens. Vnd nun meine band
die seind offen die ich erlepte in cristo vñ
die ich mich freüwe vnd frew mich vnd
ditz ist mit zü ter ewigen behaltsam. Das
selb ist geschan euch zehelffen in euwern ge
betten vnd von ter dienung tes heyligen
geysts. Es sey durch das lebn oder durch
ten todt wann mir zeleben ist eyn leben in
christo vnd sterben ein gewin. Vnd erselb
thü sein erbermd in euch das ir habt die
selben lieb vnd seyt einhellig. Darumb al
ler liebsten als ir habt gehört die voewis
senheit tes herren also behabt sy vnd thüt
sy in ter vorcht gots vnnd euch wirt das
leben ewiglich wañ got ist ö da wirckt
in euch. Vnd wölch ding ir thür die thüt
on hinterred oder on sünd. Vnd aller lieb
ste es ist das best. freüwet euch im herren

Vnd hüt euch vor aller vnreyner gewin
nung. All euwer epschung seind offenbar
bey got vnd seyt vest in tem synn christi.
Vnd die ding die da seind gancz vnd ge
wer vnd keüsch vnd zymlich vnnd recht
vnd lieblich die thüt. Vnnd die ding die
ir habt gehört vnd empfange die behabt
im hertzen. Vnd ter frid gots ter wirt mit
euch. Euch grüssent all heyligen. Die ge
nad vnsers herren ihesu christi die sey mit
euwerm geyst vnd macht die epistel zele
sen ten colosensern zü euch Amen.

¶Ein ente hatt die Epistel zü ten
Laodicern Vnnd hebt an die vor
red über die epistel zü ten ephesiern

Dhesi seid
asiani di
se da Sp
epfiengen
das wort
ö warheit
da testün
ten sy vest
in tem ge
lauben di
se lobt ter
Apostel
vnnd sch
reybt in
võ Rom

auß tem kercker bey tem ewãgelier thyteu

¶Die voered hatt ein ende. Vnnd
hebt an die epistel zü ten ephesiern

¶Das erst Capitel.

Aulus ein apostel Jhesu
christi durch ten willen
gots alle ten heyligen die
da seind ephesi vnnd ten
gelaubigen in ihesu chri
sto. Genad sey mit euch
vnd seite võ got vnserm
vatter vnnd von tem herren ihesu christo.
Got ter sey gesegent vñ ter vatter vnsers
herre ihesu christi ter vns hat gesegent in
allem geystlichen segen in ten himelischen
dingen in christo als er vns hatt erwöllt
in im selber vor ter satzüg ter welt daz wir
seyen heylig vñ vnuermeyligt in seinem

Plate 55: German Bible, Augsburg, Günther Zainer, 1475-76, (GW 4298).
Göttingen State and University Library.

ℭDie vorreden habent ein ende. Vnd hebet
an der prophet pſaias.
ℭDas erſt capitel·

Ie geſicht
pſaias des
ſun Amos
die er ſach
úb iudam
vñ úb ihe/
ruſalem in
den tagen
ozie ioath/
an Achas
vñ ezechie
der kúnig
iuda. Ir hi
mel hȯzent
vñ du erde
empfach mit den ozen· wann der herze hatt
geredt. Ich hab erzogē ſun·vñ hab ſp er hȯ
het·ab ſp haben mich verſchmäht. Der ochs
erkant ſeinen beſitzer·vnd der eſel die krúpp
ſeines herzen. Aber jſrahel der erkant mich
nit·vnd mein volck das vernam mich nit
Wee dem ſúndigen volcke· dem ſchwären
volck voz miſſetat·dem ſchalckhafftigen ſa
men·de úbeltättigen ſúnen. Sp habent ver/
lauſſen den herzen· Sp habent gelȯſteret den
hepligen iſrael·ſp ſcind abkeret hinder ſich·
Warczú ſchlach ich eúch fúrohin·die ir zú/
legent die úbergeung·ein pegklichs ſiechs
haubt·vnnd ein pegkliches traurigs hertz·

Plate 56: German Bible, Augsburg, Günther Zainer, 1475-76,
(initial showing stem of Jesse).

Plate 57: Low German Bible, Cologne, Bartholomäus von Unckel, 1478 (GW 4307), fol 2r. Göttingen State and University Library.

Plate 58: Low German Bible, Cologne, 1478, fol 5r.

Hie hebt ſich an.Geneſis das erſt buch der fünff bucher moyſi. Das erſt Capitel iſt võ der ſchöppfung der werlt vnd aller creaturen. vnd von den wercken der ſechs tag.

Jn dem anfang hat got Beſchaffen hymel vnd erden.aber dye erde was eytel vnd lere.vnd die vinſternus warn auff dē antlitz des abgrunds.vnd der geiſt gots ſwebet oder ward getragen auff dē waſſern.Vñ got der ſprach.Es werde dz liecht Vñ das liecht iſt worden.vñ got ſahe dz liecht das es gutt was.vnd er teylet das liecht võ der vinſternus.vnd das liecht hyeß er den tag.vnd die vinſternus die nacht.Vñ es ward abent vñ morgen eyn tag. Vnd got der ſprach.Es werde das firmament in dem mittel der waſſer. vñ tayle die waſſer võ dē waſſern.Vñ got machet das firmament.vnd teylet die waſſer.Sy ſo waren vnder dem firmament.von dē ſy ſo waren ob dem firmament. vnd es iſt alſo geſchehen vnd got hieß das firmament den hymel vnd es iſt der abent vñ der morgē der ander tag wordē vñ got ſprach aber.Es ſulle geſamelt werdē dy waſſer.die vnder dem hymel ſeynd.an eyn ſtatt, vñ erſcheyne die dürre. vnd es iſt alſo geſchehē Vñ got hieß die dürre dz ertreich.Vñ ſy ſamnungen der waſſer.hieß er die mere.vnd got ſahe das es was gut.vnd ſprach.Die erde gepere grunend krawt.das ſo bringe den ſamen.vnd dy öpfelbawm.dz holtz.dz ſo bringe ſy frucht nach ſeym geſchlecht . des ſame ſey in yn ſelbs auff der erde.vnd es iſt alſo geſchehen.vnd die erd bracht grunend kraut. vnd bringenden ſa

Plate 59: The ninth German Bible, Nuremberg, Anton Koberger, 1483 (GW 4303), fol 5r. Göttingen State and University Library.

also das alle ding wurden volbracht die lucas
schreybt.in dem buch actus apostolorum. Dar
nach zu de lersten gab paulus ein beschliessug
vnd ein vollendung mit seiner predig desselben
buchs. Wann den selbe der herr erwelt hat. Dar
nach als er lang het gestrytten.wider die anfech
tung des leybs. Vn wiewol das ist.Es es nütz
wer den.die so gern lesen.vn die gott den herre
suchen.Es wir de selben hete besunderlich mer
vn mer beschriben. Jedoch so wayß ich Es der
ackerman der so arbeyt des ersten soll essen vo
seinen früchten.vn darumb habe wir vermiden
öffenlich fürwitzigkeit Es wir nit ersehen wür
den.zeerzaigen den sy got wöllen.auch de wöl
len got offenbarn.die in verschmehen.

Ein ander vorrede

Jnn vil habe sich
gefliffen zeorden die rede der
ding.die so sind erfült an vns
Als vns die gegeben habe. Dy
auch sy haben gesehen.vn sind
gewesen diener der predig. Jst
auch mir gesehen worde. Der ich fleyssigkliche
von anfang alle ding begriffen hab ordenlich
zeschreyben.dir zu allerliebster Theophile.Das
zu erkennest die warheit.der wort.von den zu
bist gelert.

Die hebt an das Buch luce des euangelisten.

Das erst Capitel. wy der
engel zacharie erschine. Zacharias de engel nit
gelaubet.vn darum erstümet. Wy maria vo de
engel gegrüst ward. vn auß vermanug des en
gels elizabeth heisucht.vn grüsset. vn wy eliza
beth gepare.vn zacharie sei mud eröffent ward

S was i de
tagen hero
dis des künigs iudee
ein priester mit name
zacharias. Von dem
geschleht abia.vn sei
eweyb von den töch
tern aaron.vn ir nam was elizabeth. Wann beyd
warn sie gerecht vor got sie giengen in allen ge
rechtigkeyten.vn in den geboten des herren on

klag.vn sie hetten keinen sun.darumb Es eliza
beth was vnberhaftig.vn beyde warn sie vber
gangen in iren tagen. Vn es geschah als brau
chet zacharias die priesterschaft in d ordnung
seins ampts vor got.er gieng auß nach de lobe
das er legt das brünend opfer.vn gieng.in de
tempel des herre.vn alle menig des volcks wz
außwendig bettend zu der stund des brünen
den opfers. Vnd der engel des herren erschyn
im.steend zu der gerechten des altars des weyr

Plate 60: The ninth German Bible, Nuremberg, Koberger, 1483.
The gospel according to St Luke.

Ein neuer Spruch/ wie die Geystlicheit vnd etlich Handtwercker yber den Luther clagen.

Der geitzig clagt auß falschem müt/
Seit im abget an Eer vnd Güt.
Er Zürnet/Dobet/vnde Wüt/
In dürstet nach des grechten plůt.

Die warheit ist Got vnd sein wort/
Das pleibt ewiglich vnzerstort.
Wie ser der Gotloß auch rumort/
Gott bschützt sein diener hie vnd dort.

Der Grecht sagt die Gotlich warheit/
Wie hart man in veruolgt/verleit.
hofft er in Gott doch alle zeit/
Pleibt bstendig in der grechtigkeit.

H. R. 26

Die clag der Gotlosen.
Hör vnser clag du strenger Richter/
Vnd sey vnser zwitracht ein schlichter.
Eh wir die beid selb legen an/
Martin Luther den schedlich man/
Der hat geschriben vnd gelert/
Vnd schir das gantz Teütsch land verkert/
Mit schmehen/lestern/nach vnd weit/
Die Erwirdige Gaistlicheit.
Von iren Pfründen/ Rent vnd Zinst/
Vnd verwürfft auch iren Gotdinst/
Der Vätter gepot/ vnd auffsetz/
hayßt er vns/ vnd menschen gschwetz
helt nichts von Aplaß vnd Fegfewr/
Die Meß kům auch kain Sel zu stewr.
All Kirchen Pew/Zir/ vnd gschmuck/
Veracht er gar/ er ist nit eluck.
Des clagen die Prelaten ser/
Pfaffen/Münch/ Stationirer/
Glockengiesser vnd Organisten/
Goltschlager vnd Illuministen/
hådtmaler/ Goltschmit vñ bildschnitzer/
Ratschmit/ Glaßmaler/ seidensitzer/
Stainmetzen/ Zimerleüt Schreiner/
Paternoster/ Kartzenmacher.
Die Permenter/ Singer vnd Schreyber/
Fischer/Zopffnůn vnd Pfaffen Weyber/
Den alln ist Luther ein schwer/
Von dir wirt ein Vrteil begert.
Sunst werde wir weiter Appellieren/
Vnd dem Luther die Prend recht schirn/
Müß Pümen/ oder Reuocirn.

Antwort D. Martini.
O du armer aller hertzen/
Hör mein antwort des ist kein schertzen/
Die schreyen fast ich thůn mich freen/
Vnd wöllen doch nit Disputirn.
Sonder mich mit worten schmeckn/
In thut we das ich thu auffdeckn.
Ir grossen geytz vnd Simoney/
Ir falsch Gotdinst vnd Gleißnerey.
Ir Bannen/Auffsetz vnd gepot/
Vor aller welt zu schand vnd spott.
Mit deinem wort/ das ich dem leer/
Nun in abget an gut vnd Eer.
So kunden sy dein wort nit leiden/
Drumt mich schelten/hassen vnd neiden.
Wenn ich hett gschuben vnd gelert/
Das sich ir Reich vnd bet gemert.
So wer kein besser auff gstanden/
In langer zeit in Teütschen Landn.
Dis ist auch die vrsach ich sag/
Das gegen mir auch steit in clag.
Der Hantwercks leüt ein grosse zal/
Der auch abget in disem val.
Seyt diß Apgstterey entnimpt/
Also seynd der mich ergrimt.
Von erst des Baals Tempel knecht/
Den ir jarmarck thut nimmer recht.
Vnd Demetrius der werckman/
Dem sein handwerck zu ruck wil gan.
Her durch dein wort das ich thu schreibn/
Ir disen soll mich nit abtreibn/
Bey deinem vrteil will ich pleiben.

Actuum .1.

3. Regü.18.

Actuū.19.

Hans Sachs Schuster.

Das Vrteil Christi.
Das mein gericht das ist gerecht/
Nů merck vermaints gaistlichs gschlecht.
Was ich euch selb bevolhen han/
Das ir in die gantz welt solt gan.
Prediger aller Creatur/
Das Euangeli rain vnd pur/
Dasselbig hant ir gar veracht/
Vnd vil newer Gotdinst auff pracht.
Der ich doch kein geheissen hab/
Vnd verkaufft sie vmb gelt vnd gab.
Mit Vigil/ Jartåg vnd Selmessen/
Vnd versperrt auch das Himelreich/
Ir seyt den Doten grössern gleich.
Vñ schlacht zu dot auch mein Propheten/
Der gleich die Phariseer thetten.
Also verfolgt ir die warhait/
Die euch teglichen wirt geseit.
Vnd so ir euch nit pessern wert/
Ir vmkumen/Darumb so fert.
Von euwerm falschen widerstreit/
Dergleichen ir handtwercks leyt.
Die ir mein wort veracht mit dring/
Von wegen weiß aygen nütz.
Vnd höit doch in den worten mein/
Das ir nit solt sorgfeltig sein.
Vmb zeitlich güt/ gleich den Hayden/
Sů der sucht das Reich gots mit freuden.
Das zeitlich wirt euch wol zufalln/
Sunst wert ir in der hellen qualln/
Das ist mein vrteil zu euch alln.

Joānio.5.

Mar. vltio.

Matthei.15.

Math.23.

Luce.13.

Mathei.6.

Plate 61: Hans Sachs: Ein neuer Spruch, wie die Geistlichkeit und etlich Handwerker über den
Luther klagen (A new poem: how the clergy and certain craftsmen complain about Luther).
Broadsheet, Nuremberg, Hieronymus Höltzel, 1524, woodcut by Sebald Beham.
Nuremberg, German National Museum.

Plate 62: Martin Luther: Biblia, das ist: Die gantze Heilige Schrifft: Deudsch. Auffs New zugericht, Wittenberg, Hans Lufft, 1541. Wolfenbüttel, Herzog August Library.

Countless legends have arisen concerning the language of the Luther Bible, which the research into linguistic history of recent years makes it simpler to evaluate. It is important to keep in mind that the wide distribution of Luther's pamphlets and Bible translations, the pains he took to avoid regional dialect expressions, and his use of the printed language of south-east Germany all contributed positively to that levelling-out of language within the German empire which had already begun, and to the development of a common German printed language. Luther's own hope that the language of the Saxon chancellery would become universally understood ("Ideo ist communissima lingua Germaniae", Table-talk, 1040 and 2758) hopelessly overestimated the rôle of official language. In the southern towns his translations required a supplementary glossary of Middle German/South German words, whereas northern Germany was quickly provided with its own Low German renderings. But in tandem with this conscious striving towards standardisation, he exercised a formative stylistic influence through the new words he coined, his phraseology and his metaphorical language. Recent research has underplayed his apparently direct and "popular" address, and suggests that he was striving for a "sacral" language that was impregnated with classical rhetoric and closely matched stylistic qualities in the original text.

The influence of Luther's language and style does not go back just to the widely circulated Bible itself, but also to his theological tracts, the later writings of his pupils of which the Table-talk is an example, and eventually to the church hymns and Protestant sermons of the centuries which followed. Many authors quoted from the Luther Bible in their fictional texts, from Hans Sachs to the Historia von D. Johann Fausten (1587). The devotional literature and biblical drama of the sixteenth and seventeenth centuries used "Luther-German". Writers of the enlightenment and classical period from Hamann to Klopstock and Goethe in the eighteenth century engaged anew amongst themselves with the language of the Reformer, which resonated through Nietzsche, Thomas Mann and Brecht far into the twentieth century. The Reformation and printing are consequently first-hand participants in the emergence of a High German literary language.

Gutenberg goes electronic

Gutenberg had grasped that what was practical in the fourth decade of the fifteenth century – such procedures as impressing stamps into clay or tooling bookbindings or printing fabrics, the engraving skills of goldsmithery and the casting techniques used in bell-founding, and harnessing the power of the wine- or paper-making press to print or impress – could lead to an epoch-making new process, whereby he could cast virtually unlimited numbers of identical letters in lead, from which he could then print at will, and so create a means of multiplying information such as no earlier age had enjoyed.

This invention survived virtually unchanged down the centuries: only some four hundred years later did the development of the cylinder press give rise to new working practices, but even then there was no real departure from his principles for letterpress printing. Similarly, few fundamental changes were brought about by the Monotype or Linotype systems of mechanical composition, the introduction of reel-fed paper, or the replacement of wood-engraving for pictorial reproduction. Offset printing was the first innovative printing process that relied neither on the relief principle nor on the intaglio principle represented by copperplate-engraving, but instead used a planographic or flat printing surface. But the most significant step – the introduction of photo-typesetting – which would allow offset to supplant letterpress, still lay some decades ahead. For over five hundred years, lead had ruled supreme, and now its place was to be taken by film. Typefaces would no longer be cut and cast in metal, but their designs exposed onto film masters for photo-composition. The beginning of the end for Gutenberg's invention – quite unremarked by the press – might be dated from 1971, when the Association of German Typefounders voted to dissolve itself. The current digital revolution is superseding not only metal types and photographic film, it may even bring about an electronic alternative to paper itself. At the moment we are experiencing the digitisation of the printing process and the spread of information in electronic form at a variety of levels and in a number of emergent technologies.

Digital printing has the following characteristics:

- text and images held exclusively as digital data;
- printing directly from the author's files;
- no use of films or sensitized papers;
- creating the image by transferring it dot by dot onto the printing surface.

The digitised data is directly transferred from software onto an erasable printing cylinder, and thence, without using any carrier, onto the printing surface. The procedure of preparing the data and illustrating and scanning the work is entirely carried out on the computer. At the time of writing, electro-photography is the most successful of the various printing systems available. Its technique, which is also that applied in laser printers and photocopiers, is centred on a photo-semiconductor that immediately loses its conductivity when in the dark. A cylinder that is covered with a semiconductor of that kind is statically charged through corona radiation to the effect that it obtains an even electric charge. This charge is fully retained as long as the cylinder is kept in the dark. But as soon as it is touched by a laser beam, which is used to transfer the image to be printed from the software onto the cylinder, it will release its charge. This results in a latent image of charge on the cylinder that is then coloured with an electromagnetic toner that only adheres to the charged areas. Finally, this image is either fixed on the cylinder and then printed onto the printing surface (direct process) or first printed onto the printing surface and then fixed through pressure or heat (indirect process). In either process, the cylinder needs to be cleaned and discharged again before printing the next image.

What appears to be a work-intensive process at first sight, proves to be very advanced particularly for small and sophisticated orders, for it needs to be remembered that this process requires none of the intermediate operations of the earlier printing processes – no typesetting or photocomposition is involved, and neither do stereos or films need to be made for transfer to the printing cylinder. Hence, electrophotography facilitates interrupting the print run to introduce changes to the text or layout of individual pages.

Electro-photography has an advantage over offset printing in radically simplifying the pre-press stages. Since data is utilised just as it is received from the customer, the risk of introducing mistakes into the final printed work with each further operation is eliminated. Production costs are significantly reduced since no films or printing plates are required, thus making the process ideal for very short print runs, in contrast to offset printing which generally becomes economical only with runs of over 1000 copies. As a result, smaller editions need less storage space, and the publisher does not have to risk too high an initial edition as further tiny runs can be printed as called for. The files can easily be archived for later use, and corrected or updated at will. As touched upon before, electrophotography makes it possible to interrupt a run to insert changes or to customise pages for different users. Last but not least, the process gives publishers the chance to split a job and allocate it to different printers. This procedure is already in practice amongst larger publishing houses, where it is quicker and cheaper to mail data than printed editions.

Digital printing still fails to match the standards and output of offset printing, but for the moment it comes into its own for runs of less than 1000 copies. Since editions, particularly of technical, scientific and academic works, are progressively decreasing in size worldwide (in the USA, for example, half of all books appear in runs of fewer than 1000 copies), the market for digital printing will continue to develop and ensure that such books and journals can continue to appear in printed form.

PRINT ON DEMAND

So-called "print on demand" has recently gained an increasing importance, particularly for books, journals, dissertations, and out-of-print material of specialised interest. Whereas such publications were formerly printed in an edition and then distributed, they may now just be publicised, and printed subsequently to individual order.

As users increasingly prefer direct access to electronic data rather than receiving it in print form, librarians find themselves confronted with completely new jobs. Libraries worldwide have mounted their catalogues on the internet so that ultimately, time-consuming book searches will become history. Large libraries, such as the British Library and the Bibliothèque Nationale are even one step ahead for they have already started to make complete works available on screen. Likewise, "Project Gutenberg" in Germany aims to achieve an electronic database that will eventually contain all the most important works of world literature.

MANUSCRIPTS ON SCREEN

Although the internet is inevitably thought of as the source of the most recently updated information on any topic, it also lends itself to providing scholars with access to valuable manuscripts and early printed books. The internet has brought about a new approach to the concept of facsimile editions, thus contributing to the conservation of old and fragile originals. For example, some sixty of the most important manuscripts of our cultural heritage held by the Biblioteca Apostolica Vaticana can be read on screen: thus manuscripts such as Virgil's, which date from the fourth century, or Euclid's from the twelfth century may be studied in screen-resolutions and with high quality printouts that easily satisfy the demands for scientific research work. Accordingly, researchers are no longer under pressure to travel, say, to the Jagiellonian University in Kraków to study the most important astrological work of early modern times, the *De Revolutionibus* by Nicholas Copernicus, for they can easily find it on the University's website. Likewise, researchers or, in fact, everyone interested can find the complete facsimile edition of the *Gutenberg Bible* belonging to the Göttingen State and University Library on the internet (*www.gutenbergdigital.de*). Users are offered the chance to study all 1286 richly illuminated pages – to compare them with other copies through the Keio University of Tokyo project (*www.humi.keio.ac.jp/treasures/incunabula/B42-web*) or the British Library (*www.bl.uk/treasures/gutenberg/homepage.html*) – or simply to look at them for their beauty. Moreover, as the internet makes it possible to compare the Latin *Vulgata* text side by side with a German or English translation, or to compare passages in the illuminations with their sources in the contemporary *Göttingen Pattern Book*, this electronic facsimile edition has become a standard research tool for philologists, theologians and book historians. It is beyond doubt that the precious old book and the new medium have thus formed an impressive and invaluable symbiosis.

This new development of electronic media takes place in parallel to a stable market for book market in the western world. Production by title continues to rise, reaching new heights with, for example, some 70,000 titles annually in the German-speaking area or 300,000 titles worldwide. The Frankfurt Book Fair – the world's most important book fair – held each October, provides an important market place for hundreds of thousands of academic, non-fiction and fiction titles. The national libraries, whether in Budapest, Frankfurt or London, are moving over to the storage of electronic media as well. Whereas books, in theory, are produced to survive for centuries, the question of how best to store electronic information has long remained unsettled.

ELECTRONIC INK

Recent developments at the Massachusetts Institute of Technology of "electronic ink" or "digital paper" promise to synthesize the advantages of the traditional book with those of the internet. The team working under Joseph Jacobson in the nanotechnology department has developed a digital paper which takes Gutenberg's invention forward: whereas the latter had made it possible to print the identical text many thousands of times onto sheets of paper, the advent of digital paper makes it possible to print many thousands of constantly changing pages of information onto the same sheet of paper. The technique may be described as follows: a carrier is printed with tiny micro-encapsulated pellets ($10,000/cm^2$) filled with black electronic ink containing particles of positively charged white pigment. When the pellets are loaded with a negative charge they appear white but when they are loaded with a positive charge they immediately turn black. Similar to the pixels in newspaper printing, the digital paper can be filled with textual or graphical information of any nature.

Indicative of its ultimate goal, Joseph Jacobson calls his project "The last book". It is his vision that in the not-too-distant future every child will be given his or her "last book", which, because it has some 240 pages of digital paper, can be refilled infinitely with any desired text and so will make further books superfluous. Even the problem of receiving information on the internet will be solved in the next couple of years by means of broadband transmissions over cellular phone systems. As, in all likelihood, Joseph Jacobson's invention will give rise to a new form of communication, he and his team were awarded the Gutenberg Prize of the International Gutenberg Society in Mainz in 2000. But whatever the future will bring we may legitimately say in the twenty-first century that Gutenberg has gone electronic.

Bibliography

ABBREVIATIONS

GJ: *Gutenberg-Jahrbuch.* Founded by Aloys Ruppel (1926), edited on behalf of
        the Gutenberg-Gesellschaft by Stephan Füssel, Mainz.
GW: *Gesamtkatalog der Wiegendrucke.* Published by the Kommission für den
        Gesamtkatalog der Wiegendrucke: vols. 1–8,1 Leipzig 1925–40; second
        revised impression, vols 1–7 Stuttgart: Hiersemann 1968; vols 8ff Stuttgart:
        Hiersemann 1978 ff.
H: Hain, Ludwig: *Repertorium bibliographicum, in quo libri omnes ab arte
        typographica inventa usque ad annum MD typis expressi . . . recensentur.*
        Stuttgartiae et Lutetiae Parisorum 1826–38. Reprint, Milano: Görlich 1966.

1. BIBLIOGRAPHIES / RESEARCH REPORTS

Corsten, Severin and Reinmar Fuchs assisted by Kurt Hans Staub: *Der Buchdruck im
  15. Jahrhundert: Eine bibliographie.* 2 vols. Stuttgart: Hiersemann 1988/93.
Füssel, Stephan: "Gutenberg-Forschung Neunzehnhundert-Zweitausend" In: GJ
  2000, pp. 9–26.

2. GUTENBERG: LIFE AND WORK

Bechtel, Guy: *Gutenberg et l'invention de l'imprimerie: Une enquête.* Paris: Fayard 1992.
Davies, Martin: *The Gutenberg Bible.* London, The British Library 1996.
Davies, Martin: "Juan de Carvajal and Early Printing." In: *The Library* 18/3 (1996),
  pp. 193–215.
Dolgodrova, Tatiana: "Die Miniaturen der Leipziger Pergament-Ausgabe der
  Gutenberg-Bibel: zur Zeit in der russischen Staatsbibliothek, Moskau." In: GJ
  1997, pp. 64–75
Füssel, Stephan: "Gutenberg and the advent of printing in Western culture." In:
  Hyphen vol. 2. Athens 1998, pp. 70ff.
Füssel, Stephan: *Johannes Gutenberg in Selbstzeugnissen und Bilddokumenten.* Reinbeck:
  Rowohlt 1999. (=rororo Monographie 134).
Geldner, Ferdinand: *Der Türkenkalender.* Facsimile und commentary. Wiesbaden:
  Reichert 1975.
Hellinga, Lotte: "Das Mainzer Catholicon und Gutenbergs Nachlaß: Neudatierung
  und Auswirkungen." In: *Archiv für Geschichte des Buchwesens* 40 (1993),
  pp. 395–416.
Hoffmann, Leonhard: "Die Gutenbergbibel: Eine Kosten-und Gewinnschätzung des
  ersten Bibeldrucks auf der Grundlage zeitgenössischer Quellen." In: *Archiv für
  Geschichte des Buchwesens* 39 (1993), pp. 255–319.

Ing, Janet: *Johann Gutenberg and his Bible*. New York: The Typophiles, London: The British Library, 2nd printing 1990.

International Symposium on Printing History in East and West, edited by the Korean National Commission for Unesco. Seoul 1997.

Johannes Gutenberg: Die 42-zeilige Bibel. Commentary to the facsimile of the Burgos copy. Valencia: Vincent Garcia Editores 1997.

Johannes Gutenberg: Regionale Aspekte des frühen Buchdrucks. Papers of the international conference on the 550th anniversary of printing 1990 in Berlin. Berlin 1993 (= Beiträge aus der Staatsbibliothek zu Berlin 1).

Johannes Gutenbergs 42-zeilige Bibel. Commentary volume to the facsimile, by Paul Schwenke. Leipzig: Insel-Verlag 1923.

Johannes Gutenbergs zweiundvierzigzeilige Bibel. Facsimile of the example in the Staatsbibliothek Preußischer Kulturbesitz Berlin. Commentary volume edited by Wieland Schmidt und Friedrich Adolf Schmidt-Künsemüller. Munich: Idion-Verlag 1979.

Kapr, Albert: *Johannes Gutenberg: Persönlichkeit und Leistung*. Leipzig: Urania 1986. 2nd edn. Munich: C. H. Beck 1988.

Kapr, Albert: *Johann Gutenberg: The Man and his Invention*. Translated from the German by Douglas Martin. Aldershot: Scolar Press, Burlington Vt: Ashgate 1996.

Köhler, Johann David: *Hochverdiente und aus bewährten Urkunden wohlbeglaubte Ehren-Rettung Johann Gutenbergs (...)*. Leipzig: Fritsch 1741.

Köster, Kurt: "Gutenbergs Straßburger Aachenspiegel-Unternehmen von 1438/40." In: GJ 1983, pp 24–44.

Lehmann-Haupt, Hellmut: *The Göttingen Model Book*. Columbia: Univ. of Montana Press 1972.

Lehmann-Haupt, Hellmut: *Gutenberg and the Master of the Playing Cards*. New Haven and London: Yale Univ. Press 1966.

Lehmann-Haupt, Hellmut: *Peter Schoeffer of Gernsheim and Mainz*. Rochester, N.Y.: Leo Hart 1950.

Man, John: *The Gutenberg Revolution: The story of a technical genius and an invention that changed the world*. London, Hodder Headline, 2000.

Mazal, Otto: **Der Mainz Psalter von 1457**. Facsimile and commentary volume. Dietikon-Zürich: Stocker 1968.

McMurtrie, Douglas C.: *The Gutenberg Documents: With translations of the texts into English*. New York: Oxford Univ. Press, 1941.

Miner, Dorothy: *The Giant Bible of Mainz*. Washington D.C.: Library of Congress 1952.

Morrison, Blake: *The Justification of Johann Gutenberg: A Novel*. London: Chatto & Windus 2000.

Needham, Paul: "The Paper Supply of the Gutenberg Bible." In: *The Papers of the Bibliographical Society of America* 79 (1985), pp. 303–74 (with census).

Painter, George D.: "The untrue portraits of Johann Gutenberg." In GJ 1967, pp. 54–60.

Painter, George D.: "Gutenberg and the B36-group: A Reconsideration." In: *Essays in Honour of Victor Scholderer*. Mainz: Karl Pressler 1970, pp. 292–322.

Powitz, Gerhardt: *Die Frankfurter Gutenberg-Bibel: Ein Beitrag zum Buchwesen des 15. Jahrhunderts*. Frankfurt am Main: Klostermann 1990 (= Frankfurter Bibliotheksschriften 3).

Ruppel, Aloys: *Johannes Gutenberg: Sein Leben und Werk*. Berlin: Gebr. Mann 1939, 2nd edn. Berlin 1947, reprint Nieuwkoop: de Graaf 1967.

Ruppel, Aloys: *Gutenbergs Tod und Begräbnis*. Mainz 1968 (= Kleiner Druck der Gutenberg-Gesellschaft No 81).

Schneider, Cornelia: *Peter Schöffer: Bücher für Europa*. Mainz: Gutenberg-Museum 2003

Schneider, Heinrich. *Der Text der Gutenberg-Bibel zu ihrem 500. Jubiläum untersucht*. Bonn: Hanstein 1954 (= Bonner biblische Beiträge 7).

Schorbach, Karl: "Die urkundlichen Nachrichten über Johannes Gutenberg." In: *Festschrift zum fünfhundertjährigen Geburtstage von Johann Gutenberg*. Edited by Otto Hartwig. Mainz 1900, pp.133–256.

Schorbach, Karl: "Neue Straßburger Gutenberg-Funde." *Gutenberg-Festschrift*. Mainz 1925, pp.130–43.

Sproule, Anna and Pollard, Michael: *Johann Gutenberg: Master of Modern Printing*. Farmington Hills MI: Blackbirch Press 1999.

Stüben, Jochen: "Das Rendsburger Fragment der Gutenberg-Bibel." In: GJ 1998, pp. 56–79.

Thorpe, James E.: *The Gutenberg Bible: Landmark in Learning*. 2nd edn. San Marino: The Huntingdon Library 1999.

Widmann, Hans: *Der gegenwärtige Stand der Gutenberg-Forschung*. Stuttgart: Hiersemann 1972.

Zedler, Gottfried: *Die Mainzer Ablaßbriefe der Jahre 1454 und 1455*. Mainz 1913.

3. THE BOOK AND SOCIETY IN THE FIFTEENTH CENTURY AND LATER

Birkerts, Sven: *The Gutenberg Elegies: The fate of reading in an electronic age*. New York and London: Faber and Faber 1994.

Blockbücher der Mittelalters: Bilderfolgen als Lektüre. Exhibition monograph ed. by the Gutenberg Society and the Gutenberg Museum. Mainz 1991.

Borgman, Christine L.: *From Gutenberg to the global information infrastructure*. Cambridge MA: M.I.T. Press 2000.

Brandis, Tilo: "Die Handschrift zwischen Mittelalter und Neuzeit: Versuch einer Typologie." In GJ 1997, pp. 25–57.

Bühler, Curt F.: *The Fifteenth-Century Book: The Scribes, The Printers, the Decorators*. Philadelphia: Pennsylvania Univ. Press 1960.

Burger, Konrad: *Buchhändleranzeigen des 15. Jahrhunderts*. Leipzig 1907.

Burke, Peter: *A Social History of Knowledge: From Gutenberg to Diderot*. London: Blackwell 2000.

Clair, Colin: A History of European Printing. London, New York: Academic Press 1976.

De Hamel, Christopher: A History of Illuminated Manuscripts. 2nd edn. London: Phaidon 1994.

De Hamel, Christopher: The Book: A History of the Bible. London: Phaidon 2001.

Eisenstein, Elizabeth L.: The printing press as an agent of change. 2 vols. Cambridge and New York: Cambridge University Press, 1979.

Febvre, Lucien and Martin, Henri-Jean: L'apparition du livre. Paris 1958 (= L'évolution de l'humanité 49).

Febvre, Lucien and Martin, Henri-Jean: The Coming of the Book. London and New York: Verso 1976.

Flasch, Kurt: Nikolaus von Kues: Geschichte einer Entwicklung. Frankfurt am Main: Klostermann 1998.

Fleischmann, Isa: Metallschnitt und Teigdruck: Technik und Entstehung zur Zeit des frühen Buchdrucks. Mainz: von Zabern 1998.

Füssel, Stephan (commentary): The Luther Bible of 1534, complete facsimile edition. Cologne, London, Las Vegas, Tokyo: Taschen 2002.

Füssel, Stephan (commentary): Emperor Maximilian I: The adventures of the knight Theuerdank, complete facsimile of the 1517 edition. Cologne, London, Las Vegas, Tokyo: Taschen 2003.

Füssel, Stephan (commentary): Schedel, Hartmann: Chronicle of the World: The complete and annotated Nuremberg Chronicle of 1493. Cologne, London, Las Vegas, Tokyo: Taschen 2001.

Füssel, Stephan (ed.): Deutsche Dichter der frühen Neuzeit: ihr Leben und Werk. Berlin: Erich Schmidt 1993.

Füssel, Stephan (ed.): 500 Jahre Schedelsche Weltchronik. Nuremberg: Hans Carl 1994 (= Pirckheimer-Jahrbuch 1994).

Füssel, Stephan: "'Dem Drucker aber sage er Dank . . .' Zur wechselseitigen Bereicherung von Buchdruckerkunst und Humanismus." In: Artibus. Festschrift für Dieter Wuttke zum 65. Geburtstag. Wiesbaden: Harrassowitz 1995, pp. 167–78.

Füssel, Stephan: Die Welt im Buch: Buchkünstlerischer und humanistischer Kontext der Schedelschen Weltchronik von 1493. Mainz: Gutenberg-Gesellschaft 1996 (= Kleiner Druck der Gutenberg-Gesellschaft 111).

Füssel, Stephan and Honemann, Volker (eds.): Humanismus und früher Buchdruck. Nuremberg: Hans Carl 1997 (= Pirckheimer Jahrbuch 1996).

Geldner, Ferdinand: Inkunabelkunde: Eine Einführung in die Welt des frühesten Buchdrucks. Wiesbaden: Reichert 1978 (= Elemente des Buch- und Bibliothekswesens 5).

Gier, Helmut and Janota, Johannes: Augsburger Buchdruck und Verlagswesen. Wiesbaden: Harrassowitz 1997.

Giesecke, Michael: Der Buchdruck der frühen Neuzeit: eine historische Fallstudie über die Durchsetzung neuer Informations- und Kommunikationstechnologien. Frankfurt am Main: Suhrkamp 1991.

Grenzmann, Ludger and Stackmann, Karl (eds.): Literatur und Laienbildung im Spätmittelalter und in der Reformationszeit. Stuttgart: Metzler 1984

Grimm, Heinrich: "Die Buchführer des deutschen Kulturbereiches und ihre
    Niederlassungen in der Zeitspanne von 1450 bis um 1550." In: *Archiv für Geschichte
    des Buchwesens* 7 (1967), cols. 1153–1772.
Gumbrecht, Hans Ulrich and Pfeiffer, K. Ludwig (eds.): *Materialität der
    Kommunikation*. Frankfurt am Main: Suhrkamp 1988.
Gutenberg: *550 Jahre Buchdruck in Europa*. Exhibition catalogue of the Herzog August
    Library, edited by Paul Raabe. Wolfenbüttel 1990.
Hirsch, Rudolf: *Printing, Selling and Reading 1450–1550*. Wiesbaden: Harrassowitz,
    2nd edn. 1974.
*Inkunabel- und Einbandkunde: Beiträge des Symposions zu Ehren von Max Joseph Husung
    1995 in Helmstedt*. Wiesbaden: Harrassowitz 1996
Kind, Helmut and Rohlfing, Helmut: *Gutenberg und der europäische Frühdruck: Zur
    Erwerbungsgeschichte der Göttinger Inkunabelsammlung*. Göttingen: Wallstein 1993.
Kock, Thomas and Schlusemann, Rita: *Laienlektüre und Buchmarkt im späten Mittelalter*.
    Frankfurt am Main and Berlin 1997.
Köhler, Hans-Joachim (ed.): *Flugschriften als Massenmedien der Reformationszeit*.
    Stuttgart: 1981 (= Spätmittelalter und frühe Neuzeit 13).
Kleinschmidt, Erich: *Stadt und Literatur in der Frühen Neuzeit*. Cologne and Vienna:
    Böhlau 1982.
Krafft, Fritz and Dieter Wuttke (eds.): *Das Verhältnis der Humanisten zum Buch*.
    Boppard: Boldt 1977 (= Kommission für Humanismusforschung, Mitteilung IV).
Kunze, Horst: *Geschichte der Buchillustration in Deutschland: Das 15. Jahrhundert*. 2 vols.
    Leipzig: Insel-Verlag 1973.
Lowry, Martin: *Nicholas Jenson and the rise of Venetian publishing in Renaissance Europe*.
    Oxford: Basil Blackwell 1991.
Lowry, Martin: *The World of Aldus Manutius: Business and Scholarship in Renaissance
    Venice*. Oxford Univ. Press and Cornell Univ. Press 1979.
Ludwig, Walther: "Der Humanist und das Buch: Heinrich Rantzaus Liebeserklärung
    an seine Bücher." In: *Illinois Classical Studies* 19 (1994), pp. 265–81.
Park, Seon Re: "Six perspectives in the history of printing." In: GJ 1998, pp. 42–7.
Schmidt-Künsemüller, Friedrich Adolf: *Die Erfindung des Buchdrucks als technisches
    Phänomen*. Mainz: Gutenberg-Gesellschaft 1931 (= Kleiner Druck 48).
Scapecchi, Piero: "Subiaco 1465 oppure Bondeno 1463?: Analisi del frammento
    Parsons-Scheide." In *La Bibliofilia* Anno CIII, Disp. I., pp. 1–24.
Schedel, Hartmann: *Chronicle of the World: The complete and annotated Nuremberg
    Chronicle of 1493*, introduction and appendix by Stephan Füssel. London and New
    York: Taschen 2001.
Smith, Margaret M.: *The Title-Page: Its Early Development 1460–1510*. London: The
    British Library 2000.
Teichl, Robert: "Der Wiegendruck im Kartenbild." In: Bibliothek und Wissenschaft 1
    (1964), pp. 201–65 with 1 map.
Tiemann, Barbara (ed.): *Die Buchkultur im 15. und 16. Jahrhundert*. 2 vols. Hamburg:
    Maximilian-Gesellschaft 1995/1999.

Widmann, Hans: Der deutsche Buchhandel in Urkunden und Quellen. Hamburg: Hauswedell 1965.

Widmann, Hans: Vom Nutzen und Nachteil der Erfindung des Buchdrucks: aus der Sicht der Zeitgenossen des Erfinders. Mainz: Gutenberg-Gesellschaft 1973 (= Kleiner Druck 92).

Widmann, Hans: "Die Wirkung des Buchdrucks auf die humanistischen Zeitgenossen des Erfinders." In: Krafft and Wuttke: Das Verhältnis der Humanisten zum Buch. Boppard: Boldt 1977, pp. 63–88.

Wuttke, Dieter: "Sebastian Brant und Maximilian I: Eine Studie zu Brants Donnerstein-Flugblatt des Jahres 1492." In: Die Humanisten in ihrer politischen und sozialen Umwelt. Ed. by Otto Herding and Robert Stupperich. Boppard: Boldt 1976, pp. 141–76.

Wuttke, Dieter: Humanismus als integrative Kraft: Die Philosophia des deutschen "Erzhumanisten" Conrad Celtis. Nuremberg: Hans Carl 1985.

4. THE BOOK IN BRITAIN

Davies, Martin: "Incunabula." In Studies in Fifteenth-Century Printed Books presented to Lotte Hellinga. London: The British Library 1999.

De la Mere, A. C. and Hellinga, Lotte: "The First Book Printed in Oxford: The Exposition Symboli of Rufinus." In Transactions of the Cambridge Bibliographical Society 7 (1977–80), pp. 184–244.

Early English Printing: A Series of Facsimiles of all the Types used in England during the XVth Century. With an Introduction by Edward Gordon Duff. London: 1896. Reprint Hildesheim and New York: Georg Olms Verlag 1974.

Feather, John: A History of British Publishing. London and New York: Croom Helm 1988.

Hellinga, Lotte: Caxton in Focus: The Beginning of Printing in England. London: The British Library 1982.

Hellinga, Lotte and Trapp, J. B. (eds): The Cambridge History of the Book in Britain. Vol III: 1400–1557. Cambridge University Press 1999.

Hellinga, Lotte and Härtel, Helmar: "Book and Text in the Fifteenth Century." Proceedings of a conference held in the Herzog August Library Wolfenbüttel. Hamburg: Hauswedell 1981.

Painter, George D.: William Caxton: A Quincentenary Biography of England's First Printer. London: Chatto & Windus 1976.

William Caxton: An Exhibition to Commemorate the Quincentenary of the Introduction of Printing into England. The British Library 1976.

PICTURE CREDITS

The author and publisher would like to thank the following libraries for their permission to reproduce works in their collections. Most of the illustrations were kindly provided by the Staats- und Universitäts Bibliothek Göttingen, plates 6–11, 15, 17, 18, 22–30, 32–36, 39, 40, 49, 54–60. The Biblioteca Pública in Burgos supplied plate 5; the Universitätsbibliothek in Leipzig, plates 19, 20, 37, 45; the Gutenberg-Museum in Mainz, plates 1, 13, 16; the Germanische Nationalmuseum in Nuremberg, plate 61; the Universitätsbibliothek in Tübingen, plate 50; the Library of Congress in Washington, plate 4; and the Herzog August Bibliothek in Wolfenbüttel, plates 14, 31, 42, 43, 48, 51, 62. The other plates are taken from facsimile sources with acknowledgement as appropriate.

Index

(References to illustrations are in **bold**)